Language Smugglers

Literatures, Cultures, Translation

Literatures, Cultures, Translation presents books that engage central issues in translation studies such as history, politics, and gender in and of literary translation, as well as books that open new avenues for study. Volumes in the series follow two main strands of inquiry: one strand brings a wider context to translation through an interdisciplinary interrogation, while the other hones in on the history and politics of the translation of seminal works in literary and intellectual history.

Series Editors

Brian James Baer, Kent State University, USA
Michelle Woods, The State University of New York, New Paltz, USA

Editorial Board

Paul Bandia, Professeur titulaire, Concordia University, Canada, and Senior Fellow, the W. E. B. Du Bois Institute for African American Research, Harvard University, USA
Susan Bassnett, Professor of Comparative Literature, Warwick University, UK
Leo Tak-hung Chan, Guangxi University, Hong Kong, China
Michael Cronin, Dublin City University, Republic of Ireland
Edwin Gentzler, University of Massachusetts Amherst, USA
Denise Merkle, Moncton University, Canada
Michaela Wolf, University of Graz, Austria

Volumes in the Series

Translation and the Making of Modern Russian Literature
Brian James Baer

Interpreting in Nazi Concentration Camps
Edited by Michaela Wolf

Exorcising Translation: Towards an Intercivilizational Turn
Douglas Robinson

Literary Translation and the Making of Originals
Karen Emmerich

The Translator on Stage
Geraldine Brodie

Transgender, Translation, Translingual Address
Douglas Robinson

Western Theory in East Asian Contexts: Translation and Translingual Writing
Leo Tak-hung Chan

The Translator's Visibility: Scenes from Contemporary Latin American Fiction
Heather Cleary

The Relocation of Culture: Translations, Migrations, Borders
Simona Bertacco and Nicoletta Vallorani

The Art of Translation in Light of Bakhtin's Re-accentuation
Edited by Slav Gratchev and Margarita Marinova

Migration and Mutation: New Perspectives on the Sonnet in Translation
Edited by Carole Birkan-Berz, Oriane Monthéard,
and Erin Cunningham

This Is a Classic: Translators on Making Writers Global
Edited by Regina Galasso

Language Smugglers: Postlingual Literatures and Translation within the Canadian Context
Arianne Des Rochers

Language Smugglers

Postlingual Literatures and Translation within the Canadian Context

Arianne Des Rochers

BLOOMSBURY ACADEMIC
NEW YORK • LONDON • OXFORD • NEW DELHI • SYDNEY

BLOOMSBURY ACADEMIC
Bloomsbury Publishing Inc
1385 Broadway, New York, NY 10018, USA
50 Bedford Square, London, WC1B 3DP, UK

BLOOMSBURY, BLOOMSBURY ACADEMIC and the Diana logo are trademarks of
Bloomsbury Publishing Plc

First published in the United States of America 2023
This paperback edition published 2025

Copyright © Arianne Des Rochers, 2023

For legal purposes the Acknowledgments on p. viii constitute an extension
of this copyright page.

Cover design by Daniel Benneworth-Gray
Cover image from Through the heart of Patagonia (1902)
by Hesketh Vernon Hesketh-Prichard, John Guille Millais, and James Britten

All rights reserved. No part of this publication may be reproduced or transmitted in any form or by any means, electronic or mechanical, including photocopying, recording, or any information storage or retrieval system, without prior permission in writing from the publishers.

Bloomsbury Publishing Inc does not have any control over, or responsibility for, any third-party websites referred to or in this book. All internet addresses given in this book were correct at the time of going to press. The author and publisher regret any inconvenience caused if addresses have changed or sites have ceased to exist, but can accept no responsibility for any such changes.

Whilst every effort has been made to locate copyright holders the publishers would be grateful to hear from any person(s) not here acknowledged.

Library of Congress Cataloging-in-Publication Data

Names: Des Rochers, Arianne, 1989- author.
Title: Language smugglers : postlingual literatures and translation within the Canadian context / Arianne Des Rochers.
Description: New York: Bloomsbury Academic, 2023. | Series: Literatures, cultures, translation | Includes bibliographical references and index. | Summary: "Challenges and contextualizes the standard language used in translation theory and comparative literature within the unique linguistic and translational context of the Canadian nation-state"– Provided by publisher.
Identifiers: LCCN 2023002899 (print) | LCCN 2023002900 (ebook) | ISBN 9781501394119 (hardback) | ISBN 9781501394157 (paperback) | ISBN 9781501394126 (ebook) | ISBN 9781501394133 (pdf) | ISBN 9781501394140 (ebook other)
Subjects: LCSH: Translating and interpreting–Political aspects–Québec (Province) | Translating and interpreting–Social aspects–Québec (Province) | Multilingualism and literature–Québec (Province) | Standard language–Québec (Province)
Classification: LCC P306.8.C2 D47 2023 (print) | LCC P306.8.C2 (ebook) |
DDC 418/.02–dc23/eng/20230313
LC record available at https://lccn.loc.gov/2023002899
LC ebook record available at https://lccn.loc.gov/2023002900

ISBN: HB: 978-1-5013-9411-9
PB: 978-1-5013-9415-7
ePDF: 978-1-5013-9413-3
eBook: 978-1-5013-9412-6

Typeset by Deanta Global Publishing Services, Chennai, India

To find out more about our authors and books visit www.bloomsbury.com and sign up for our newsletters.

Contents

Acknowledgments	viii
Note on Translations	x

Introduction: Linguistic Borders, Nationalism, and Translation
   in Quebec and Canada   1

1 Translation as Mapping: Denaturalizing National Cartographies
   of Language   21

2 Against Standardization: Gregory Scofield and France Daigle
   Talk Back   65

3 The Linguistic Abject: The Queering of Language in Kevin
   Lambert and Joshua Whitehead   111

4 Motherless Tongues: The Unfamiliar Writings and Translations
   of Oana Avasilichioaei and Nathanaël   161

Conclusion: Toward a Postlingual Approach to Translation:
   Translating (in) the Twenty-First Century   205

Works Cited	223
Index	235

Acknowledgments

This book is indebted to the work of countless others who came before me. Perhaps most obviously, I am grateful to the poets and writers I discuss in these pages: Gregory Scofield, France Daigle, Kevin Lambert, Joshua Whitehead, Oana Avasilichioaei, Nathanaël, Leanne Betasamosake Simpson, and Georgette LeBlanc. Thank you for writing and translating in ways that have disrupted and transformed how I practice and think about translation. I am especially grateful for the generosity of Leanne, Kevin, Joshua, Nathanaël, and Georgette, with whom I have had the chance to share thoughts and ideas around postlingual literary expression and its challenges for translation. This book would not exist without your radical, queer, and decolonial poetics.

This book would be a lot less rigorous and sophisticated without the guidance of Neil ten Kortenaar, Monica Heller, and Smaro Kamboureli. Thank you for engaging with earlier versions of this work with such enthusiasm and curiosity and for challenging me to always dig deeper. I also want to thank Sarah Dowling for her attentive comments and unwavering support and Sherry Simon for believing in this project, at times more than I did myself. Having such inspiring and empowering mentors in my corner as I wrote and rewrote and revised and edited this book has meant the world to me.

This book took form in a close-knit ecosystem of students, scholars, and professors at the Centre for Comparative Literature at the University of Toronto between 2016 and 2019. I want to thank every colleague I have shared space, time, and ideas with there, especially my dear friends Amelia Bailey, Matthew Larocque-Coulas, Nathaniel Harrington, Rob Twiss, Julia Irion Martins, and Talia Isaacson for brightening my stay in Toronto and for providing me with a safe yet always demanding intellectual environment. Thank you to Aphrodite Gardner, Bao Nguyen, Ann Komaromi, and Jill Ross for their support and kindness and to the various professors who have helped shape my intellectual trajectory, most notably Elizabeth Povinelli, Neil ten Kortenaar, Thomas Lahusen, Eva-Lynn Jagoe, Barbara Havercroft, Jesook Song, and Alejandro Paz.

This book would not exist without the web of translators with whom I share a passion, a practice, and a politics. I am eternally indebted to Alex Gauthier, Natasha Kanapé Fontaine, Kama La Mackerel, and Edith Bélanger for agreeing to translate, sometimes in experimental, inventive, and postlingual ways, with me. Thank you for bringing your ideas, thoughts, and values to my table and for helping me grow. Thank you, also, to the many translators who have listened to me talk about the ideas behind this book, especially Sonya Malaborza, Geneviève Robichaud, Luba Markovskaia, Georgette LeBlanc, Catherine Ego, Aimee Wall, Bilal Hashmi, Olivia Tapiero, and Kama La Mackerel. To be able to evolve, both as a translator and as a person, within our wonderful translation community is truly a blessing.

I also want to thank every author who has trusted me with the translation of their books, particularly Leanne Betasamosake Simpson, Joshua Whitehead, Kate Briggs, and Billy-Ray Belcourt. Thank you for the worlds that you create and for letting me translate them. Thank you for trusting me with such responsibility.

In terms of the making of this book, I am indebted to Nathaniel Harrington and Anne Malena for their generous and helpful comments and edits on my manuscript. Thank you to Brian James Baer and Michelle Woods, the editors of the Literatures, Cultures, Translation series; I am honored to be featured alongside such innovative and critical voices. I am also extremely grateful for Haaris Naqvi, Rachel Moore, Hali Han, and everyone at Bloomsbury Academic for their dedication and care throughout the editorial process.

Finally, I want to thank Vincent for his support, dedication, and love all through the years it took me to write this book and Dominique for their uplifting and reassuring presence when I needed it most.

Note on Translations

Unless otherwise stated, all English translations of quoted citations and excerpts are by the author. Excerpts from primary sources appear in the original phrasing when the point is to highlight the interplay of linguistic forms in literary works under study, while excerpts appear in translation when the point is the content of the passage under discussion. When applicable and relevant, the source quotations are provided in footnotes for comparative purposes.

Introduction

Linguistic Borders, Nationalism, and Translation in Quebec and Canada

In a seminal 1985 essay, Jacques Derrida famously asks: "How is a text written in several languages at a time to be translated?"[1] Considering that translation is commonly known as the rendering of a text from *one* language into *another*, it is indeed a question worth asking, one that has caught the attention of translation and literary scholars these last few decades. What can, and what should, translators do when faced with a text that appears to be written in more than one language? Translate in several different languages as well? Perhaps. But, as Derrida also asks later on, "translating with several languages at a time, will that be called translating?"[2]

Perhaps these questions are rigged from the start, due to their very formulation, centered on the idea of distinct, countable languages. Trying to find practical answers to these questions implies taking the existence of distinct, bounded languages for granted. Perhaps the classification of linguistic practices (including writing) into categories such as English and French is but one narrative, one way of framing linguistic expression, one that has been hiding other potential narratives about language use. Perhaps these classifications (English, French, but also monolingual, bilingual, multilingual) tell us more about our dominant modes of perception when it comes to language and less about the empirical linguistic nature of the texts we interact with as scholars, translators, and readers. This book, then, asks: how do texts that are seemingly "written in more than one language" challenge the entire differential regime of translation? What would translation look like if we left the idea of "languages" as countable, fixed systems behind? Is translation without linguistic borders possible?

This book points to a new, alternative language consciousness that looks beyond the predetermined linguistic borders we tend to take for granted. It is inspired by a series of texts written by contemporary authors who are

---

[1] Jacques Derrida, "Des Tours de Babel," in *Difference in Translation*, ed. and trans. Joseph F. Graham (Ithaca: Cornell University Press, 1985), 171.
[2] Ibid.

invested in undoing the normative and violent borders of colonial and patriarchal categories (such as race and gender) that are often used against them. Importantly, the writers featured in this study are, as the title of the book suggests, language smugglers: they deliberately "smuggle" foreign, unwanted, disruptive linguistic elements into an official, sedimented, and dominant language, much as people all around the world smuggle "illegal" people or commodities across national borders throughout the world. As such, smugglers constantly reveal the porosity, artificiality, and precarity of borders, at the same time as they experience their very real, material violence. Even though the degree of this violence varies greatly depending on the kind of border one is transgressing, geographical borders and linguistic borders are part of the same regime of bordering, which main function is to produce relations of exclusion and dominance. From a linguistic standpoint, an individual or group threatening the "purity" or the "integrity" of a national language can be met with ostracization, discrimination, and exclusion. In other words, within a nation-state's geographical borders, linguistic borders often serve to create, reproduce, and justify social and political exclusions on the grounds of language.

Guided by a number of language smugglers who enact a complete disregard of linguistic borders, this book explores possible ways in which translation can, and should, enact a similar refusal of linguistic categories. Echoing recent calls to counter liberal conceptions of translation as exclusively positive[3]—as peaceful and desirable mediation between cultures, as building bridges, and so on—this book sees dominant modes of translation as intimately tied to the needs of a capitalist and colonial world order. In this light, crossing (linguistic) borders is not enough, as it keeps borders intact—and, as Harsha Walia reminds us, borders are "less about a politics of movement per se and [are] better understood as a key method of imperial state formation, hierarchical social ordering, labor control, and xenophobic nationalism."[4] Rather, we must undo the borders that bound language, order social hierarchies along linguistic lines, and limit our linguistic imaginaries, practices, and solidarities.

It is also important to note that this book stems from a particular positionality within a politically and culturally specific location: that of Canada, and more specifically its only monolingually French province,

---

[3] See, for instance, Tiphaine Samoyault, *Traduction et violence* (Paris: Éditions du Seuil, 2020) and Federico Italiano's edited volume *The Dark Side of Translation* (London/New York: Routledge, 2020).

[4] Harsha Walia, *Border & Rule: Global Migration, Capitalism, and the Rise of Racist Nationalism* (Halifax/Winnipeg: Fernwood Publishing, 2021), 2.

Quebec, two settler colonial societies that lie on the unceded, colonized territories of numerous Indigenous nations. I was born in a Montreal suburb to white, lower-middle-class, cis-heterosexual, and francophone parents in 1989, at a time when the independence movement was at its height, a few years before it would be crushed by the negative outcome of the second independence referendum in 1995. After 1995, what was once a more pluralistic, socialist, and progressive nationalist movement based on the (admittedly colonial and problematic) notion of a shared territory started to shift, embracing a more ethnic, identitarian definition of the Québécois nation based on shared customs (such as the French language and so-called secularism), reminiscent of the ways in which the French Canadian "race" was defined before the Quiet Revolution, that is, on religious, linguistic, and cultural grounds. Today, Quebec nationalism has taken a deeply conservative turn and uses the French language (its protection, its imposition, its "survival") as the main defining feature of Québécois identity, determining who can claim it and who cannot.[5]

As a white, francophone settler who very much fits the ethnolinguistic description of the "historical French majority" and who benefits from such identitarian articulations of the Québécois "nation," I see it as my responsibility to actively question and undermine the linguistic constructs that allow for the reproduction and the justification of social inequalities in the settler colonial context where I live and work. Further, my formal, university training in translation as well as my practice as a translator have made me conscious of the ways in which linguistic borders and linguistic purism are constantly reproduced and preserved, both in those fields and in dominant discourses in the public sphere. This book, therefore, is my individual attempt to push back against a fundamentally nationalist—and therefore colonial and patriarchal—understanding of language that permeates both the field of translation and our daily lives in present-day Quebec and Canada. It is an attempt to look beyond our linguistic present and to shape the ways in which we practice and theorize translation according to a decolonial, queer, inclusive, always evolving linguistic horizon.

---

[5] For critiques of twenty-first-century Québécois nationalism, see Dalie Giroux, *L'oeil du maître* (Montréal: Mémoire d'encrier, 2021); Jean-Marc Piotte and Jean-Pierre Couture, *Les Nouveaux visages du nationalisme conservateur au Québec* (Montréal: Québec-Amérique, 2012); Francine Pelletier, *La bataille pour l'âme du Québec* (Périphéria, https://ici.tou.tv/bataille-pour-lame-du-quebec, 2022). For an examination of the importance of linguistic purism for Quebec nationalism throughout time, see Stanley Aléong, "Discours nationalistes et purisme linguistique au Québec," *Culture* 1, no. 2 (1981): 31–41; and Chantal Bouchard, *La langue et le nombril : Une obsession québécoise* (Montréal: Fides, 1998).

Language Politics in Quebec: The Debate Around Franglais

This book takes as its starting point a province-wide debate on the use of "Franglais," or Frenglish, in 2014, sparked by the publication of an opinion piece by prominent columnist Christian Rioux in one of Quebec's most prominent newspapers, *Le Devoir*.[6] In his piece, Rioux deplores the degraded quality of the French language he supposedly observes in Quebec and, most importantly, points a finger at Dead Obies, a Montreal-based rap group whose lyrics are composed of what Rioux frames as a "suicidal" mix of French and English or, as he also puts it elsewhere, a "sublanguage spoken by handicapped beings in the process of being assimilated."[7] According to him, users of Franglais, or Frenglish, and especially its representatives in the cultural and artistic sphere, are obliviously (or worse, willfully) contributing to the assimilation of the Québécois nation by contaminating French, its true and only correct mode of expression, with English, which historically symbolizes the oppressor in the Québécois collective imagination.

This is not the first column Rioux wrote on the topic; he used the same tactic—demonizing and belittling musicians who sing in a nonmonolingual, "improper" way—in 2013 and 2012 when he criticized Acadian artists Lisa LeBlanc and Radio Radio for contributing to the "slow but certain disintegration of the one and only matrix that Quebec possesses,"[8] apparently forgetting that these artists are not even, in fact, Québécois but from the neighboring provinces of New Brunswick and Nova Scotia, respectively. If the 2012 and 2013 columns engendered few public responses, the 2014 article was the straw that broke the camel's back. Many commentators and public intellectuals weighed in on the matter, including former Dead Obies member Yes McCan, who signed a scathing response in *Voir* magazine titled "Dead Obies and Frenglish: A Reply to Those Offended."[9]

On one side, Rioux's brand of cultural nationalism centered on the purity and prominence of French as distinct from and threatened by the demonized English language of the Canadian majority; on the other, scholars, activists, and artists interrogated what they saw as the exclusionary mechanisms of the

---

[6] Christian Rioux, "J'rape un suicide...," *Le Devoir* (Montréal, QC), July 18, 2014, https://www.ledevoir.com/opinion/chroniques/413795/j-rape-un-suicide.
[7] Christian Rioux, "Radio Radio," *Le Devoir* (Montréal, QC), October 26, 2012, https://www.ledevoir.com/opinion/chroniques/362441/radio-radio.
[8] Ibid.
[9] Yes McCan, "Dead Obies et le franglais: La réplique aux offusqués," *Voir* (Montréal, QC), July 23, 2014, https://voir.ca/jepenseque/2014/07/23/la-replique-aux-offusques/.

monolingual model of Québécois nationalism and as a moral panic whose primary function is to reposition the French majority as a victim within the very province it governs. The debate around linguistic normativity, the purity of French, and most importantly its centrality in the articulation of the Québécois nation and the movement for separation and sovereignty of the second half of the twentieth century was not new in itself. Indeed, these questions often emerge in public discourse in Quebec, the now infamous 2014 debate on Franglais being but one significant example.

Rioux's rhetoric and its focus on the sacrosanct purity of language, which frames French as a victimized, precarious language under threat in Quebec, can seem surprising given that the French language benefits from tremendous institutional and state support in Quebec and in Canada as compared to, say, Indigenous languages—most notably, through the Office québécois de la langue française (OQLF) and the Canadian policy of official bilingualism. For example, in September 2020 the government of Quebec made the controversial announcement that it would allocate $5 million to enforce its French language charter, in the middle of the Covid-19 pandemic, while hospitals remained underfunded through this unprecedented health crisis. If French was once a minoritized language within the territory we now call Quebec, decades of political activism have led to its official recognition, as well as to its sedimentation, institutional and otherwise, as Quebec's official, dominant language. This is what Myriam Suchet calls "the posture of domination that has become the white, francophone culture"[10] in Quebec.

Nevertheless, the preservation of French in Quebec is often presented as pressing and necessary and framed in terms of having to protect it from outside contamination at all costs. For instance, in the spring of 2021, columnist Gilles Proulx published three articles where he characterized the English language as a "virus" and the anglicization of Montreal as a "pandemic," suggesting that if we do not act, the French language will find itself in "intensive care."[11] In fact, we routinely see in Quebec media a heightened moral panic around the supposed decline of French in the province—a moral panic that has been circulating intermittently for at least the last forty years. This panic often translates into reactionary xenophobia, anti-immigration sentiment, and racism, as its proponents self-victimize through an exaggerated fear of the linguistic Other. The French language is

---

[10] Myriam Suchet, *L'horizon est ici: Pour une prolifération des modes de relations* (Paris: éditions du commun, 2019), 110.
[11] Gilles Proulx, "L'anglicisation, cette autre épidémie," *Le Journal de Montréal* (Montréal, QC), January 28, 2021, https://www.journaldemontreal.com/2021/01/28/langlicisation-cette-autre-epidemie.

framed as a living and breathing thing that we must protect from surrounding threats at all costs, including at the expense of the actual lives, needs, and dignity of other linguistic groups.[12]

This framing of English or linguistic forms associated with other languages as a foreign invasion clearly reveals a function of nation-building, as shown by the objectives of Bill 96, "An Act respecting French, the official and common language of Quebec," adopted in May 2022. The objectives of the bill include "to confirm the status of French as the common language; the language allowing adherence and participation in the distinct culture of the Québécois nation" and "making the French language an invariable priority of the Quebec government."[13] Indeed, French nationalism in Quebec heavily relies on the constant exclusion of other languages as well as on a kind of linguistic purism, both of which are not, as we will see throughout this book, without social consequences. Language—its "mastery," one's status as a legitimate speaker—becomes one of the grounds on which the national body excludes and discriminates in order to produce and reproduce its borders along racial, ethnic, linguistic lines. In spite of this anxiety, it becomes clear that "pure" French is more a prescriptive ideal than an empirical reality when the contemporary cultural, social, and political realities of present-day Montreal, Quebec, and Canada as a whole are considered.

How is all this related to, or relevant for, translation? If linguistic purism is at the heart of present-day articulations of Québécois nationalism, it is also at the very heart of what translators do in their everyday tasks. The practice of translation shares one thing with Québécois nationalism:

---

[12] For instance, in the spring of 2022, the Quebec government used the notwithstanding clause, which allows a province to override basic freedoms guaranteed by the Canadian Charter of Rights and Freedoms, to adopt a contentious language bill. The bill, large in scope, limits the use of English in the courts and public services, which will undoubtedly infringe on the ability of individuals who do not speak French, such as certain Indigenous communities, immigrants, and the anglophone minority, to access vital services such as health care. According to this bill, an anonymous tip-off allows the Office québécois de la langue française, a linguistic institution, to enter any building and room (other than a private residence) and to seize documents, including confidential medical records, to verify that these documents and supporting interactions were conducted in French. The adoption of the bill has been heavily protested, notably by English-speaking Kanien'keha:ka and Cree Nations, and Julius Grey, a prominent human rights lawyer in the province, called it "the most gratuitous use of power" he's ever seen. See Ian Austen, "Law Requiring French in Quebec Becomes Stricter," *The New York Times* (New York, NY), May 24, 2022, https://www.nytimes.com/2022/05/24/world/canada/quebec-language-bill-96.html.

[13] See Quebec Government. "Projet de loi sur la langue officielle et commune du Québec, le français," 2022, http://www2.publicationsduquebec.gouv.qc.ca/dynamicSearch/telecharge.php?type=5&file=2022C14F.PDF.

the idea that languages (in the case of Quebec, the French language specifically) are fixed, bounded, distinct systems that are and that must stay mutually exclusive. From the "chasse aux anglicismes" and the general condemnation of "linguistic interference" to repeated observations about the "genius of the language" or the "naturalness" of this or that expression in this or that language to the very prescriptive ways in which we evaluate, revise, and correct translations—simply put, according to the number of "mistakes" they contain—professional translation training and practices are for the most part articulated around the goal of attaining and maintaining linguistic purity, to the point where translators are seen as the holders of the legitimate norm.[14] As Sherry Simon puts it, "a significant portion of translation has this primary function: to guarantee the citizens' unilingualism. Translation establishes and confirms the norms of proper, acceptable French."[15]

This book emerges out of the realization that translation creates, reproduces, and solidifies the linguistic borders that are mobilized in order to enforce and justify exclusions from a national community and from the rights, resources, and privileges that come with it. How can we reconcile translation, a practice typically centered on linguistic normativity, with growing concerns for social justice and the political conviction that linguistic borders create an exclusionary mechanism that produces and reproduces social inequalities on the basis of language? This book explores the ways in which translation theory and the practice of translation are involved in the production and the reproduction of unjust linguistic "systems" rooted in the policing of social hierarchies disguised as ahistorical and apolitical linguistic categories. In other words, its aim is to explore how day-to-day, small-scale decisions, such as labeling a word an "anglicism" and condemning that word as such, are connected to "supralinguistic concepts that become disguised as linguistic ones."[16] Choices translators make every day are thus both the products of these linguistic ideologies and the tools that serve to produce, maintain, and reinforce them.

To explore the impact of linguistic normativity within the fields of translation theory and practice, this book turns to contemporary literary works published in Canada that are written in decidedly nonnormative, nonmonolingual ways. Whether these texts are written in what we tend

---

[14] Matthieu LeBlanc, "Traduction, bilinguisme et langue de travail: une étude de cas au sein de la fonction publique fédérale canadienne," *Meta* 59, no. 1 (2014): 537–56.
[15] Sherry Simon, *Le trafic des langues: traduction et culture dans la littérature québécoise* (Montréal: Boréal, 1994), 51.
[16] Thomas Bonfiglio, *Mother Tongues and Nations: The Invention of the Native Speaker* (Berlin: De Gruyter Mouton, 2010), 1.

to recognize as several "languages," "registers," or "dialects," they all offer linguistic landscapes that do not correspond to the conventional, predominant mapping of languages along ethnonational lines (for instance, German, Italian, English, French). The notion of linguistic cartography refers to the mapping, onto fluid and disordered linguistic practices, of not only relatively fixed and ordered linguistic categories, such as "English" or "French," but also "African American Vernacular English," "Québécois French," "Acadian French," and even literary "registers" such as "formal" and "informal." The concept of "enregisterment" is useful here in thinking about the ways in which communicative practices come to index styles, identities, genres, dialects, and even languages. As Asif Agha argues, "to speak of 'registers' is to speak of a sociohistorical-snapshot of a process of enregisterment,"[17] rather than of a fixed and natural category of linguistic forms. Enregisterment is understood as a social process whereby linguistic items are analyzed and organized as cultural models of action, as "behaviors capable of indexing stereotypic characteristics of incumbents of particular interactional roles."[18] Whenever the notions of "languages" or "registers" are used throughout this book, they refer to the naturalized products of a specific process of enregisterment, or linguistic mapping, rather than to a reified linguistic category or system.

As we will see in the first chapter, the dominant linguistic cartographies with which we grapple today are intricately connected to the demands of the modern nation-state. Indeed, the "one nation, one language" model led, particularly in the nineteenth century, to the creation of national languages through the conceptual mapping of sets of linguistic practices along national lines. This, this book argues, is what makes possible the structural understanding of translation as a kind of rewriting that renders a text from "one language" to "another." The texts analyzed in the following chapters, however, present us with linguistic forms and elements not usually associated with the national languages of French or English—the two official, colonial languages of the Canadian state, which also figure as the two dominant languages of (monolingual) literary publication in Canada. What other kinds of linguistic mapping, outside of this colonial and national cartography of language(s), then, do these texts point to? And is it not possible, and in fact desirable, for translation to follow these alternative, postnational cartographies of language?

---

[17] Asif Agha, "Enregisterment and Communication in Social History," *Registers of Communication* 18 (2015): 27.
[18] Ibid.

Writing and Translating in Settler Colonial Canada

The Canadian linguistic context offers an interesting ground for asking and thinking about these questions, for several reasons. First, Canada is known for its policies of official bilingualism at the federal level, which grant official recognition, state support and institutionalization, and public visibility and legitimacy to the French and English languages, despite the immense linguistic diversity the Canadian state hosts. As Eve Haque has shown, official bilingualism in the Canadian context is a policy that "extends collective language rights only to official-language groups, justified through the purported openness of language and the [individual] 'freedom' of other ethnic groups to integrate by way of official-language competence."[19] In that sense, it is a tool of "state management of populations on the terrain of language"[20] central to the white settler nation-building project. Furthermore, official bilingualism at the state level does not translate, for the most part, into bilingualism at the provincial, local, or individual levels: as Denise Merkle and Gillian Lane-Mercier observe, the local level is generally characterized by official and public monolingualism, which is what gives rise to the idea of the "two solitudes," supposedly coexisting side by side.[21] We see this clearly in the context of largely monolingual (French) Quebec or largely monolingual (English) Ontario, as well as in the monolingual logics that largely define the two distinct (French/English) literary industries in so-called[22] Canada. Almost all publishers, distributors, and bookstores in Canada indeed operate monolingually, publishing a number of writers from different linguistic

---

[19] Eve Haque, *Multiculturalism within a Bilingual Framework: Language, Race, and Belonging in Canada* (Toronto: University of Toronto Press, 2012), 237.

[20] Monica Heller, "Socioeconomic Junctures, Theoretical Shifts: A Genealogy of Language Policy and Planning Research," in *The Oxford Handbook of Language Policy and Planning*, ed. James W. Tollefson and Miguel Pérez-Milans (Oxford Handbooks Online, 2018), https://www.oxfordhandbooks.com/view/10.1093/oxfordhb/9780190458898.001.0001/oxfordhb-9780190458898-e-6.

[21] Denise Merkle and Gillian Lane-Mercier, "Towards an Ethos of Diversity," in *Minority Languages, National Languages, and Official Language Policies*, ed. Denise Merkle, Gillian Lane-Mercier, and Jane Koustas (Montreal/Kingston: McGill-Queen's University Press, 2018), 9.

[22] The expression "so-called Canada" is used to bring attention to the colonial, artificial, and ideological nature of the name "Canada" when used to describe a territory or variety of territories that have been named and continue to be named differently, most notably by Indigenous peoples. Indeed, the territory we know today as Canada already bore various Indigenous names that were erased, negated, and replaced as European powers and settlers claimed the land for themselves. As such, the name "Canada" itself reveals a colonial perspective; the qualifier "so-called" is used throughout this book to make that perspective visible as well as to challenge the perceived objectivity or neutrality of dominant, colonial placenames we tend to take for granted.

backgrounds and packaging a vast array of linguistic practices under the homogeneous umbrella of either "English" or "French."

What's more, official bilingualism (re)produces English and French as fundamentally, ontologically, naturally distinct. This is because the very notion of bilingualism—or multilingualism—conceives of languages as fixed, delineated, and mutually exclusive codes. This supposedly a priori and natural linguistic differentiation is precisely what makes translation both possible and necessary. It thus comes as no surprise that, with translation programs in at least twelve universities countrywide, a federal Translation Bureau that employs hundreds of translators, and a variety of translation grants, professional orders, and publications, conferences, and events on translation, Canada is one of the world's leading countries when it comes to translation—training, technology, theory, professional activity, and so on. Thus, bilingualism and translation go hand in hand in Canada: on the one hand, as the focus on the coexistence of two bounded linguistic systems, bilingualism is what makes translation possible; on the other, translation, commonly understood as the rendering of an utterance from one language to another, in turn makes state bilingualism possible by (re)producing monolingual texts and, consequently, subjects.

Third, both Canada and Quebec are currently the stage of strong challenges to their national narratives and accompanying language politics presented by Indigenous people, francophone communities outside of and anglophone communities within Quebec, and high levels of immigration. Not only does the ever-diversifying population of Canada and Quebec challenge the exclusive association of the nation with one (or two) language(s), but also Indigenous critiques of settler colonialism are increasingly putting into question the very legitimacy of the Canadian state and its various orders of government. On the grounds of language alone, Indigenous communities rightly remind us that English and French were brought to and forcefully imposed on Turtle Island through genocidal and assimilationist practices, and that neither is the "only linguistic matrix" of this land, as Rioux would have it. In fact, what some of us call Canada has always been a highly complex linguistic region, with numerous languages and great linguistic diversity, including over seventy recognized Indigenous languages falling into twelve different language families, many of which are endangered because of a history of colonial policies such as the *Indian Act* and residential "schools" that denigrated and prohibited the speaking of these languages until as late as 1997. As an example, the number of fluent speakers of the Wolastoqey language is currently estimated at less than 100—out of roughly 9,000 registered members of the Wolastoqey nation, whose unceded lands the province of New Brunswick occupies today.

For context, the ravages brought by the residential school system upon Indigenous communities are such that in 2007, the Truth and Reconciliation Commission of Canada (TRC)[23] was established in response to the Indian Residential Schools Settlement Agreement—an agreement between the Government of Canada and approximately 86,000 Indigenous individuals who at some point were enrolled in the residential school system. After it provided those directly or indirectly affected by the legacy of residential schools with an opportunity to share their stories and experiences, the TRC released its six-volume report in 2015, including ninety-four calls to action to further "reconciliation" between settler Canadians and Indigenous peoples. Out of these ninety-four calls to action, only thirteen have been completed as of December 2022, according to the CBC.[24] For instance, the Indigenous Languages Act, which is aimed at restoring and maintaining fluency in Indigenous languages, was passed in 2019 in response to Call to Action 14, even though sufficient funding and initiatives, as well as tangible results, have yet to follow. At the university where I teach in Moncton, New Brunswick, the Call to Action 16, which calls upon postsecondary institution to create degree programs in Aboriginal languages, has not yet been implemented. In any case, there are many areas where government work is falling short, notably when it comes to language rights, funding, and politics. Further, as the Yellowhead Institute has observed, "no meaningful plans have been implemented that promise to reverse the disproportionate number of Indigenous peoples in Canada's prisons or, for that matter, to close the health care gap that leads to shorter life expectancy for Indigenous peoples."[25] And so, while the TRC has been key in educating a lot of Canadians on the topic of the history and legacy of the residential school system, as well as in shifting the national conversation in meaningful ways, tangible changes and improvements in the lives and

---

[23] Since the focus of this book in no way relates to state-sanctioned efforts toward reconciliation with Indigenous peoples, this very brief discussion of the TRC is provided here merely to introduce unfamiliar readers to the Canadian context and is far from exhaustive. To anyone interested in learning more about the history and legacy of the residential school system and of genocidal and assimilationist practices and policies toward Indigenous people in Canada, I strongly recommend the reading of the TRC's official reports, which can be found on the National Centre for Truth and Reconciliation website: https://nctr.ca/records/reports/.
[24] Canadian Broadcast Corporation, "Beyond 94," updated June 8, 2022, https://www.cbc.ca/newsinteractives/beyond-94?&cta=1. The number of completed calls to action is even lower (eleven) according to two independent organizations, the Yellowhead Institute and the Indigenous Watchdog.
[25] Eva Jewell and Ian Mosby, "Calls to Action Accountability: A Status Update on Reconciliation," The Yellowhead Institute, December 17, 2019, https://yellowheadinstitute.org/2019/12/17/calls-to-action-accountability-a-status-update-on-reconciliation/.

material conditions of Indigenous peoples across the country remain, for the most part, to be seen. As such, past and ongoing state negligence and outright violence toward Indigenous peoples serve as a reminder that the Canadian nation-state is perhaps not the benevolent, friendly place it is often portrayed as.

Echoing the empirical plurality of voices and linguistic practices found on this territory, as well as the challenges made to a "unified," "legitimate" view of the Canadian (or Québécois) nation, more and more literary texts published within the confines of the Canadian state transgress the "one text, one language" model of writing. Indeed, in recent years many books of fiction and poetry published in Canada, especially by queer, racialized, and Indigenous writers, have challenged the structural notions of linguistic autonomy and singularity that underlie not only the formation of the nation-state but also the bulk of Western translation theory and the field of comparative literature. Such is the case, for instance, of Leanne Betasamosake Simpson, a Michi Saagiig Nishnaabeg writer from Alderville First Nation, and of Joshua Whitehead, an Oji-Cree writer from Peguis First Nation, who "smuggle" unauthorized linguistic forms into their official language of publication, English.

It is no coincidence that writers such as Simpson and Whitehead challenge us to reconsider the traditional monolingual logics of writing. As Indigenous writers, they are particularly attuned to the monologic, colonial mechanisms of exclusion and assimilation on which the settler state relies, including on the terrain of language, to justify its ongoing dispossession of Indigenous peoples. By infusing a colonial language with various linguistic forms associated with other languages and creating effects of illegibility and opacity, these writers enact a refusal to be good, monolingually intelligible national subjects. It is also worth noting that, to my knowledge, all writers analyzed in this book but one are openly queer, and they all write from the margin(s) of the nation-state in one way or another: Gregory Scofield is a gay Métis poet, France Daigle a queer Acadian novelist from Moncton, Kevin Lambert a gay writer from rural Quebec, Joshua Whitehead a Two-Spirit writer from Peguis First Nation, Nathanaël a genderqueer writer, Oana Avasilichioaei a queer Romanian immigrant living in Quebec, Leanne Betasamosake Simpson an Anishinaabe writer and scholar, and Georgette LeBlanc an Acadian poet from Saint-Mary's Bay, a small francophone community in Nova Scotia.

Unsurprisingly, this shared experience of queerness and marginalization within a corpus centered on nonnormative ways of writing echoes a number of theoretical interventions, which suggest that queer writers have a particularly fraught relationship with linguistic norms and normativity, and that sexuality shapes what is said and how it is said.[26] Given that (nonconformist) queer writers tend to actively transgress gender and sexual norms to various extents, it is not surprising that they would be more inclined to subvert normativity on other fronts, for example, on the grounds of language.[27] As a result, the linguistic assemblages that make up their works do not follow national lines, and this makes it impossible to locate a linguistic border that translation would simply cross. What to do, then, with such texts in translation? If translation is commonly understood as the rendering of a text from one language to another, what happens when the text one is translating is not written in "one language"?

In fact, what if *no* text is ever written in a single language? What if "English"—or "French" or "bilingualism" or "multilingual writing"—were simply "only one perspective on a more complex set of practices which draw on linguistic resources that have been conventionally thought of as belonging to separate systems because of our dominant linguistic ideologies?"[28] What do linguistic categories such as English and French hide when we apply them uncritically to texts that are, perhaps, not at all written according to these categories' logics? What if these languages are the order that editors, readers, and translators impose, more or less successfully, on the linguistic forms and resources they work with, and not the other way around?

The works that will be analyzed throughout this book would all be typically labeled "multilingual," that is, they draw on linguistic resources and forms that are considered to fall "outside" of their conventional language of publication, be it English or French. These works were all published between 2005 and 2020; as such, they are contemporary to the debate on Franglais discussed earlier. Furthermore, they were all published by Canadian publishing houses, which means that they are produced, published, and marketed within

---

[26] An entire field is dedicated to the relationship between language use and the construction and display of sexual identities, usually organized under the terms "Language and Sexuality" or "Language and Gender." See, for instance, Deborah Cameron and Don Kulick, *Language and Sexuality* (Cambridge: Cambridge University Press, 2003), for a thorough review of the field, and Kira Hall and Rusty Barrett (eds.), *The Oxford Handbook of Language and Sexuality* (New York: Oxford University Press, 2018), for various case studies, approaches, and interventions.

[27] That is not to say that all queer and transgender writers are critical of social norms, be they linguistic or sexual. Of course, members of the LGBTQ+ community can live deeply normative lives and abide by certain norms (e.g., marriage, the gender binary, etc.), and some queer writers do write in completely monolingual, normative ways. The argument here is that nonnormative queer writers, those who actively and deliberately disrupt sexual and gendered norms in their daily lives and in their works, will tend to be more critical of all kinds of norms, including linguistic ones.

[28] Monica Heller, "Bilingualism as Ideology and Practice," in *Bilingualism: A Social Approach*, ed. Monica Heller (London: Palgrave Macmillan, 2007), 15.

the same national, settler colonial, bi/monolingual framework. Be they Indigenous, immigrants, working class, racialized, or queer, the writers who appear throughout this book fail, in one way or another, at being the good white, heterosexual settler subject of the Canadian nation-state. Importantly for the argument of this book, they *deliberately* fail at being a monolingually intelligible subject in their writings. Above all else, this refusal of transparent legibility according to the monolingual logics of the state is what these writers have in common—not French or English. Despite their differences, Gregory Scofield, France Daigle, Kevin Lambert, Joshua Whitehead, Nathanaël, Oana Avasilichioaei, Leanne Betasamosake Simpson, and Georgette LeBlanc reveal the work of linguistic differentiation (and, consequently, of translation) as normative, hierarchical, and violent, inasmuch as it imposes a linguistic order on texts that explicitly refuse to conform to that order.

Rather than asking how we can translate the "vernacular" aspects or the presence of "languages" or "registers" other than the standard ones in these texts, as others have done,[29] this book turns to literary works to problematize the very foundations of translation, an activity theorized as taking place *between languages* and, as such, as dependent on reified linguistic difference. For this reason, this book turns its gaze away from the field of translation studies, as well as the actual activity of translation, because, as will be shown in the first chapter, these two fields are deeply defined according to a structural understanding of language as a fixed, bounded system. As such, this book is not strictly about translation or translation studies per se— with the exception of the concluding chapter—but about what is revealed when we refuse to take the national cartographies of language, and more generally the notion of language as bounded system, as givens. Hence, the texts featured in the subsequent chapters will be analyzed not from the point of view, strictly speaking, of translation but as texts that raise fundamental questions about the borders of language—especially with regard to particular subject positions—and, as such, about the very understanding of translation.

This book, in short, takes the form of literary critique and asks a twofold question: Why do these writers, from their own subject positions, write in nonmonolingual ways? And, what is hidden when we approach, label,

---

[29] See, for instance, Ellen Jones, *Literature in Motion: Translating Multilingualism Across the Americas* (New York: Columbia University Press, 2022); Remy Attig, "Transnational Translation: Reflections on Translating from Judeo-Spanish and Spanglish," *TTR* 32, no. 2 (2019): 61–80; Alex Gauthier, "These foreign c*nts've goat trouble wi the Queen's f*ckin English, ken, our é-énoncer la voix scots de *Trainspotting* au moyen du Québec et de la (socio-)linguistique," *TTR* 28, no. 1–2 (2017): 207–37; Anick Chapdelaine and Gillian Lane-Mercier, *Faulkner: Une expérience de retraduction* (Montréal: Presses de l'Université de Montreal, 2001).

and treat nonmonolingual texts as monolingual? The aim is, through the invocation of literary texts deployed as deductive tools, to reconsider the undemocratic underpinnings of translation, an activity governed by the idea that languages are distinct and should be kept so, as well as to discover what other kinds of linguistic mappings translation can produce and enact. The texts that make up this book's corpus are thus considered not only as objects of knowledge but also as sources, or producers, of knowledge. As such, the objective is not to merely apply theoretical frameworks to literary texts but also to gain theoretical insight from these texts by treating them "as formative in their own right, as representations that summon up new ways of seeing rather than as echoes or distortions of predetermined political truths."[30]

Outline of the Book

This book is comprised of five chapters. Chapter 1 sets the theoretical grounds for the following chapters by deconstructing the analytical and linguistic categories that make a structural understanding of language and translation possible. It begins by reviewing the conventional perception of language in the field of translation by describing the formally trained Canadian translator's habitus and reveals a strong attachment, both in translation training and in translation theory, to the structural understanding of language. As will be illustrated in this first chapter, in the field of translation this understanding takes the form of three axioms, which go as follows: (1) translation is only possible between "standard" varieties of language, (2) translation is the rendering of a text from one (bounded) language to another, and (3) the ideal directionality of translation is from one's "second language" to one's "native language." The rest of the chapter is concerned with the theoretical deconstruction of these axioms and the structural linguistic mapping that supports them, drawing on a range of sociolinguistic accounts, queer theories, and literary criticism that will reveal several major concepts—such as "standard language" or "mother tongue"—to be fundamentally ideological rather than empirical. The chapter also engages with theoretical interventions in the field of translation studies with regard to "multilingual," "heterolingual," or "translingual" texts, from which this book both draws and departs in its framing of these texts as explicitly heteroglossic, deterritorialized, and postlingual. As we will see, approaching literary texts without falling back on the notion of language as system forces us to give

---

[30] Rita Felski, *Uses of Literature* (Hoboken: Wiley-Blackwell, 2008), 9–10.

up the field of translation as it is currently constituted and to reimagine it on altogether different grounds. Moreover, seeing translation as a practice of linguistic mapping in itself suggests that it is possible to (re)map linguistic practices otherwise, beyond the normative linguistic categories we are used to. To help us imagine alternative configurations for translation, the following three chapters each tackle one of the three translation axioms by engaging with some of the postnational, anti-colonial, and queer linguistic mappings that contemporary literary works published in Canada have to offer.

Chapter 2 addresses axiom 1: "translation is only possible between standard varieties of language," tackling the idea of "standard language" by turning to the poems (2005–16) of Gregory Scofield, a Métis of Cree and Scottish descent, as well as to the novel *Pour sûr* (2010) by France Daigle, an Acadian writer from Moncton, New Brunswick. Scofield's and Daigle's writings grapple, both thematically and formally, with the forces and pressures of standard language ideology. Both writers construct an explicitly normative, homogeneous, and oppressive linguistic standard, which they pit against fluid, diverse, and fundamentally social linguistic practices. In other words, their texts thematize the clash between norm and usage, highlighting both the deeply problematic nature of the cult of the standard in terms of its social and material consequences and the fact that written linguistic practices, including translation practices, are themselves a fundamentally and primarily social phenomenon. Both writers signal a move away from the abstraction of language and toward the localized embodiment of linguistic practices in writing. By addressing the oppressive nature of unitary, standardized language—in terms of its silencing of Indigenous voices in Scofield and in terms of the linguistic insecurity and dispossession it causes in Daigle—both writers ask translation to leave linguistic normativity behind and to draw instead on the rich variability and fluidity of linguistic practices, observable or imagined. They point to an understanding of translation as a fundamentally social practice, which involves seeing both the source and the target texts as drawing from a set of linguistic and expressive resources that circulate in specific social and discursive spaces and whose meaning and value are socially constructed under particular historical, cultural, and political conditions that are to be taken into account.

Chapter 3 addresses axiom 2: "translation is the rendering of a text from one language to another," as it explores the notion of linguistic difference in Chicoutimi-born writer Kevin Lambert's novel *Querelle de Roberval* (2018) and in Oji-Cree writer Joshua Whitehead's novel *Jonny Appleseed* (2018) and poetry collection *full-metal indigiqueer* (2017). With a focus on the notion of explicitly heteroglossic writing as writing that embraces the linguistic abject (i.e., linguistic forms considered foreign, corrupt, threatening), this chapter shows that both writers thematically and materially smuggle the linguistic abject into the imperial language in which they respectively publish, thus calling for the perpetual "queering," or disrupting, of any normative language understood as bounded entity. Much like the queer, for Lambert and Whitehead language is "never fully owned, but always and only redeployed, twisted, queered from a prior usage and in the direction of urgent and expanding political purposes."[31] Bringing the linguistic abject into a dominant, normative language functions first as a strategy that refuses to participate in the reproduction of fixed, established, often oppressive linguistic categories by deliberately "contaminating" them. But welcoming the linguistic abject also points to a gesture of inclusion rather than exclusion: in Lambert's and Whitehead's works, less normative, more inclusive cartographies of language emerge through an address that does not prioritize transparent communication to a homogenous linguistic community. As we will see, Whitehead's heteroglossic language introduces various linguistically abject elements into English, creating an effect of illegibility which produces for the reader a kind of failure, that is, a "failure to assimilate the Other into cultural and political discourses that appropriate its difference."[32] On the other hand, the rural and working-class Québécois linguistic forms in *Querelle de Roberval*, while they certainly function as normative, metropolitan French's linguistic abject, occupy a fraught structural position in Quebec because of their relation to ethnolinguistic nationalism there. In that sense, Lambert's novel reads as a cautionary tale that previously abjected practices can also become a new norm in themselves, excluding other forms of linguistic life in the process. For both writers, the welcoming of the linguistic abject is best seen not as an end in itself but as the constant and never-ending necessity of the queering of language, which implies that translation should never rely on fixed linguistic categories and has to constantly reinvent the borders it creates.

Chapter 4 addresses axiom 3, "the ideal directionality of translation is from one's second language to one's native language," exploring the notion of "mother tongue" in the works of two Montreal writers, Nathanaël and Oana Avasilichioaei. Montreal has a long-standing history of (more or less violent) language contact, leading to an experience of the city and its linguistic practices that make its inhabitants particularly aware of the fraught nature of the ethnonational categories which underlie linguistic categories, especially the notion of "native speaker." The writers in this chapter complicate their

---

[31] Judith Butler, *Bodies That Matter* (New York: Routledge, 2011), 237.
[32] Smaro Kamboureli, *Scandalous Bodies: Diasporic Literature in English Canada* (Waterloo: Wilfrid Laurier University Press, 2009), 130.

relationship to their assigned "mother tongue" by appropriating languages that supposedly do not belong to them. Not only do their works complicate the inherent directionality of translation as movement from one language to another, as they are not written in one singular, recognizable, unitary language, but they also force a redefinition of what it means to belong to a language and to refuse the concepts of "domestic" and "foreign." Their texts make it impossible for translation to follow its traditional, prescriptive directionality, which espouses a movement from the Other toward the Self, as the traditional foundations on which this binary rests come undone. Through the concept of "motherless tongues," this chapter shows that by breaking the association between a given language and the social group (or territory) to which it is said to belong—be it on biological or national grounds or according to an assessment of linguistic competence—the grounds on which languages were created and constructed come undone, as these grounds were never linguistic in the first place. Nathanaël and Avasilichioaei, whether they reappropriate certain ways of writing for themselves or challenge their own supposed proprietary control over a language, point to an understanding of language as a collective process, rather than as a fixed product that can be commodified and owned. Here, language is not only deterritorialized, it is also de-spatialized, making it difficult to fix and, consequently, to own.

Drawing on the previous deconstructions of all three axioms, the concluding chapter develops a postlingual approach to translation, where translation is understood as the rendering, or rewriting, of a text not from one language to another but from one linguistic, cultural, social *landscape* to another. The "trans" in translation remains, but the idea of movement or displacement concerns actual (or imagined) physical, material, or virtual places, rather than abstract languages. The "carrying across" of translation needs not occur across a linguistic border; *across* can also be understood as "from one end of something to the other," where the thing to be "crossed" is not a border but a distance. The idea becomes to draw from the resources that make up our immediate linguistic, communicative, and expressive environment, regardless of whether or not they are assigned to a given linguistic system, in order to produce translations that will resonate in that place at the same time that they reproduce the source text's heteroglossia and undermine the (national) language of publication's monopoly and dominance. This will be illustrated by several examples from my own translation practice, taken from my (co)translations of Leanne Betasamosake Simpson's books, as well as from Acadian poet Georgette LeBlanc's translation of Sue Goyette's *Ocean*.

Ultimately, this book points to a general undoing of languages understood as distinct and unitary and urges us to move away from imagined communities that are based on an abstract "language" that we—readers, publics, communities—supposedly share. The writers who have instigated this undoing refuse national mappings of language because these mappings create exclusions by drawing a line between linguistic practices and speakers who are deemed legitimate, and those who are not, and by using that line to justify the exclusion of the latter. Pierre Bourdieu has argued, for instance, that the relationship between the linguistic product performed by a socially positioned speaker and the products simultaneously available in the surrounding social setting is one of value.[33] The legitimate language is constituted by the forms that are the most valued and thus functions as linguistic capital, which evidently translates into economic, social, cultural, and symbolic capital.

The texts analyzed throughout the book take us away from the idea of legitimate language by representing in their works various positions of enunciation typically associated with linguistic illegitimacy. They do so, this book suggests, in order to create a space for practices and speakers that are excluded from the public space of the nation and, thus, from capital. They explore, through writing, alternative ways to address, create, and maintain communities that do not reproduce the exclusions they write against. Written "in anticipation of a future that radically departs from the present" and "signaling something more than the cheap limits of what is possible,"[34] these texts show that it is possible to exist as a community without a "shared language" that is fixed, policed, and exclusionary. Their authors do so by writing from various, fluid, and changing positions of enunciation, revealing the inherent heterogeneity of both individuals and collectivities and suggesting that what we share is not a common language but a condition of partial illegibility, opacity, and difference.

The fugitive-like aspect of language in the works analyzed in the following chapters—their constant queering, their playful qualities, their lack of resolution, their refusal to master language—suggests the possibility—the end goal, perhaps—of producing translations that are also unrecognizable as a distinct, unitary language and thus unintelligible to settler colonial monolingualism. Rather than translating "from English" and "into French," seeing the source text as being constituted from a variety of socially meaningful resources picked by the writers from their own linguistic surroundings allows us to replicate this heteroglossia in translation as well, whether or not it complies with the rules of any target language. This move

---

[33] Pierre Bourdieu, *Langage et pouvoir symbolique* (Paris: Éditions du Seuil, [2001] 2014).
[34] Sarah Dowling, "Conflicting Englishes: Cheap Signaling and Vernacular Poetry," *Jacket2*, January 20, 2015, https://jacket2.org/commentary/conflicting-englishes.

away from idealized, abstract languages in the gesture of translation, in turn, forces a focus on the singularity and the relationality of the encounters, both between the translator and the text they are translating and between the translator and their linguistic surroundings or landscape or, in other words, their community. This leads us to a decidedly more localized, subjective practice of translation that draws on the translator's specific embodied and territorialized experience.

Ultimately, the deconstruction of the notion of language as a fixed, bounded system leads us to consider a postlingual approach to translation, understood as the rendering or rewriting of a text not from one language to another but from one linguistic *landscape* to another. A postlingual approach to translation does not impose normative linguistic categories on linguistic practices that are inherently heteroglossic and fluid, positing instead that translation does not necessarily need to happen along the lines of "different languages." Translation is best understood as a social practice which deals with and draws from (at least) two sets of socially meaningful linguistic, communicative, and expressive resources that can (and often do) overlap. To use the famous phrasing, then, the task of the translator is to produce the same, yet always different, positions of enunciation the author chose to represent on the page, within the set of linguistic resources that are available to them, rather than reproducing normative linguistic categories.

1

Translation as Mapping

Denaturalizing National Cartographies of Language

> Never let constructions of language and tradition masquerade as cartographies for the real.
> —Richard Bauman and Charles L. Briggs, *Voices of Modernity*

This chapter deconstructs the analytical categories that make a structural understanding of language and translation possible by calling for the denaturalization of the linguistic systems (French, English, etc.) as we know them today. First, it reviews the conventional perception of language in the field of translation by describing the formally trained Canadian translator's habitus, which will reveal a strong attachment, both in translation training and in translation theory, to the structural understanding of language as well as to naturalized linguistic categories. Concretely, I suggest that this attachment takes the form of the three following axioms in translation theory and practice: (1) translation is only possible between "standard" varieties of language, (2) translation is the rendering of a text from one language to another, and (3) the ideal directionality of translation is from one's "second language" to one's "native language." Drawing on sociolinguistic accounts and on queer theory's use of the concept of abjection, these axioms will be deconstructed one at a time and exposed as fundamentally ideological. The chapter then engages with the field of translation studies and its notions of "multilingual," "heterolingual," or "translingual" texts, from which this book departs in its framing of these texts as explicitly heteroglossic and deterritorialized, drawing on the work of Naoki Sakai, Mikhail Bakhtin, and Gilles Deleuze and Félix Guattari. Whereas most accounts in translation studies frame linguistically diverse texts as a problem for translation, this chapter turns such logic on its head, suggesting that the problem lies not in said texts but, rather, in the structural definition of translation we have been working with all along. As we will see, approaching literary texts without falling back on the notion of language as system forces us to give up the field of translation as it is currently constituted and to reimagine it on different grounds. Ultimately, translation will be considered as a practice of linguistic mapping, suggesting that it is possible, perhaps even ideal, to map linguistic practices differently through translation.

Becoming a Translator

The scholarly field of translation studies is, of course, intricately connected to the actual, on the ground practice of translation, as it often analyzes and explores actual translations written by practitioners. Much of translation studies, indeed, relies on translators as the producers of its objects of study. Thus, translators' practice of translation, informed by the field of translation studies, in turn, becomes the basis of that field. In order to better understand the common (mis)conceptions of language that have come to populate the field, this chapter starts at the beginning of the production chain: the formal training of professional translators, as described by various translation textbooks (English to French) that are widely used in translation programs in Canada. A discursive analysis of these textbooks will show that they are deeply informed by (at times blatant) linguistic ideologies rather than empirical or verifiable linguistic realities.

Often, these textbooks present their readers with observations about the nature of translation or the nature of the French language that are far from substantiated. For instance, the introduction of the twice republished *En français dans le texte*, by Robert Dubuc, reads more like Christian Rioux's panicked, knee-jerk reaction to Franglais than like an empirical examination of the actual state of French in Quebec:

> The purpose of this work is to serve as *a clear and definitive corrective to the French spoken and written in Quebec and Canada*. . . . Our objective is to promote the use of correct French in our written communication. Linguists, in general, evidently do not hold this corrective effort in high esteem. But the law of live and let live that has been established has led us to the threshold of *intellectual bankruptcy*.
>
> Graduate students are often unable to compose dissertations or theses in comprehensible language. Engineers and other liberal professionals get caught up in the difficulty of editing reports, which have become illegible in *the absence of any minimal amount of linguistic correctness*. Businesses are, morally, tearing their hair out in the face of the

impossibility of ensuring even a minimal effectiveness in internal written communication. . . . It is necessary to take a sharp turn.

This modest work does not claim, in and of itself, to correct a situation that will require other powerful tools. Although it does not aspire to reconstruct the whole building, it does come bearing a few stones.[1]

In Dubuc's introduction, French as it is spoken and written in Canada is presented as deviant, in dire need of correction. Apparently, the situation is such that no one understands anyone else anymore; the state of affairs Dubuc describes—without providing any evidence—is one of complete linguistic chaos. French appears as a destroyed edifice that we must reconstruct; and Dubuc's modest contribution, centered on "la chasse aux brebis galeuses"[2] (literally, "the pursuit of mangy sheep," the term he uses to refer to anglicisms), is a move designed to address this apparently pressing matter. Concerns about the supposed decline or corruption of French aside, the burden of linguistic preservation seems to fall on the shoulders of individual speakers, understood here specifically as translators. This attitude is evident in most, if not all, French translation textbooks in Canada, which are explicitly corrective and prescriptive in nature.

These attitudes imply that taking the institutionalized, formal road to professional translation training involves becoming familiar with a deeply ingrained structural understanding of language, according to which languages are self-contained, self-regulating systems comprised of interconnected units and delimited by relatively fixed boundaries. This view of translation suggests a highly prescriptive, purist vision of language such as the one described earlier, as it frames linguistic rules as neutral and objective, even natural, since they are thought to emanate from the linguistic system itself. It is also this understanding of language which supports the understanding of translation as "the activity or process of changing the words of one language into the words in another language that have the same meaning."[3] According to this definition, which corresponds to the commonplace understanding in translation training and practice at large, languages are naturally distinct entities, or systems, separated by a border which the translator crosses.

---

[1] Robert Dubuc, *En français dans le texte* (Montréal: Linguatech, 2000), xviii. Emphasis added.
[2] The sheep metaphor also points to the idea of *pure laine* (literally, pure wool), which refers to individuals whose ancestry is exclusively French Canadian. The notion of "pure" breeding is applied here to linguistic use, suggesting that "sick" elements can compromise the integrity and lineage of French.
[3] Cambridge Dictionary Online, https://dictionary.cambridge.org/dictionary/english/translation.

An interesting illustration of this understanding of translation as the rendering of a text *from one language to another language* is the image gracing the cover of the third edition of *La traduction raisonnée: Manuel d'initiation à la traduction professionnelle de l'anglais vers le français* (first published in 1993, now in its third edition published in 2013), the leading translation textbook used in French translation programs across Canada, as shown in Figure 1.1.

Figure 1.1 The cover of *La traduction raisonnée* (2013). Reproduced with the permission of the University of Ottawa Press.

The cover shows a human figure walking on a tightrope, holding a long pole in its hands, metaphorically presenting the translator as walking, carefully and skillfully, on the line between two languages. This image brings to mind the notion of translator as mediator between two separate entities as well as the pitfalls of failing to follow the traditional scripts of translation according to a clear linguistic boundary. In the blue, abstract background, two wavy lines—one red, one yellow on the original cover, here reproduced in different shades of grey—cut across the cover, beginning and ending at the same spots at the opposite edges of the cover, following similar curves, even crossing on two occasions, but always remaining discrete. The lines function as a metaphor for languages, texts, or people (the author/translator pair, perhaps); in any case, they appear as already autonomous entities following a similar trajectory but always remaining discrete.

The idea of the border is indeed central to common contemporary understandings of translation. As Sherry Simon puts it, "an operation of translation can only be made if there is a border to cross. The border guarantees a language's internal coherence, and makes possible its reproduction in another linguistic and cultural area."[4] In translation textbooks and in most of Western translation theory, linguistic boundaries appear as ahistorical, apolitical borders which translators must identify and respect. The following example, taken from another textbook taught in translation programs, sprinkles the idea of a natural-like state of linguistic difference, along with a good dose of personification and linguistic relativity: "This text to be translated is in English, a language that does not see reality with the same lens as French. The student must be aware of the differences between these two linguistic systems (linguistic and stylistic features). Such is the task of the translator."[5]

Differences between two given linguistic systems appear as given and unquestioned facts, while the translator's task is to learn to recognize and identify them. *La traduction raisonnée* tells the same story, as author and translation scholar Jean Delisle states that the first and most important of the translator's four fundamental abilities is "the ability to dissociate languages (to know how to avoid interferences)."[6] Languages are given, ontologically distinct entities delineated by what is imagined to be a fixed, clear line that the translator needs to learn to locate and to cross in a way that reifies

---

[4] Simon, *Le trafic des langues*, 112.
[5] Maurice Rouleau, *Pratique de la traduction: L'approche par questionnement* (Montréal: Linguatech, 2007), xiv.
[6] Jean Delisle, *La traduction raisonnée. Manuel d'initiation à la traduction professionnelle de l'anglais vers le français* (Ottawa: Presses de l'Université d'Ottawa, 2013), 19.

what are taken to be the fundamental differences between languages, that is, without practicing linguistic "interference"—without transferring an item, a rule, or a pattern from one language to the other. In short, linguistic difference precedes translation. This is the widespread Babelian paradigm of translation.[7]

In fact, the pedagogy of translation in Canada still draws massively on the contrastive approach of early translation theory developed in the 1950s and 1960s, which focused on the study of two languages by identifying and contrasting their general and specific differences. Such rule-based, contrastive, and systematic approaches can be explained by the interest in machine translation at the time, notably in the context of the Cold War. Jean-Paul Vinay and Jean Darbelnet's influential *Stylistique comparée du français et de l'anglais* (1958) is a classic example of this linguistics-oriented approach, which has had a tremendous impact on the creation of translation theory as a field. Rohan Anthony Lewis sums up the emergence of translation theory as follows:

> The contrastive approach was particularly influential during the postwar period, when structural linguistics were playing a key role in the development of translation studies. Since translation was understood as an operation on language, conceived in terms of linguistic form (the Saussurean *langue*) rather than linguistic usage (the Saussurean *parole*) (Beaugrande 1994, 9), it seemed natural that structural linguistics could tackle theoretical questions related to translation. Translation was thus defined in relation to languages: source language and target language. However, this definition relied on the structuralist division of languages in "systems," each one distinct from the others.[8]

The idea behind this contrastive approach is to "extract" the differences between languages from a bilingual corpus; the "observed" patterns then turn into a set of prescriptive rules as to what to do and what not to do when writing and/or translating in one or the other. For instance, the authors of

---

[7] See, for instance, George Steiner, *After Babel: Aspects of Language and Translation* (Oxford: Oxford University Press, 1975). The story of the Tower of Babel, at the origins of the multiplicity of languages, posits the fact that different linguistic groups, which are unable to communicate with one another, exist, as they were created by God in order to punish them—which implies, on the other hand, the ideal of a single, common language. It is only from this point on, according to the story, that translation is needed. Thus, translation is framed as the solution to linguistic multiplicity—as a solution that comes after the fact of linguistic differentiation and that seeks to overcome it.

[8] Rohan Anthony Lewis, "Langue métissée et traduction: quelques enjeux théoriques," *Meta* 48, no. 3 (2003): 412.

Stylistique comparée du français et de l'anglais observe bilingual road signs in Montreal, on which, they say, the French has been inadequately translated: "These signs are perfectly clear, but that is not how one would write them in French."[9] One example they give is "Ne pas entrer" in order to translate "Do Not Enter," rather than the more "frequent," and thus "proper," "Défense d'entrer." Here, the guiding principle for accurate translation is not clear communication—as was seemingly Dubuc's concern earlier—since, as the authors point out, these signs do a perfectly good job at making their meanings clear. Rather, the idea is that translation simply should reflect the "natural" laws and patterns of the target language, which seemingly exist beyond human agency.

In short, for many translation theorists at the time, translation was an interlingual process that relied on the supposed symmetry of two languages understood as preexisting and equal entities. Since then, poststructuralist theories have attempted to focus on the notions of source text and target text, rather than source language and target language, and on *parole* rather than *langue*. However, as Lewis explains, the distinction among languages remains crucial for the *trans* in translation theory: indeed, linguistic difference functions as an important marker without which it would be impossible to distinguish between "translation proper" and other similar practices, such as adaptation or rewriting. Roman Jakobson's 1959 typology of translation is a good case in point of how the idea of linguistic difference was central to delineating the field and its object of study in the first place. Jakobson identifies three kinds of translation: (1) intralingual translation, meaning the interpretation of verbal signs by means of other signs *of the same language*; (2) interlingual translation or "translation proper," that is, the interpretation of verbal signs by means of signs *from another language*; and (3) intersemiotic translation, the interpretation of verbal signs by means of a nonverbal sign system such as music.[10] Following Jakobson, translation proper, which is the focus of translation studies and translation theory as opposed to adaptation or rewriting, involves two equivalent messages in "two different codes."[11]

---

[9] Jean-Paul Vinay and Jean Darbelnet, *Stylistique comparée du français et de l'anglais* (Montréal: Beauchemin, 1958), 17. The circular nature of such reasoning is painfully obvious: these textbooks are written in what we recognize as proper French, therefore whatever they say is proper, because they are written in proper French.
[10] Roman Jakobson, "On Linguistic Aspects of Translation," in *On Translation*, ed. Reuben A. Bower (Cambridge, MA: Harvard University Press, 1959), 233.
[11] Ibid.

The understanding of translation as happening between two languages naturally relies on the "notion of linguistic autonomy,"[12] whereby meaning is transferred from one bounded linguistic system to the other. As Reine Meylaerts observes, even in the contemporary field of translation studies and translation theory, "[i]mplicitly or explicitly, translation is still approached as the *full* transposition of *one* (monolingual) source code into *another* (monolingual) target code for the benefit of a *monolingual* target public."[13] She further observes that, since the 1980s, so-called Descriptive Translation Studies has used a "largely binary cultural model in which translations take place between cultures, which are conceived as geographically separate from each other. The general assumption was one of a more or less absolute language barrier between cultures."[14] Supposedly descriptive studies within the field are thus revealed to retain strong ideological attachments to nationalistic and prescriptive views on language and culture and to participate in the creation of the linguistic reality it purports to merely describe. Today, both in translation theory and in translation practice, this inherited understanding of translation and language from decades of scholarship is so ingrained that it is hard to imagine translation differently.

While major theories of translation do not display the same anxiety about threats to linguistic purity that we find in Christian Rioux and Robert Dubuc, the structural understanding of language, which makes possible their purist views, still defines the field to a large extent. As we saw, a view of language as a closed system quickly and quite deeply forms part of the translator's habitus, especially among Canadian translators who work "from English" and "into French," given the fraught historical power imbalances between the social groups associated with these languages in so-called Canada and the widespread idea that the French language is under threat and needs to be constantly protected. The structural understanding of language described earlier is what makes possible a number of assumptions about the nature of translation that circulate widely in translation training, practice, and theorizing. Most evidently, the naturalization of a structural understanding of language takes three major forms within the field, presented here in the form of three axioms:

---

[12] Rusty Barrett, "The Emergence of the Unmarked: Queer Theory, Language Ideology, and Formal Linguistics," in *Queer Excursions: Retheorizing Binaries in Language, Gender, and Sexuality*, ed. Jenny L. Davis, Lil Zimman, and Joshua Raclaw (Oxford: Oxford University Press, 2014), 200.

[13] Reine Meylaerts, "Heterolingualism in/and Translation: How Legitimate Are the Other and His/Her Language?," *Target* 18, no. 1 (2006): 5.

[14] Ibid., 6.

1. Translation is the rendering of a text or utterance from *one language* to *another*, where the two are understood as distinct, that is, as separated by a relatively stable and locatable border. Linguistic difference thus precedes translation and is, in fact, its Babelian prerequisite.
2. Translation is possible only between two linguistic systems of equal value; such linguistic symmetry can only be achieved between *standard languages*. Hence, in translation theory "language" is shorthand for "standard language." This focus on standard languages posits any slippage away from standard forms (think "dialect," "regional," "vernacular," "slang") as a *problem* for translation.
3. Translators should translate into their dominant language, more often than not understood as their "native" language. Translation, because it is understood as a spatial movement *from* and *to* two different languages, is directional, and the prescribed directionality of translation suggests that one should translate from one's "second language" into one's "first language."

At the heart of these three axioms is the notion of a linguistic border, central to the categorization of language into different entities. Yet, this structural understanding of language cannot be the objective description of an empirically observable reality, since no one has ever succeeded in "discovering" the exact location of the boundary between, say, French and English. Instead, the illusion of a border is *created*. For instance, bilingual dictionaries, by their very nature, construct a very material border between an English word and its French equivalent. The same can be said of some literary works, where "foreign" words are italicized, creating a visible border in print. Outside of print, however, linguistic borders are unmarked and thus do not exist, for a border that is not marked or recognized cannot be said to exist. Rather, the notion of language as system as well as the corollary notions of linguistic boundaries and differences are the product of a complex and historical process of bordering,[15] a set of ideological *assumptions* we have come to believe to be true about the workings of language—and which compels you, the reader of this sentence, to register said sentence as written in English. The interconnected axioms described earlier may seem like they are linguistic in nature, but as we delve into the narratives and assumptions that make them possible, it will become clear that they have less to do with

---

[15] The term "bordering" is borrowed from Harsha Walia, who interrogates the formation and function of borders as a spatial and material power structure. She states: "Borders are not fixed or static lines; they are productive regimes concurrently generated by and producing social relations of dominance." Walia, *Border & Rule*, 6.

language and more to do with ethnonationalist power connected to the interests of capital.[16]

As we will see, the kind of normativity, prescriptivism, and purism that populates the field of translation—and which can turn into linguistic delegitimization and social stigmatization, as we will see throughout this chapter—rests on an understanding of language that is rooted in sociohistorical processes which created and naturalized languages as distinct, countable, bounded systems, rather than based on any empirically verifiable existence of these systems. If we have come to understand languages as mappable—that is, understood spatially as bounded systems—it is not because they naturally exist as such; rather, they are the product of a certain kind of mapping,[17] in other words of an active process of boundary making informed by social, ideological, and political forces. It is the borders drawn through this particular mapping that we end up following uncritically in the field of translation when we say, for instance, that a text has been translated from English into French. There is a pressing need, within translation studies and beyond, to expose the naturalization of linguistic categories and to call for their denaturalization as part of a broader project of contesting white supremacy, colonialism, and nationalism. The following section looks into the political and ideological causes and workings of this particular inherited mapping of linguistic practices into distinct, bounded categories, in order to challenge our ingrained attachment to this historical understanding of language, most notably as it plays out in distinguishing between "native" and "non-native" speakers.

The Making of a Language

When Rioux accuses Dead Obies of speaking "a mediocre and shapeless creole," "a non-language,"[18] or when Dubuc equates the supposedly poor quality of French in Canada with an intellectual bankruptcy, they simply reiterate a preexisting value judgment against a kind of linguistic practice that is identified as falling outside the realm of "proper" language (equated with reason, modernity, and progress). Rioux, for instance, pits the "non-language" of Dead Obies against the French and English languages, which

---

[16] See, on this last point, Heller, *Socioeconomic Junctures*, online.
[17] The concept of mapping is inspired by the invocation of "the mapping aspect of language and of translation" in Don Mee Choi's *Translation Is a Mode: Translation Is an Anti-Neocolonial Mode* (Brooklyn: Ugly Duckling Press, 2020).
[18] Rioux, "J'rape," online.

are, he suggests, "great languages of culture." But what counts as a language and what does not? What are the discursive conditions that make it possible for Rioux to make such a claim? As we will see, languages as distinct and delineated entities are the result of an active, deliberate, and politically driven process of linguistic mapping.

The following sections focus on the historical, social, and political conditions and processes that led to the cartographies of language we know today, which identify certain linguistic practices with the label of a given language, while at the same time categorizing other practices as falling outside that label. As we will see in the following pages, imperial languages as we know them—French, English, Spanish—had to undergo a long, complex, and sometimes violent process of sedimentation, which involved, in interconnected ways, the differentiation of linguistic practices, the consecration of certain linguistic forms through their standardization, and the appropriation of these forms by specific social groups. These processes and the resulting notion of language as system are underpinned by an ideological assemblage composed of entangled concepts, processes, and conditions—most notably, modernity, the emergence and consolidation of the nation-state, colonialism, the notion of civilizational progress, the notions of boundedness and purity, Enlightenment rationality, Romantic authenticity, and the idea of mother tongue—which are detailed later in the text.

Constructing the "Proper" Language: Language Standardization

The idea of standard languages is a concept central to translation, one that is rarely questioned or historicized within translation studies. The contributors to the volume *Standard English: The Widening Debate*, although their analyses differ in many key aspects, all seem to achieve consensus on the following observation: the concept of a standard language is a confused and confusing one, and no one really seems to know what, in this case, standard English actually looks like as a linguistic object. According to Hailey Davis, since the seventeenth century the notion has referred to many different things, such as "a 'common core of language,' an ideal or value to be met, the 'true' meanings behind words, the language of the literati, and those items of vocabulary listed in the *Oxford English Dictionary* (*OED*)."[19] In most cases, the word "standard"

---

[19] Hailey Davis, "Typography, Lexicography and the Development of the Idea of 'Standard English,'" in *Standard English: The Widening Debate*, ed. Tony Bex and Richard J. Watts (London: Routledge, Taylor & Francis e-library, 2002), 86.

is typically presented as the desirable level of usage that all users should aspire to achieve, often if not always equated with notions of correctness and excellence. Most importantly, according to James Milroy, standard languages are "fixed and uniform-state idealisations," not empirically verified or verifiable realities.[20] In fact, variationist and sociolinguistic studies alike have shown many times that all languages, including major languages that would appear to be relatively fixed, are variable and volatile phenomena. In other words, languages are, empirically speaking, the opposite of uniform and thus do not exist as distinct entities—which suggests that we merely conventionalize the use of various communicative resources as "different." Yet, the idea that languages exist in static, invariant, and bounded forms still plagues many disciplinary discussions today, even the field of linguistics.[21]

A good way to start unpacking the notion of a standard language is to use the term *standardized* to describe a variety or form of language, which allows us to see it not as a self-contained product but as an arbitrary form that is created and maintained through the continual *process* of standardization. Hence, if we seek to critically engage with the notion of the standard language, it is first and foremost the ideology of standardization as a process that is relevant, not the product-oriented taxonomic labeling of certain forms of speech as standard or nonstandard.[22] According to Tony Bex and Richard J. Watts, "standardisation is best seen as a process driven by spokespeople who have successfully articulated a particular set of social values."[23] Richard Watts has described it as a "deeply entrenched tradition" and as a "social institution."[24] Standardization is a major aspect of state-driven language planning, defined by José Del Valle and Luis Gabriel-Stheeman as "a goal-oriented activity intended to influence people's linguistic behavior and attitudes" as well as to promote a unity of language within a certain population and/or territory in order to govern said territory more easily.[25]

---

[20] James Milroy, "The Consequences of Standardisation in Descriptive Linguistics," in *Standard English: The Widening Debate*, ed. Tony Bex and Richard J. Watts (London: Routledge, Taylor & Francis e-library, 2002), 18.

[21] See Tony Bex and Richard J. Watts, Introduction to *Standard English: The Widening Debate*, ed. Tony Bex and Richard J. Watts (London: Routledge, Taylor & Francis e-library, 2002), 1–15; and José Del Valle and Luis Gabriel-Stheeman, "Nationalism, Hispanismo, and Monoglossic Culture," in *The Battle Over Spanish between 1800 and 2000: Language Ideologies and Hispanic Intellectuals*, ed. José Del Valle and Luis Gabriel-Stheeman (London: Routledge, 2002), 1–13.

[22] Milroy, "The Consequences," 24.

[23] Bex and Watts, Introduction to *Standard English*, 13.

[24] Richard J. Watts, "The Social Construction of Standard English: Grammar Writers as a 'Discourse Community,'" in *Standard English: The Widening Debate*, ed. Tony Bex and Richard J. Watts (London: Routledge, Taylor & Francis e-library, 2002), 66.

[25] Del Valle and Gabriel-Stheeman, "Nationalism," 8.

The process of standardization has by now been studied and researched by numerous scholars, some of whom have suggested that it typically follows a certain trajectory. For instance, Peter Trudgill's taxonomy includes three stages: first, the determination of which forms are deemed to be standard, second, the codification of said forms, and third, their stabilization through prescriptive methods.[26] The first stage entails the selection of existing features that will serve as the model, and the second stage codifies and fixes the chosen forms through the development of descriptive and prescriptive grammar, lexicography, orthography, and "accent." Finally, the third stage ensures that the selected and codified form is socially stabilized, mostly through its circulation in public education, the media, and so on, and, if we consider another typology developed by Susan Gal, with significant help from a consenting or participating population. Gal similarly identifies five stages: "(a) selection or invention of a linguistic variety as a source of norms; (b) codification of the norms; (c) elaboration of norms, especially in literature but also in signage, schooling and government; (d) building prestige for the norms, and (e) acceptance of the norms by a significant portion of a community for a significant portion of daily activities."[27] Trudgill's stabilization stage can be said to include Gal's last three, although Gal's model highlights the role of the population's participation and consent in the success (or failure) of a given standardization project. Finally, as Del Valle and Gabriel-Stheeman observe, these stages do not always occur in a strict sequence and can coincide in time.[28]

Another point on which there is relative consensus is the idea that large-scale standardization and the resulting notion of standard languages are fairly recent phenomena. For instance, Davis observes that the first attestation of the expression "Standard English" appeared in the original proposal for the *OED* in 1858.[29] Bex and Watts have observed that the detailed codification of English in grammars began at the end of the eighteenth century,[30] while Susan Gal has located the large-scale project of monolingual language standardization in Europe primarily in the nineteenth century.[31] On the side of France, Renée Balibar identifies the stabilization of French as we now

---

[26] Peter Trudgill, "Standard English: What It Isn't," in *Standard English: The Widening Debate*, ed. Tony Bex and Richard J. Watts (London: Routledge, Taylor & Francis e-library, 2002), 117.

[27] Susan Gal, "Sociolinguistic Regimes and the Management of 'Diversity,'" in *Language in Late Capitalism: Pride and Profit*, ed. Monica Heller and Alexandre Duchêne (London: Routledge, 2012), 29.

[28] Del Valle and Gabriel-Stheeman, "Nationalism," 7–8.

[29] Davis, "Typography," 71.

[30] Bex and Watts, Introduction to *Standard English*, 13.

[31] Gal, "Sociolinguistic Régimes," 28–9.

know it ("la langue républicaine") as an effect of the French Revolution and similarly locates the practices leading to the unification and homogenization of French in the nineteenth century.[32] Of course, these processes, even though they became prominent in the eighteenth and nineteenth centuries, were made possible by earlier discursive, political, and ideological processes, dating back to the early modern period.[33]

The fact that the project of monolingual language standardization overlaps with the rise of nationalism in the nineteenth century is no coincidence: according to Eric Hobsbawm, the "identification of the state with one nation... implied a homogenization and standardization of its inhabitants, essentially, by means of a written 'national language.'"[34] The process of unification that nation-building entails required homogenization, which called for the minimization of internal differences within the nation; hence, linguistic standardization was undertaken in order to eradicate the many linguistic differences and varieties within the nation and to create and implement one "common language" that would unite the nation. As Monica Heller and Bonnie McElhinny have observed, standardization efforts intensified greatly in the nineteenth and twentieth centuries, as "[t]he construction of a common, shared, national language was a key tool for ensuring participation in a shared discursive space and a disciplined orientation toward when and how to communicate."[35] This was made possible in large part because of the development of printing, which brings me to one last, but not least, observation about the process of standardization: it is widely recognized that the concept of standard languages was largely developed in relation to the written form.

Writing could do for standardization what oral speech could not: "fix" linguistic forms and suppress linguistic variability, which are important characteristics of oral practices. It is the development of printing and specifically the activity of lexicography that institutionalized words, that is,

---

[32] Renée Balibar, *Les français fictifs: Le rapport des styles littéraires au français national* (Paris: Hachette, 1974).
[33] Bonfiglio, *Mother Tongues*, 5. These developments from the early modern period can also be seen as an acceleration and broadening of already existing tendencies in writing that predate the development of printing. For instance, Sumerian, Akkadian, Middle Egyptian, Koine Greek, Classical Arabic, and Classical Chinese all had active lexicographical traditions, established grammars, set curricula of texts and written signs, and so on. Debates around the "correct usage" in both Ancient Greek and Latin also illustrate that practices of standardization have existed for thousands of years, if only in smaller-scale, literary, and administrative settings.
[34] Eric Hobsbawm, *Nations and Nationalism since 1780: Programme, Myth, Reality* (Cambridge: Cambridge University Press, 1990), 93.
[35] Monica Heller and Bonnie McElhinny, *Language, Capitalism, Colonialism* (Toronto: University of Toronto Press, 2017), 104.

that gave words a relatively fixed form, assigned them a specific meaning, and associated them with a "correct" use.³⁶ Indeed, Benedict Anderson has shown that the technology of communications that is print played a fundamental role, along capitalism, in the creation of monoglot mass reading publics as well as in the fixing of print languages and the differentiation of status between them.³⁷ Therefore, writing and standardization have radically transformed what we understand language to be: by drawing a distinction between language and speech, standardization ultimately destroyed the equation of language with speech, equating it instead exclusively with the written, that is, standardized, form. Taken to its extreme, this understanding does not recognize the languageness of nonstandard forms.³⁸ This is precisely what happens in translation theory when nonstandard forms are deemed untranslatable or at the very least are framed as a problem for translation.³⁹

If standard languages are not a natural phenomenon but the naturalized product of a now widely documented process, this means that there are actors in charge of selecting, defining, and maintaining the standard. The question of who is "assigned the task of determining the legitimate forms of speech and of developing mechanisms that influence people's linguistic behavior and attitudes" is a significant one.⁴⁰ Research shows that power over language is usually, if not always, a crucial aspect of power tout court. In her study of the institutionalization of the French language in France, Renée Balibar has thoroughly demonstrated that language is one terrain on which to struggle over, exert, and resist power. Balibar's research shows that those in power, or at least those who have significant representational power, have been the ones determining the legitimate forms that the national language ought to take throughout the history of the French modern state: the aristocracy prior to 1789; then the bourgeoisie and more specifically the "Revolution's spokespeople," that is, the National Assembly representatives, until 1880; and the "schoolteachers" after that.⁴¹ More recently, Chantal Bouchard has echoed Balibar's claim that the legitimate, national language is the exclusive property of the minority holding power:

---

[36] Davis, "Typography," 76.
[37] Benedict Anderson, *Imagined Communities: Reflections on the Origins and Spread of Nationalism* (New York: Verso, [1983] 2016), 42–6.
[38] See Jonathan Rosa, *Looking Like a Language, Sounding Like a Race: Raciolinguistic Ideologies and the Learning of Latinidad* (Oxford: Oxford University Press, 2019).
[39] See Madeleine Stratford, "Au tour de Babel! Les défis multiples du multilinguisme," *Meta* 53, no. 3 (2008): 457–70.
[40] Del Valle and Gabriel-Stheeman, "Nationalism," 7.
[41] See Renée Balibar, *L'Institution du français: Le colinguisme des Carolingiens à la République* (Paris: Presses Universitaires de France, 1985), 411.

In a given society, it is the dominant subgroup, the ruling class, who defines the markers of prestige by attributing more value to its own customs, clothing, housing, behavior and language than it does to other subgroups in the same realms. . . . Language contributes to this hierarchical system, in the sense that the norm, i.e. the linguistic variety that comes to be associated with prestige among all the varieties which coexist in a society, is defined by the ruling class.[42]

Thus, language becomes a mechanism of discrimination, used to justify social inequalities and the unequal distribution of resources. To borrow Susan Gal's words, "recent scholarship sees standardization as an ideological project of differentiation and hierarchization"[43] in the service of the modern nation-state, a project necessarily connected to the interests of colonialism and capitalism. It should thus be clear by now that standardization is not innocent or neutral, objective, or universal; it is an ideologically fraught and politically driven process. A "standard language" is in fact a *standardized* set of linguistic practices constructed by agents of state-building and rendered valuable because it is used by these agents to exercise power, access resources, and exploit certain groups.

It follows, then, that any discussion in translation studies or practice cannot uncritically invoke it without problematizing, historicizing, and politicizing it. Lewis goes as far as to suggest that "prescriptive translation theory cannot productively generate conceptions of translation without assessing the historical, social, cultural and political context that shaped the core concerns upon which translation is based."[44] Standard language ideology is indeed deeply ingrained in the field of translation studies. Lewis has shown that linguistic standardization and normalization have played and continue to play "an extremely important role in determining how the core concepts used in translation derive their meaning, particularly in contexts in which Western models of language dominate."[45] Translation, as it is both practiced and theorized, relies on an idea of linguistic symmetry, which requires a conceived equality between a source language and a target language. This idea of linguistic symmetry implies that the goal of translation is to find equivalences between two existing and presumably stable linguistic systems that have corresponding resources to produce the same meanings.

---

[42] Chantal Bouchard, *Méchante langue: La légitimité linguistique du français parlé au Québec* (Montréal: Presses de l'Université de Montréal, 2012), 21.
[43] Gal, "Sociolinguistic Régimes," 29.
[44] Rohan Anthony Lewis, *Creolising Translation, Translating Creolisation* (doctoral thesis, Université de Montréal, 2004), viii.
[45] Ibid., 229.

This symmetry, Lewis suggests, can only be achieved between languages that have been standardized, since they are the only ones that have been "fixed." This is what allows prominent French theorist Antoine Berman to proclaim, somehow unabashedly, that "'cultivated' languages are the only ones that can translate."[46]

This idea of "cultivated languages" is rooted in Enlightenment ideologies, which associate modernity with the idea of "purified," "universal" language. As Richard Bauman and Charles L. Briggs, discussing Locke,[47] argue, language could only become modern and be freed of its "natural imperfections" once it was redefined as the center of a new realm of governmentality—after which practices of purification became the measure of each individual's modernity. Supposedly stripped of ties to particular social locations and interests and freed of all forms of social difference and conflict, language came to constitute the abstract, general, and certain basis for generating knowledge, in other words, a perfect embodiment of logic and rationality. It is worth noting that the association between "purified" or "cultivated" language and reason is especially strong in France, given the legacy of the French Revolution. Indeed, much has been written on the policy of linguistic uniformity enacted in the wake of the Revolution as an attempt to distinguish the "clear" and "rational" language of the new revolutionary order from the "decadent" and "corrupt" language of the aristocracy on the one hand and to homogenize the language of the masses so that the nation could address them in one language on the other hand—to the point where speakers of "patois" were seen as counterrevolutionaries and thus against reason.[48]

To be sure, translation, as an institutionalized activity that has been centered on writing for the past centuries, has played an important role in the process of "purification" and standardization. The most telling case in point is that of Martin Luther, who in the sixteenth century famously translated the Bible into a German vernacular and who is often celebrated for paving the

---

[46] Antoine Berman, "La traduction comme épreuve de l'étranger," Texte 4, no. 1 (1985): 69.
[47] Richard Bauman and Charles L. Briggs, Voices of Modernity: Language Ideologies and the Politics of Inequality (Cambridge: Cambridge University Press, 2003), 59.
[48] On the policy of linguistic uniformity enacted in the wake of the Revolution, see Peter Flaherty, "Langue nationale/Langue naturelle: The Politics of Linguistic Uniformity during the French Revolution," Historical Reflections/Réflexions historiques 14, no. 2 (1987): 311–28. On the distinction between the rational language of the revolutionary movement and the corrupt language of the aristocracy, see Pierre Swiggers, "Ideology and the 'Clarity' of French," in Ideologies of Language, ed. John E. Joseph and Talbot J. Taylor (London: Routledge, 1990), 112–30. For the labeling of patois speakers as counterrevolutionary, see Patrice L.-R. Higonnet, "The Politics of Linguistic Terrorism and Grammatical Hegemony during the French Revolution," Social History 5, no. 1 (1980): 42.

way for the creation of what we now know as the standard German language. For centuries, translators have played an important part in the process of standardization and in the reproduction of the standard language ideology as language watchdogs or guardians. It could be argued, moreover, that the structural understanding of translation as the rendering of meaning from one bounded language to another is precisely tied to the emergence of the liberal "democratic" nation-state as the fundamental and predominant unit of political and economic organization. According to Heller, trade between imperial powers as well as between metropoles and colonies required the engineering of the forms of bilingualism that would allow international cooperation without threatening the integrity of the nation-state. Such elite forms of bilingualism are understood as "a restricted good, acquirable through private means (governesses, grand tours), and limited to turning in performances of standard languages each in their whole, bounded form, with no traces of contact—or what I have called elsewhere 'parallel monolingualisms.'"[49]

Indeed, the notion of "parallel monolingualisms" strongly resembles the understanding of translation described in the previous section as well as the role translation has played within the context of official bilingualism in so-called Canada. Hence, the making of distinct "standard" languages, in the making of the social order in which nation-states are the new, dominant, and normative form of political organization, is what actually gives rise to the entire professionalization of translation—as one way to manage national boundaries in the context of international trade and relations. But translation can and has taken multiple forms, including oral ones—oral interpretation and theatre translation are but two examples—and has been taking place as an activity for millennia, way before the emergence of the modern nation-state. So while it would be naive and uncritical to dismiss the role that translation has played and continues to play in the definition, implementation, and prescription of linguistic standardization, it would be equally uncritical and anachronistic to imply that translation has functioned, always and everywhere, according to the belief that languages must exist in some authoritative, invariant form, since, as Milroy observes, this belief is not a linguistic universal. As he states, the "notion of correctness, the belief in the value of 'pure' dialects and the insistence on uniformity are all part of the ideology of standardisation."[50] The focus on standard languages in Western translation practice and theory is thus the product of standard language ideology—placing tremendous value on a given standard language and identifying it with language as a whole—for which translation and

[49] Heller, "Socioeconomic Junctures," online.
[50] Milroy, "The Consequences," 35.

translation studies have also historically played a crucial role. Hence, it is neither a question of whether we can or cannot translate nonstandard forms nor that of how we can translate them. It is, rather, a matter of engaging critically with the notion of the standard, recognizing that it is the product of centuries-long processes and political projects, and asking ourselves if there is any other way to conceive of language and translation beyond these parameters, without ignoring the fact that standardization has important, real-world materialities and consequences.

Drawing a Language's Boundaries: The Notion of Linguistic Abjection

At the very basis of the structural understanding of language underlying the common definition of translation lie the ideas of linguistic difference and linguistic boundaries. Conceiving of languages as bounded systems implies a spatial understanding of language, brought about by the organization of linguistic forms and practices into different systems not unlike geographically bounded territories. For instance, translators often encounter comments and edits on the part of their editors who simply say something along the lines of "this is not French" or "this is not how we say this in French," implying that these forms fall outside of the category of French, which is often presented in itself as giving sufficient reason not to use a certain formulation or a word. But what exactly counts as "French," and how and where does one draw the line?

In order to circumscribe the terrain of French, one needs first and foremost to differentiate it from *what it is not*. Thus, to have such things as "the French language," a foundational process of exclusion is needed to delineate a language's limits in the first place. To quote Rusty Barrett, "the notion of linguistic autonomy places clear boundaries around languages so that certain forms are marginalized or entirely *excluded* from the assumed bounded structure associated with a given language."[51] As Hailey Davis has shown, for instance, dictionaries play a crucial role in establishing what belongs and does not belong "inside" a given language: "[t]he principle underlying the OED, as it underlies Saussurean theory, is that it is a repository of all the words in the [English] language."[52] What is not in the dictionary, therefore, appears as falling outside of English. Elements deemed uncivilized, not modern enough—archaisms, obsolete spellings, peasant

---

[51] Barrett, "The Emergence," 200.
[52] Davis, "Typography," 77.

speech, regional vocabulary, and so on—are either excluded altogether or get labeled as such in dictionaries—regional, obsolete, vulgar, informal, and so on.[53] Most importantly, foreign elements considered to come from "outside" the language at a given time are also de facto rejected, such as so-called anglicisms in French. This is tied to the notion of social and moral order within the nation and the subsequent production of "deviancy" by the dominant ideology. The nation's order, as we saw earlier, was equated with one single language, and the presence of more than one language—bilingualism, be it national or individual—was framed as disorderly.

Hence, at the very foundation of the creation of "a language" understood as a bounded system lies a foundational process of exclusion without which the language in question cannot be delineated. Indeed, boundary making is always central to the formation of categories; in that sense, categories are always relational and co-constitutive, which means that we must examine the relational process which underlies the construction of any given category. In other words, what is excluded from a category is as important as what is included. Interesting parallels between linguistic normativity and other kinds of normativity—for example, sexual—emerge, as all social categories are an attempt to construct and reproduce a specific social (and moral) order. In queer theory, for instance, gender binarism is seen not as an essential and basic distinction between the fixed categories of female and male but rather as a "form of normativity that forces individuals to fall into one side of this binary and marginalizes those who fail to adhere to normative assumptions about gender oppositions."[54] In this light, norms are fundamental mechanisms that contribute to "policing the boundaries of essentialist identity categories."[55] In queer theory, queerness has been shown to be a *structural position* in a hierarchy determined by heteronormative social norms and without which heterosexuality cannot be defined. Of interest here is the implication that

---

[53] As the editors of the second edition of the *OED* stated in 1989, "[t]he aim is to present in alphabetical series the words that have formed the English vocabulary from the time of the earliest records down to the present day, with all the relevant facts concerning their form, sense history, pronunciation, and etymology. It embraces not only the standard language of literature and conversation, whether current at the moment or obsolete, or archaic, but also the main technical vocabulary, and a large measure of dialectal usage and slang" (quoted in Davis, "Typography," 88). Another phenomenon to consider is that neologisms—internet, tweet, selfie—are added every year, reflecting the changing nature of the world around us.

[54] Barrett, "The Emergence," 210.

[55] Heiko Motschenbacher, "Language and Sexual Normativity," in *The Oxford Handbook of Language and Sexuality*, ed. Kira Hall and Rusty Barrett (Oxford Handbooks Online, 2018), 5, https://www.oxfordhandbooks.com/view/10.1093/oxfordhb/9780190212926.001.0001/oxfordhb-9780190212926-e-14.

exclusion from the heteronormative order has been largely theorized in queer theory and gender studies through the notion of abjection.

In *Pouvoirs de l'horreur*, Julia Kristeva associates the psychological and discursive processes of subject formation and identification with the fundamental physiological reaction that is abjection, as both entail a similar process of exclusion. In simple terms, individuals become discrete subjects only insofar as they reject things they believe they are not: this "originary repulsion" is what defines human subjectivity according to Kristeva. In other words, the construction of the "I" depends on the expulsion of the "not-I" to establish the boundaries of its physical body, which function as the first contours of the subject. Similar processes of rejection also take place in the social realm, where abjection takes a more "imaginary form" and is used to exclude people and practices within a given discursive, cultural, social, or political order, such as the nation-state.[56] Abjection becomes a discursive tool to signify the limits of a given human universe, both in the individual and in the social sense.[57]

Judith Butler famously used the notion to analyze the discursive formation of gender identities as well as sex- and gender-based stigmatization in the 1990s. In *Gender Trouble*, they argue that

> the operation of repulsion can consolidate "identities" founded on the instituting of the "Other" or a set of Others through exclusion and domination. What constitutes through division the "inner" and "outer" worlds of the subject is a border and boundary tenuously maintained for the purposes of social regulation and control. The boundary between the inner and outer is confounded by those excremental passages in which the inner effectively becomes outer, and this excreting function becomes, as it were, the model by which other forms of identity-differentiation are accomplished. In effect, this is the mode by which Others become shit.[58]

---

[56] Georges Bataille, in 1934, was the first to discuss the idea of social abjection, in a short but dense essay titled "L'abjection et les formes misérables," where he argued that abjection is the imperative force of sovereignty. According to Bataille, abjection is in fact sovereignty's founding exclusion, as it constitutes a segment of the population as moral outcasts and outsiders, thus delineating the community's borders: "the miserable population, exploited for production and pushed to the outskirts of life by a prohibition of contact, is represented from the outside, with disgust, as the dregs of the people, as rabble and gutter" (Georges Bataille, *Œuvres complètes, tome II, Écrits posthumes 1922-1940* (Paris: Gallimard, 1970), 218.) Abjection in the social realm is a complex tool of social "segmentation" that distinguishes between "noble" people and "miserable" people, the latter being discursively rejected as being excremental and as existing on the outskirts of proper society.
[57] See Julia Kristeva, *Pouvoirs de l'horreur* (Paris: Éditions du Seuil, collection Points, 1980), 18.
[58] Judith Butler, *Gender Trouble* (New York: Routledge, [1990] 2008), 182.

Identity is always differentially constructed, that is, constructed in opposition to identities that become other and abject through their very rejection. Thus, consolidating identity categories entails delineating them with clear boundaries that need constant maintenance and reproduction, through the repeated mechanism of abjection. This leads Butler to draw a clear parallel between the notion of exclusion qua abjection and any kind of boundary making: "the repudiation of bodies for their sex, sexuality, and/or color is an 'expulsion' followed by a 'repulsion' that founds and consolidates culturally hegemonic identities along sex/race/sexuality axes of differentiation."[59]

In short, the construction of the human is a "differential operation" that produces the more and the less "human," the inhuman, and the humanly unthinkable. These exclusionary sites come to delimit the "human" as its constitutive outside, at the same time that they haunt those boundaries as the persistent possibility of their disruption and rearticulation. Butler uses abjection to discuss the formation of clear, bounded sexual and gender identities as well as the discrimination against certain groups and bodies— such as transgender bodies or queer sexualities—precisely on the grounds that they do not easily fit in those categories, which follow a "heterosexualizing imperative."[60] In turn, they argue that these categories depend precisely on their abject counterparts to be constructed, reproduced, and maintained in the first place. Sexual identities as we know them are revealed as relational and codependent, and it is through differentiation from their excluded Other that normative categories constitute themselves. In the social realm, this exclusion translates into the delegitimization and stigmatization of and discrimination against the identities, elements, or beings that are made abject through the process.

The notion of abjection is a productive lens through which to analyze the creation of distinct languages, since, as we saw earlier, languages as we know them operate according to a similar exclusionary logic. If queer bodies and practices constitute the heteronormative order's abject, nonnormative linguistic practices, for example, "hybrid" linguistic forms, can be conceived as a given linguistic order's abject. As we saw with the discourses of Rioux and Dubuc, nonmonolingual linguistic practices are seen as monstrous cases of "contaminated," "corrupted," "infected" French, while Simon contrasts "mixed languages" with "intact languages."[61] "Anglicisms" and other examples of so-called linguistic interference in French do indeed create a certain sense of horror—or, at least, of shock and discomfort—as reactions

---

[59] Ibid.
[60] Butler, *Bodies That Matter*, xxx.
[61] Simon, *Le trafic des langues*, 113. Simon uses the expression "les langues intègres."

to the use of Franglais in Quebec show. The linguistic abject, much like the queer abject, is found in a structural position, always in relation to something that is considered normal, proper, appropriate, in this case, an established, standardized language such as French. As Balibar observes, "as soon as a norm—the 'French language'—exists, this in itself disturbs all practices, since any linguistic practice, within a society governed by established and legitimized powers, exists in relation (if only indirectly) with the language of the powerful," pointing to the structural position of nonnormative linguistic practices.[62]

Languages are thus created and formed through a process of ordering and cleansing. As Mary Douglas reminds us, "Eliminating [dirt] is not a negative movement, but a positive effort to organise the environment."[63] The environment here is, of course, a given language, and dirt is that language's abject. The integrity of French, for instance, relies on the constant expulsion of what it constructs as "other," as "different"; linguistic practices that fail to operate this "cleansing" are deemed abject. As Douglas observes, "ideas about separating, purifying, demarcating and punishing transgressions have as their main function to impose system on an inherently untidy experience. It is only by exaggerating the difference between within and without... that a semblance of order is created."[64] A language such as French or English is best described as a linguistic *order* or regime that seeks to create uniformity out of linguistic plurality, rather than as a purely linguistic (and thus apolitical) sovereign system. Acknowledging that linguistic systems—French, English, and so on—are the products of an active and deliberate process of exclusion qua abjection leads us to understand, first, that languages are not neutral entities, but that they emerge out of a specific kind of *mapping* of linguistic practices, which primarily takes the form of inclusion/exclusion on the basis of difference and on the subsequent abjection of linguistic practices that are judged not to "belong."

Second, it allows for an understanding that the differentiation of languages and their idealization out of context is an inherently antidemocratic process. This has significant implications if we attend to the social consequences of linguistic abjection; if certain linguistic practices are delegitimized, stigmatized, and discriminated against, so are the individuals who are associated with them at any given time. As with queer abjection, the problem with linguistic abjection lies in the fact that the norms of standard

---

[62] Balibar, *L'Institution*, 411.
[63] Mary Douglas, *Purity and Danger: An Analysis of Concepts of Pollution and Taboo* (London: Routledge, Taylor & Francis e-library, [1966] 2001), 2.
[64] Ibid., 4.

languages are created and policed by the powerful and become a tool for the justification of social exclusions and stigmatization. For instance, writer Kevin Lambert speaks of the ways in which the concept of "mal-écrire," or "bad writing," is often mobilized in order to denigrate certain voices without giving any other justification.[65] This is precisely what we saw happening with Christian Rioux, who solely engages with the linguistic *form* of Dead Obies, rather than with what they have to say, and delegitimizes the group on that basis only. Mela Sarkar has called this delegitimizing mechanism "the monolingualism principle" and sees it as a "homogenization attempt according to the dominant society's criteria, a phenomenon that is in itself exclusionary towards linguistic and racial minorities."[66]

Any approach to the practice of translation must recognize that the "integrity" of the languages at play depends on fraught processes of abjection that have social and material consequences, and that the production and reproduction of linguistic categories such as French or English are inherently political. In the same vein, framing the policing of linguistic boundaries we observe in the field of translation as part of the abjection of certain linguistic forms and practices makes clear that translation as an activity, because it constantly has to expel certain elements and mark them as undesirable, actively participates in the mapping of languages as distinct. The notion of linguistic abjection points to the dynamic and political nature of such mapping and takes us away from the notion of language as a fixed, apolitical, and ahistorical bounded system. Translation practiced according to predetermined linguistic boundaries appears as a form of mapping in itself, one that reiterates normative and exclusionary categories.

Owning a Language: The Notion of Mother Tongue

As we saw earlier, modern linguistic standardization and differentiation are actively and deliberately achieved by specific political actors with specific political objectives in mind—namely, the justification, on linguistic grounds, of social inequalities within a capitalist and colonial world order. Linguistic standardization and boundary making are part of what Heller calls "linguistic engineering" as a means of making imperial subjects. One of the goals of standardization was that of "commensuration," referring to the processes of

---

[65] Kevin Lambert, "Faut-il 'bien' écrire?" (Centre de recherche interuniversitaire en sociocritique des textes, Université de Montréal, 2017), http://oic.uqam.ca/fr/communications/faut-il-bien-ecrire.

[66] Mela Sarkar, "'Ousqu'on chill à soir?' Pratiques multilingues comme stratégies identitaires dans la communauté hip-hop Montréalaise," *Diversité urbaine*, Special Issue (2008): 40.

making the languages of the metropole comparable to the languages of the colony so that they could be hierarchized: "practically this usually meant constructing the main languages of interaction, whether standardized, pidgins, or creoles. . . . It also meant using the ideologies of difference and inequality, most often racialized versions of social Darwinism, to devalue colonial languages, and to limit the legitimacy of colonial subjects as speakers of the imperial language."[67]

A third important aspect of this process of linguistic mapping—parallel to the delegitimizing of nonstandard linguistic forms—is the *legitimization* of a standard dialect and, most importantly, of the stranglehold of a particular group on the official, standard, national language. In other words, the social group in power needs to justify its control of and authority over the set of linguistic forms that is equated with the standard language at a given time, in order to legitimize the inequalities fundamental to the making of profit under capitalism. This legitimacy is usually achieved through metaphors of nativity and organicism applied to the realm of language under the guise of concepts like "mother tongue," "native language," and, often, "first language" or "L1." These metaphors have been crucial in setting the ground for the appropriation of the standard language as a domain, or property, that belongs only to certain speakers. The concept of mother tongue, however, hardly points to an empirical or verifiable reality. It remains vague and ill-defined, drawing on a variety of criteria such as origin, competence, and identification, both internal and external, depending on the context or the theory.[68]

Thomas Bonfiglio traces the appearance of metaphors of motherhood and nativity in the discourse surrounding language to the early modern period, along with the emergence of nation-states.[69] He argues that the nascent linguistic nationalism of the time "alloyed to the grand imperialism of first wave European colonialism," as the image of a national language created a vehicle for and articulation of conquest.[70] Hence, the idea of "mother tongue" is closely related to that of "national tongue," the mother being the conduit for the transmission of national and linguistic filiation. The ethnolinguistic concept of "mother tongue" as we know it today—closely related to national or regional identity formation—sedimented in the course of the eighteenth century in the context of the appearance of what Yasemin Yildiz has called

---

[67] Heller, "Socioeconomic Junctures," online. See also Frantz Fanon, *Peau noire, masques blancs* (Paris: Éditions du Seuil, [1952] 1971), 14–32.
[68] See Giulio Lepschy, *Mother Tongues and Other Reflections on the Italian Language* (Toronto: University of Toronto Press, 2002); Nike Pokorn, *Challenging the Traditional Axioms: Translation into a Non-Mother Tongue* (Amsterdam: John Benjamins, 2005), 3.
[69] Bonfiglio, *Mother Tongues*, 5.
[70] Ibid., 81.

the monolingual paradigm.⁷¹ As is now well documented, language played an important part in the discursive making of European nation-states as the ideal convergence of "one language, one culture, one history, and one territory." Benedict Anderson also speaks of a "conception of nation-ness as linked to a private-property language,"⁷² and indeed, as we saw in the previous sections, during this period various standardization projects sought to fix and delineate linguistic practices according to strict boundaries that would correspond to those of European nations, through an organicist approach which derives both linguistic and national identity from the local soil as a private property.

In this context, the notion of "mother tongue" emerged as a "unique, irreplaceable, unchangeable biological origin that situates the individual automatically in a kinship network and by extension the nation," stressing a linear mode of belonging to the national community that consequently makes national subjects eligible to own the land.⁷³ In her analysis of the metaphorical biologization of language, Yildiz shows that this fabricated proximity between the mother and language constitutes a condensed *narrative* about origin and identity. The notion of the unique mother tongue, she argues, "insists on the predetermined and socially sanctioned language as the single locus of affect and attachment and thus attempts to obscure the possibility that languages other than the first or even primary one can take on emotional meaning."⁷⁴

Thus, the organic conception of language imagined as "mother tongue" leads to a prescriptive claim of originality and authenticity; other languages, because they are presumed not to be biologically tied to the speaker, are necessarily seen as secondary languages of distance and detachment at best and of alienation at worst.⁷⁵ As Rey Chow has argued, for instance, the colonized subject's encounter with the colonizer's language "has typically been represented in postcolonial studies in negative terms, as the severance of an original connection (the mother tongue) and as the deprivation of linguistic autonomy, spontaneity, and integrity."⁷⁶ Hence the widely accepted

---

71. Yasemin Yildiz, *Beyond the Mother Tongue: The Postmonolingual Condition* (New York: Fordham University Press, 2011).
72. Anderson, *Imagined Communities*, 68.
73. Yildiz, *Beyond the Mother Tongue*, 9.
74. Ibid., 13.
75. Bonfiglio shows that this distinction between natural and artificial, especially as it pertains to first and second language, was introduced by Dante and was ideologically generated (*Mother Tongues*, 73).
76. Rey Chow, *Not Like a Native Speaker: On Languaging as a Postcolonial Experience* (New York: Columbia University Press, 2014), 14.

disavowal of the possibility of *writing* in a language other than the "mother tongue."⁷⁷

Reviewing major historical philosophies of language, Steven G. Kellman observes that there seems to be "something not only painful but unnatural, almost matricidal, about an author who abandons the *Muttersprache*, and it is instructive that the most universally venerated of all authors, William Shakespeare, never left England or English."⁷⁸ The idea that one can properly think, feel, and express oneself only in the "mother tongue" is especially rooted in the writings of major German philosophers such as Schleiermacher, who in fact applies the claim that people can only create in their mother tongue to the practice of translation in "On the Different Methods of Translating."⁷⁹ Of course, many authors have proven the idea wrong, having excelled in a "second" or even a "third" language.⁸⁰ But in spite of all the modernist, postcolonial, and contemporary subjects who have had successful careers in languages other than their "mother tongue," the conception of language, origin, and identity that "mother tongue" marks is still very much in effect, even when the term itself is not explicitly invoked.

It is at any rate very much present, if only latently, in translation theory, where translation into non-native languages is seen as a secondary, often undesirable, type of translation—as illustrated by the expressions "inverse

---

⁷⁷ An exception is the celebratory reclamation of creoles by Caribbean writers; see, most notably, Jean Bernabé, Patrick Chamoiseau, and Raphaël Confiant, *Éloge de la créolité* (Paris: Gallimard, 1989); and Lambert-Félix Prudent, *Des baragouins à la langue antillaise* (Paris: L'Harmattan, 1999).

⁷⁸ Steven G. Kellman, *The Translingual Imagination* (Lincoln: University of Nebraska Press, 2000), 3.

⁷⁹ Friedrich Schleiermacher, "On the Different Methods of Translating," trans. Susan Bernofsky, in *The Translation Studies Reader*, ed. Lawrence Venuti (London/New York: Routledge, 2012), 43–63.

⁸⁰ Such is the case of colonized and postcolonial writers, who often have no choice but to write in the language of the colonizer—writers such as Chinua Achebe, Kateb Yacine, and Wole Soyinka. Other writers who emigrated as children and familiarized themselves with a new language at a young age are also good examples: Clarice Lispector, Eva Hoffman, and Edwidge Danticat. Moreover, some writers choose a different language of writing as adults; such is the case of Joseph Conrad, Samuel Beckett, and Nancy Huston. Further, writers such as Josephus, Erasmus, and Thomas More wrote in Latin, which was not their "mother tongue." In all these examples, although there are different levels of freedom and different sociopolitical circumstances involved, the "mastery" of language is distinct from ideas of lineage. For instance, Eva C. Karpinski has used the metaphor of "borrowed tongues" to refer to writing in a language which is perceived as not one's own, a language "on loan" by migrants, immigrants, or various displaced subjects. For Indigenous and postcolonial subjects, writing in a borrowed tongue often means using the language of colonial oppression and domination while at the same time trying to challenge cultural imperialism and the dominance of standard English through the use of various local "englishes." Eva C. Karpinski, *Borrowed Tongues: Life Writing, Migration, and Translation* (Waterloo: Wilfrid Laurier University Press, 2012), 2.

translation" and "translation into a non-mother tongue" in Nike Pokorn's account,[81] as opposed to translation tout court. In short, the assumption that translation should only take place from a foreign tongue to one's mother tongue, since it emphasizes the superiority of "native" translators, insists on the "unattainability of the hidden essence of the target community, a Romantic mystification of language and identification of the nation."[82] This linguistic gatekeeping—declaring who can write, who can translate into this or that language—thus relies on an understanding of language as essentially biologically inherited. This is a useful conception for so-called native speakers of major languages, who can refuse the status of native speakership to those who were not "born into" a language but who learned it later in life, thus safeguarding their own authority and prestige. According to this understanding of language, only certain people, who are thought to "belong" to a certain language by virtue of their birth or origin, can claim its ownership, thus leading to the categorization of certain linguistic practices—such as writing or translating in a language other than one's mother tongue—as illegitimate. Bonfiglio has called this confluence of folkloric notions of ethnicity, nativity, maternality, and exclusive ownership in the discourse of the national language "ethnolinguistic nationalism."[83]

Furthermore, Bonfiglio has shown that the ostensibly innocent expression "native speaker," which is invariably taken to indicate an objective description of someone possessing natural authority over a language, contains notions of race and ethnicity: "Unlike the dress, food, or music of the other, which can be comfortably enjoyed by the empowered majority, and which are not perceived as contaminative, the language of the other is no mere accessory; it is surreptitiously perceived as a metonym of race and thus serves as a surrogate arena for ethnic conflict."[84] According to Bonfiglio, it is the invocation of the vocabulary of kinship and genealogy within the realm of language that enables this racialization of language. In relation to the construction of race, he observes: "Race is a folkish notion created *a priori* by a desire to identify a majority within a nation as essentially in *natural* possession of national character, as well as to identify a minority as an other, as *naturally* different, and then to exclude that minority as

---

[81] Pokorn, *Challenging the Traditional Axioms*.
[82] Ibid., 119.
[83] See Thomas Bonfiglio, "Language, Racism, Ethnicity," in *The Handbook of Language and Communication: Diversity and Change*, ed. Marlis Hellinger and Anne Pauwels (Berlin: De Gruyter Mouton, 2007), 619–50.
[84] Bonfiglio, "Language, Racism, Ethnicity," 645; see also Rosa, *Looking Like a Language, Sounding Like a Race*.

foreign to the configuration of national character."[85] Jonathan Rosa and Nelson Flores have also discussed the conaturalization of race and language, revealing the construction and naturalization of the concept of race, as well as the construction and naturalization of languages as bounded and separate objects associated with particular racial groups, as two central components of European colonial formation of modernity.[86] As Bonfiglio puts it:

> The inclusion of language in the discourse of race is made possible by the *racializing* of language, by grafting onto language the folkish notions of consanguinity and inheritance that make racism itself possible in the first place. Crucial to this matrix are the concepts of "native language" and "mother tongue," especially as they inform the representation of nation and national language.[87]

In the Canadian context, for instance, Eve Haque has shown that, since the implementation of the Canadian Multiculturalism Act in Canada's bilingual framework in the 1970s, language has replaced the previous category of race to become the primary site for articulating and justifying ongoing political exclusions in Canada. The Canadian nation-building project, at least since the 1960s, has sought the depoliticization, management, commodification, and, in some cases, erasure of the cultures and languages not associated with French or English, always according to the disciplinary gaze of the dominant society.[88] Utilizing a contradictory dis/articulation between language and culture, Canadian multiculturalism identifies language as a fundamental element of culture for the so-called founding races, making the French and English languages worthy of institutional protection and promotion in the public sphere, while it conceives of language as a private and peripheral element of culture for any other "ethnic" group. As Haque observes, "[l]anguage provides a convenient basis for racial differentiation because, even as the universal nature of language is claimed, the deterministic and immutable origins of separate languages provide the basis for dividing and

---

[85] Bonfiglio, "Language, Racism, Ethnicity," 620, italics original.
[86] Jonathan Rosa and Nelson Flores, "Unsettling Language and Race: Towards a Raciolinguistic Perspective," *Language in Society* 46, no. 5 (2017): 621–47.
[87] Bonfiglio, "Language, Racism, Ethnicity," 620.
[88] Haque, *Multiculturalism within a Bilingual Framework*. See also May Chazan et al., "Labour, Lands, Bodies," in *Home and the Native Land: Unsettling Multiculturalism in Canada*, ed. May Chazan, Lisa Helps, Anna Stanley, and Sonali Thakkar (Toronto: Between the Lines, 2011), 1–11; Kamboureli, *Scandalous Bodies*, 110; Eva Mackey, *The House of Difference: Cultural Politics and National Identity in Canada* (Toronto: University of Toronto Press, 2002), 83, 164.

hierarchizing groups of people along cultural and racialized lines."[89] One terrain where that is easily observed is that of the phonetic accent. Rey Chow calls accents "skin tones," building on Frantz Fanon's observation in *Black Skin, White Masks* that colonial language possession can be translated by the colonized into more valued tones of skin color, while Eva C. Karpinski has observed, in relation to Eva Hoffman's acute awareness of her own accent, that "accented speech is capable of betrayal only when the 'white' body speaks."[90]

On the one hand, state bilingualism guarantees the rights of the two official-language groups, English and French, to receive government services and education in their own language. On the other hand, its nonrecognition of Indigenous languages reinforces colonial characterizations of Indigenous languages as premodern and precarious and works from the assumption that the assimilation of Indigenous groups into French or English communities is a necessary precondition for modernization and for addressing social and economic inequality. This policy, which views English and French as languages of culture and instruction, and all other tongues as simply curricular subjects, is tied to ideologies of "racial and linguistic inferiority," "primitiveness," and the need for assimilation into dominant language groups at the expense of Indigenous language use and support.[91] Along the same lines, Christian Rioux and Robert Dubuc mobilize a similar rationale that draws on ableist characterizations of language when they use the qualifiers "subaltern language of handicapped beings" and "intellectual bankruptcy" to describe the lyrics of Lisa Leblanc, Radio Radio, and Dead Obies.

This circles back to the idea of linguistic abjection, which, it should be clear by now, operates hand in hand with national and racial exclusions. As I argued in the previous sections, language should be understood to be a highly normative and prescriptive domain, and this normativity is deeply racialized, ideological, and political. Talbot J. Taylor reminds us that "[t]he perspective from which linguistic form appears is not statistical, biological, abstract, chronological, logical, or psychological: it is a normative perspective."[92] From

[89] Haque, *Multiculturalism within a Bilingual Framework*, 15.
[90] Karpinski, *Borrowed Tongues*, 171.
[91] See Deborah Shadd, "Language, Education, and the Structuring of Canada's Social Sphere," in *Minority Languages, National Languages, and Official Language Policies*, ed. Denise Merkle, Gillian Lane-Mercier, and Jane Koustas (Montreal/Kingston: McGill-Queen's University Press, 2018), 194; Donna Patrick, "Indigenizing Language Policy in Canada: Redressing Racial Hierarchies in Language and Education," in *Minority Languages, National Languages, and Official Language Policies*, ed. Denise Merkle, Gillian Lane-Mercier, and Jane Koustas (Montreal/Kingston: McGill-Queen's University Press, 2018), 218.
[92] Talbot J. Taylor, "Normativity and Linguistic Form," in *Redefining Linguistics*, ed. Talbot J. Taylor and H. G. Davis (London: Routledge, 1990), 118.

spelling rules to value judgments on "good" and "bad" writing, from regional accents to swear words, there is relative social consensus around "proper" ways to speak and write in any language. To quote Taylor once again:

> [T]o speak of the norms of language is thus to speak of the metalinguistic practices within which we hold people morally responsible for their linguistic performance. In so doing we draw attention to the role of language in the moral/political fabric that is everyday social interaction. We expect people to obey our norms; and if they do not, we look for a reason why. If no reason is forthcoming, we may well label those people "confused," "deviant," "mistaken," or the like. Consistent non-conformity will probably lead not only to the application of such disapproving labels, but also to social ostracism. Part of being "one of us" is submitting to the sort of coercive practices that make linguistic interaction a normative phenomenon.[93]

These individual exclusions, in turn, translate into larger, systemic exclusions, as Barrett argues:

> Such marginalization of nonstandard English structures reinforces the marginal status of speakers of nonstandard varieties by treating their language as something other than English. . . . The assumption that language is an autonomous system thus forces speakers of nonstandard dialects into distinct linguistic groups based on regional or ethnic identity categories, or some combination of the two. Research in syntax thus separates speakers of "English" from speakers of "African American English," "Chicano English," or "Southern White Vernacular English." Of course, speakers of these nonstandard varieties are also speakers of English, but their language is marginalized and indexically linked to identity categories, reproducing the social marginalization of these groups. Just as Butler (2004) argues that definitions of *human* are always marginalizing because they exclude certain individuals, definitions of *English* exclude certain speakers from the broader category of English speakers.[94]

Prescriptive norms, in particular, since they delineate how people *should* behave, stigmatize nonconforming behavior as deviant and thus are a central

---

[93] Talbot J. Taylor, *Theorizing Language: Analysis, Normativity, Rhetoric, History* (Oxford: Pergamon, 1997), 156.
[94] Barrett, "The Emergence," 204.

component of drawing the line between the acceptable and the unacceptable, between "us" and "them." If social norms participate in the creation of a social and moral order—distinguishing between what is acceptable and unacceptable, normal or deviant, and so on—and if exclusion is inherent to the creation of boundaries, then it follows that prescriptive norms and exclusion go hand in hand—or, at the very least, that social exclusion is a direct result of prescriptive norms and normativity, including in the linguistic realm. Practiced and theorized a certain way, translation thus becomes an important mechanism for the production and reproduction of exclusions on the basis of language.

The Regime of Translation: The Real "Problem" of Linguistic Diversity in Translation?

The sedimentation and naturalization of this mapping of linguistic practices along (ethno)national and racial lines have had a significant influence on the practice and the theory of translation as a process. Naoki Sakai recognizes that it is "extremely difficult to comprehend what we perform in translation outside the discourse of the modern nation-state, and this difficulty only teaches us how massively we are confined within the discourse regulated by the idea of the national language."[95] But, as Sakai shows, it is not merely that translators follow fraught, normative, and exclusionary linguistic borders that they perhaps should not; rather, his point is that these borders are also the direct *product* of translation. According to Sakai, it is not because two different "language unities" are given that we have to translate from one and into another; instead it is because "translation *articulates* languages so that we may postulate the two unities of the translating and the translated languages as if they were autonomous and closed entities through *a certain representation of translation*."[96] This echoes Benedict Anderson's argument that the representation of the modern nation-state as a community is made possible by the creation of a common language as opposed to other vernaculars; in other words, linguistic differentiation is a prerequisite for—not a result of—the formation of nation-states.[97]

---

[95] Naoki Sakai, *Translation and Subjectivity: On Japan and Cultural Nationalism* (Minneapolis: University of Minnesota Press, 1997), 3.
[96] Ibid., 2.
[97] Anderson, *Imagined Communities*, 43–4.

Sakai explains:

> Only in the representation of translation can we construe the process of translation as a transfer of some message from "this" side to "that" side, as a dialogue between one person and another, between one group and another, as if dialogue should necessarily take place according to the model of communication. Thus the representation of translation also enables the representation of ethnic or national subjects, and, in spite of the presence of the translator who is always in between, translation, no longer as difference or repetition but as representation, is made to discriminatorily posit one language unity against another (and one "cultural" unity against another). In this sense, the representation of translation transforms *difference in repetition* into *species difference* (diaphora) between two specific identities, and helps constitute the putative unities of national languages, and thereby reinscribes the initial difference and incommensurability as a specific, that is, commensurate and conceptual, difference between two particular languages within the continuity of the generality of Language. As a result of this displacement, translation is represented as a form of communication between two fully formed, different but *comparable*, language communities.[98]

In short, what makes it possible to represent linguistic difference as an already determined difference between one language unity and another is the work of translation itself. Linguistic difference does not precede translation: translation is what constructs linguistic difference as such, as the translational gesture draws a line where there was not necessarily one in the first place. Translation, then, is best understood as an act of mapping that both emanates from ideological and historical processes of linguistic differentiation, standardization, and hierarchization and is an integral part of these processes. The question raised here is: would it be possible, or desirable, to translate without (re)constructing abstract and representational linguistic difference, knowing that this difference reproduces social exclusions on the basis of language?

Following Sakai's argument, the conventional understanding of translation represents translation abstractly, following the logics of the homolingual address, that is, a regime where the translator is "representative of a putatively homogeneous language society and relates to the general addressees, who are also representative of an equally homogeneous language community."[99] Here

---

[98] Sakai, *Translation and Subjectivity*, 15, italics original.
[99] Ibid., 4.

we can observe a radical abstraction of the bodies and texts actually involved in the translation process, which come to represent imagined, homogeneous linguistic communities as a whole. The homolingual address presumes the normalcy of transparent communication between two homogeneous mediums, which means that the conventional understanding of translation does not make sense outside of this configuration. In contrast, says Sakai, "the heterolingual address does not abide by the normalcy of reciprocal and transparent communication, but instead assumes that every utterance can fail to communicate because heterogeneity is inherent in any medium, linguistic or otherwise."[100] The "heterolingual address" is thus illegible from the standpoint of the dual representation of translation.

This explains why nonnormative ways of writing—be it what is often called vernaculars, dialects, regionalisms, slang, or so-called multilingual writing—are repeatedly framed as a problem for translation within translation studies. Indeed, Chiara Denti notes that "heterolingualism" has seldom been taken into account in the field of translation studies, despite its longtime existence in literary history—which should not come as a surprise, since translation's role, as we have seen, has largely been to keep things monoglossic and monolingual.[101] It is true that recent research has begun to question the traditional dichotomies of translation theory, including source language and target language, as well as many other structural notions such as fidelity and equivalence. However, as Reine Meylaerts and others have noted, analyses of so-called bilingual or multilingual texts in translation theory remain largely framed in terms of translation problems and even untranslatability.[102]

For instance, the same year that Derrida was calling for a reconsideration of the strictly bilingual model in translation, French translation theorist Antoine Berman provided a good example of the framing of linguistic diversity as a dead end for translation in his seminal and influential paper "La traduction comme l'épreuve de l'étranger." In the article, Berman recognizes that literary works are first and foremost characterized by a plurality of languages, voices, and vernaculars:

> Literary prose collects, reassembles, and intermingles the polylingual space of a community. It mobilizes and activates the totality of "languages" that coexist in any language. This can be seen in Balzac,

[100] Ibid., 8.
[101] Chiara Denti, "L'hétérolinguisme ou penser autrement la traduction," *Meta* 62, no. 3 (2017): 521–37.
[102] Meylaerts, "Heterolingualism in/and Translation." For an excellent overview of the pessimistic approaches to the translation of "multilingual" texts in translation studies throughout time, see also Stratford, "Au tour de Babel."

Proust, Joyce, Faulkner, Augusto Antonio Roa Bastos.... Hence, from a formal point of view, the language-based cosmos that is prose, especially the novel, is characterized by a certain shapelessness, which results from the enormous brew of languages and linguistic systems that operate in the work.... The Babelian proliferation of languages in novels poses specific difficulties for translation.... [T]he principal problem of translating the novel is to respect its shapeless polylogic and avoid an arbitrary homogenization.[103]

Here linguistic diversity (in terms of languages per se but also in terms of registers, varieties, individual voices, etc.) is seen as a problem for translation, much as linguistic variability was deemed a problem for nineteenth-century nationalist projects. The process of linguistic standardization created the "problem" of whatever did not correspond to the standard, requiring strategies of containment, among them translation as it is currently understood. To be sure, Berman believes that the erasure of vernaculars and of the juxtaposition of different languages is a serious offence against the textuality of literary works in prose, suggesting that the linguistic diversity of literary texts is something translators should attempt to preserve, not eradicate. But he is also dedicated to actively maintaining the distinction between vernacular languages and "cultivated languages," and he concludes the section of his article on the translation of vernaculars with a somewhat fatalistic dead end: vernaculars cannot be translated, only standard languages can be. The only two options for translating vernaculars, both of which Berman considers unsatisfactory, would be translation into another local, "equivalent" vernacular, which "ridicules" the original, or translation into a standard language, which erases its (cultural, political) attachment to a local vernacular. Berman's view on the translation of nonstandardized forms can thus be summarized as follows: nonstandard forms (dialects, vernaculars, individual voices, etc.) pose a *problem* for translation; yet, because there apparently exists no satisfying solution to this problem, vernaculars cannot be translated, therefore only standard languages can translate and be translated.

How can Berman be so aware of the polyphonic nature of prose yet at the same time caught in a conception of language and translation that does not leave any room for the variability and heteroglossia contained in literary texts? He seems trapped, from the very start, in a preconceived, unquestioned view of language—detached from social life, equated with writing, and oblivious to the political nature of the process of standardization—that prevents him

---

[103] Antoine Berman, "Translation and the Trials of the Foreign," trans. Lawrence Venuti, *The Translation Studies Reader*, ed. Lawrence Venuti (London: Routledge, 2000), 287.

from imagining other possibilities than standard and nonstandard, as if these were ontological categories that we had no other choice but to work with. Berman's reasoning only makes sense if we believe that there exists a strict, clear boundary between standard and nonstandard forms and if we subscribe to the normative belief that written/standard forms are superior to oral/nonstandard forms.

This kind of conclusion, prevalent in translation studies and practice, is reliant upon a highly abstracted, idealized, and unitary view of language, seeing it as a fixed norm, but actual linguistic practices, including poetry and novels, are variable and social phenomena that are both historically determined and individually, creatively constituted. If we begin to think about the activity of translation as something other than a neutral operation aimed at the transfer of fixed meanings between languages qua stable systems, the beliefs described earlier are simply untenable. The "problem" does not lie in nonnormative ways of writing but in the structural mindset with which we approach this writing and the categories we impose on it. The question remains: why do we continue to base current understandings of translation on available linguistic categories, rather than opening up the field to a range of possibilities? Given that translation needs some kind of border to exist but that it also creates and constructs precisely the border on which it depends, could translation not create other kinds of borders? Would it not be possible to practice translation as different kinds of mapping—decolonial, relational, interpersonal, affective, temporal—so as to escape the exclusions that the notion of language as fixed, bounded system reproduces in the social sphere? To begin answering this question, a good starting point is to look at how we approach, read, and categorize texts in the first place, before we even get to translating them.

Beyond the "Lingual": Heteroglossia, Deterritorialization, and Postnational Cartographies of Language

The typologies used to describe nonnormative ways of writing in the field of translation studies (and elsewhere, for instance in literary studies) reproduce in similar ways the problem of the construction and the reproduction of linguistic differentiation. Rainier Grutman is known as perhaps the first translation scholar to theorize, in the 1990s, the translation of what he calls "heterolingual" texts. The neologism proposed by Grutman, "hétérolinguisme," refers to the "presence, within one text, of foreign idioms, in whatever form, as well as of (social, regional, chronological) varieties of the main language."[104] For Grutman, the choice of *hetero*lingual, rather than *multi-* or *pluri*lingual, places the emphasis on linguistic difference, rather than on the number of languages at play in any given text.

Since then, several important contributions have been made to this subfield, including Catherine Leclerc's *Des langues en partage? Cohabitation du français et de l'anglais en littérature contemporaine* (2010) and Myriam Suchet's *L'imaginaire hétérolingue : ce que nous apprennent les textes à la croisée des langues* (2014). Leclerc elaborates the notion of "colinguisme," referring to an imagined equal cohabitation of two languages (here, French and English) within the same text, a feat she concludes no text has achieved up until now.[105] Grutman's and Leclerc's interventions are good examples of the imposition of predetermined linguistic categories on textual practices within the field: their concepts of heterolingualism and colingualism presume and rely on the existence of different languages and conceive of linguistic practices as the mimetic textual representation of these already existing linguistic categories somewhere outside the texts they study. Suchet, meanwhile, repositions the concept of "heterolingualism" in literary texts as follows:

> If we take a closer look, "the presence, within one text, of foreign idioms" reveals itself to be the product of a construction, the result of a staging. We realize that the alterity of a "foreign idiom . . ." depends less on its "true" foreignness, and more on a calibrated work of differentiation. This work of differentiation operates in each text by means of discursive devices that draw specific dividing lines. I therefore suggest a redefinition of heterolingualism as the staging of a language as more or less foreign, on the spectrum of alterity that is constructed in and by a given discourse (or text).[106]

While the constructed nature of linguistic differentiation, in other words its staging, is acknowledged, Suchet suggests that the texts she studies participate in the work of linguistic differentiation by, basically, differentiating languages formally and textually on the page. But, in light of the extent to which linguistic differentiation is orchestrated and naturalized, we have to wonder if the interpretation of most textual practices as belonging to one language

---

[104] Rainer Grutman, *Des langues qui résonnent. L'hétérolinguisme au XIXe siècle québécois* (Montréal: Fides-CÉTUQ, 1997), 37.
[105] Catherine Leclerc, *Des langues en partage? Cohabitation du français et de l'anglais en littérature contemporaine* (Montréal: XYZ, 2010).
[106] Myriam Suchet, *L'imaginaire hétérolingue : Ce que nous apprennent les textes à la croisée des langues* (Paris: Classiques Garnier, 2014), 19.

or another is, perhaps, not entirely imposed by the scholar's interpretation of said practices, *after their iteration*. While Suchet's intervention is certainly a move in the direction this book is taking, in that she acknowledges, as she has stated elsewhere, that the French language does not exist outside of its very active and constant construction and reproduction, we might want to ask if this kind of categorization (*heterolingualism*, *multilingual* texts, *colinguisme*) is not, in fact, an entirely exogenous, nonempirical way to conventionalize linguistic practices.

The same goes for other emerging labels, such as "translingual" and "translanguaging." Sarah Dowling, for instance, uses the term "translingual" to describe the capacity of languages to interact, influence, and transform one another, compared to "multilingual," which simply describes the coexistence of languages in space and time while being silent about the relationships and conflicts between them.[107] Similarly, Douglas Robinson has coined the notion of "translingual address," which implies substantial exposure to and experience of at least two cultures and the resulting ability to shift one's attitude or perspective when moving from one to the other.[108] But while these two accounts underline the transformations and shifts that happen between languages or cultures, they both rely on a preexisting border or difference that, as we saw earlier, is not empirical but ideological. As with "heterolingual" and "multilingual," the term "translingual" presupposes the existence of countable languages, as seen in the root adjective "lingual" they all share.

As for "translanguaging," which moves away from said root in promising ways, it was first developed to move away from previous notions of bilingualism, where speakers were believed to add whole autonomous language-systems to their initial one (additive bilingualism) or to eventually replace their initial language system with another (subtractive bilingualism). Initially the term referred to the speaking practices of bilinguals and to pedagogical efforts to promote the languages they learn and speak at home or at school, focusing largely on the case of Latinx immigrant children in the United States. The notion of translanguaging first considered the linguistic practices of bilinguals as constituting only one linguistic repertoire, which happens to contain features that have been socially constructed as belonging to two separate "languages." According to this school of thought, speakers treat all available codes as a single repertoire, rather than as distinct according

---

[107] Sarah Dowling, *Translingual Poetics: Writing Personhood under Settler Colonialism* (Iowa City: University of Iowa Press, 2018), 4–5.
[108] Douglas Robinson, *Transgender, Translation, Translingual Address* (London/New York: Bloomsbury, 2019), xi.

to the labels we assign to them.[109] The current definition no longer mentions bilinguals, suggesting that every speaker takes part in translanguaging: "Translanguaging is the deployment of a speaker's full linguistic repertoire without regard for watchful adherence to the socially and politically defined boundaries of named (and usually national and state) languages."[110] While this definition very much echoes the perspective applied in this book to so-called multilingual texts, it refers first and foremost to a mental process rather than to a more or less fixed final product, such as a printed book. Further, if all speakers do practice translanguaging, one has to wonder why it is called *trans*languaging and not, simply, languaging. The presence of the prefix "trans" betrays the notion's origins in and reliance on differentiated linguistic categories,[111] from which this book actively seeks to move away.

However one wants to call them, texts written in nonnormative ways currently pose a significant challenge for translators, who often see their work through the lens of a structural understanding of language and of translation, particularly in the form of the three axioms presented earlier in this chapter. Such texts challenge the foundational assumptions that translation happens from one language to another, that only standard forms can be translated, and that translation should take place in a specific direction. Because they are not written in a single unitary language, they call into question the very idea that the translator's most important task is to differentiate between *two* languages, and that translation is therefore a purely linguistic activity. They complicate the notion that a written text should address itself in a homolingual fashion to an imagined community that is linguistically homogeneous, as they refuse to be completely legible in the eyes of that imagined community. Because they smudge the more or less neat boundaries between languages and refuse to perform unitary language, perhaps these texts would be better framed as being "postlingual." A postlingual paradigm not only acknowledges that named languages do not exist in an empirical sense, but also moves away

---

[109] See Ofelia García and Li Wei, *Translanguaging: Language, Bilingualism and Education* (London: Palgrave Macmillan, 2014); Suresh Canagarajah, *Translingual Practice: Global English and Cosmopolitan Relations* (New York: Routledge, 2013).

[110] Ricardo Otheguy, Ofelia García, and Wallis Reid, "Clarifying Translanguaging and Deconstructing Named Languages: A Perspective from Linguistics," *Applied Linguistics Review* 6, no. 3 (2015): 283.

[111] A case in point is Mike Baynham and Tong King Lee's recent volume, titled *Translation and Translanguaging*, which exclusively discusses as examples of "translanguaging" speech acts and texts that mobilize more than one recognizable language. This shows that even if the notion theoretically applies to any utterance or any speaker, only the ones traditionally seen as "bilingual" or "multilingual" are studied under the umbrella of translanguaging. See Mike Baynham and Tong King Lee, *Translation and Translanguaging* (New York: Routledge, 2019).

from the notion of linguistic system altogether. According to Rebecca Walkowitz and yasser elhariry, "postlingualism has been with us for a while, residing just on the other side of the disciplinary, political, methodological, and translational trappings of extensively debated critical paradigms such as translingualism, multilingualism, plurilingualism, and bilingualism."[112] In other words, our present time is full of postlingual expression that is simply framed in -lingual terms, under the influence of the monolingual paradigm. A postlingual perspective signals that there is—that there might already be—something beyond or *after* (mono)lingualism, without denying the (mono)lingual paradigm and the legacy of structural linguistics and its effects on the ways in which we grapple with language, identity, and belonging.

In fact, linguistic heterogeneity within a given text is a problem for translation only if translation is understood in monolingual terms, which posit linguistic homogeneity as the norm. When confronted by that "problem" upon translating the works, for instance, of Leanne Betasamosake Simpson or Joshua Whitehead, supposedly from English into French, it is difficult, if not impossible, to come up with "solutions" within the tools that conventional translation studies offer, since the very categories with which we approach textual practices can only lead to the reiteration of the idea that standard forms are the ideal, imperative norm and that anything that falls outside of them is a marginal phenomenon or a problem. Refusing to see these Indigenous writers' linguistic practices as marginal, or as a problem to be solved, from the standpoint of translation, necessarily involves the refusal of the very categories that allow for the categorization of these practices as problems. Perhaps the "problem" does not lie in the ways in which these texts are written but in the colonial mode of perception that is the basic understanding of translation as happening between languages. From this angle, there is a need to rethink translation outside of the structurally defined linguistic categories we have inherited from the linguistic mapping historicized in this chapter.

This book thus takes as its premise the idea that texts written in nonmonolingual, nonstandard, nonnormative ways, whatever form these may take, need to be theorized differently, on their own terms, without the imposition of the demands and the constraints of predetermined, ethnonational linguistic categories. Much like translation, then, framing a text as being "heterolingual" or "translingual" ultimately (re)produces the differentiation of languages; in other words, it becomes in itself an act of conventional, imperial linguistic mapping. What if, rather than having been

---

[112] Rebecca Walkowitz and yasser elhariry, "The Postlingual Turn," *SubStance* 50, no. 1 (2021): 4.

written in different languages, these texts studied by Grutman, Leclerc, and Dowling pointed to new and different ways of mapping linguistic practices? What would happen if we were to attend to these texts without automatically resorting to hierarchizing linguistic categories?

This book shifts from seeing linguistic diversity, or heterogeneity, as a problem that needs to be solved with the tools we already have to using textual instances where (constructed) linguistic borders, old and new, are mobilized as the grounds on which translation can be reconceived in new, inventive ways. Doing so involves framing the texts that will be analyzed in the following chapters differently than through the label "multilingual" or some other variation that imposes a linguistically differentiated grid on textual practices that might be otherwise interpreted. A useful concept to engage with the linguistic diversity of the texts studied in the following chapters is that of heteroglossia, as developed by Mikhaïl Bakhtin, understood as the inherent plurality of any given "language." Linguistic practices, since they are a social phenomenon, can never amount to a "unitary language," since in any given novel, speech act, or community, different linguistic uses are seen as an extension of social relations and conflicts. Bakhtin stresses the fundamentally social aspect of language and opposes "heteroglossia" to the abstracted notion of unitary language:

> Unitary language constitutes the theoretical expression of the historical processes of linguistic unification and centralization, an expression of the centripetal forces of language. A unitary language is not something given (*dan*) but is always in essence posited (*zadan*), and at every moment of its linguistic life it is opposed to the realities of heteroglossia. But at the same time it makes its real presence felt as a force for overcoming this heteroglossia, imposing specific limits to it. A common unitary language is a system of linguistic norms.[113]

The writers who will appear throughout this book refuse to defend the "already formed languages" that define the Canadian literary market, tapping into the inherent heteroglossia of social life rather than taming it through a mimetic representation of a unitary language. Furthermore, these published works are only the tip of the iceberg when it comes to nonstandard or heteroglossic writing (published and unpublished) and linguistic practices generally.

The recognition of heteroglossia as a fundamentally social aspect of language allows us to move away from the notion of linguistic diversity and

---

[113] Mikhaïl Bakhtin, *The Dialogic Imagination: Four Essays*, trans. Caryl Emerson and Michael Holquist (Austin: University of Texas Press, 1981), 270.

linguistic difference: "this stratification [of language] and heteroglossia, once realized, is not only a static invariant of linguistic life, but also what insures its dynamics: stratification and heteroglossia widen and deepen as long as language is alive and developing," in other words as long as it is spoken and written.[114] To portray what is widely known in multilingual writing as "heteroglossic" would then be a truism, since Bakhtin states that heteroglossia is an invariable part of linguistic life, that is, that any utterance, text, or speech act is, by its very social nature, heteroglossic. To use Bakhtin's word, nonstandard writing is perhaps best seen as a "centrifugal" strategy that takes language(s) away from the norm, away from its/their purported, authoritative center. It would be better, then, to categorize texts that refuse to participate in "centripetal" efforts that lead to the homogenization of social and linguistic life as textual instances which explicitly and deliberately embrace, celebrate, and promote heteroglossia, rather than erasing it, since they participate in the "uninterrupted processes of decentralization and disunification."[115] Writing in an explicitly heteroglossic way is thus both a gesture that refuses to endorse the unitary language of a given society (or nation) at a given time and a creative gesture that imagines social and linguistic configurations otherwise, suggesting new ways of relating to linguistic borders, entities, and affiliations. The notion of heteroglossia, then, is helpful in highlighting the fact that no text can exist in a pure, monolingual form, and that the distinction between "monolingual" and "multi- or heterolingual" is ideologically constructed so as to always posit the latter as an aberration.

The texts to which we will shortly turn "map" linguistic practices otherwise, that is, not necessarily according to imperial, ethnonationalistic cartographies of language. To borrow Gilles Deleuze and Félix Guattari's term, these texts operate as a "deterritorialization" not only of the "major language" in which they are written, be it English or French, but also of linguistic practices and forms in general. Deterritorialization here refers to the uncoupling of writing from national language, brought about by the use of a "major" language by a national minority in Deleuze and Guattari's account.[116] On the one hand, it means using linguistic resources that reside outside of nationalistic linguistic configurations—in other words, it refers to the weakening of the ties between a language and a place, typically the nation. On the other hand, through their heteroglossic assemblages, these texts provide us with their own linguistic cartographies, at times echoing the linguistic maps we are accustomed to, but

---

[114] Ibid., 272.
[115] Ibid.
[116] Gilles Deleuze and Félix Guattari, *Kafka: Pour une littérature mineure* (Paris: Éditions de Minuit, 1975), 29.

from a critical standpoint, and at other times suggesting new and altogether different ways of mapping linguistic practices. Thus, explicitly heteroglossic writing strategies do not only *deterritorialize* dominant languages in which literary works are published; they also imagine new linguistic territorialities, whose fluid (non)borders are often drawn in unexpected places. Most importantly, if we learn to read these texts without resorting to predetermined linguistic maps, they can teach us that translation, too, can take part in the alternative linguistic (un/re)mappings they point to.

If languages as bounded systems are the products of a certain kind of political, historical, and ideological linguistic mapping centered on the needs of the nation-state, as this chapter has demonstrated, then it follows that we can certainly *unmap* these entities and reorganize linguistic practices differently in the work of translation, especially in settler colonial contexts such as Canada, where most professional translators typically work in official, imperial, dominant languages. The task of (literary) translation is therefore not to follow uncritically the normative cartographies of language that have become naturalized, since that would amount to looking at heteroglossic texts and voices through a Eurocentric, colonial gaze—or, in James C. Scott's words, to "seeing like a State."[117] As Seneca scholar Mishuana Goeman suggests through her Native feminist discursive method of (re)mapping:[118]

> Unlike Western maps whose intent is often to represent the "real," Native maps often conflict, perhaps add to the story, or only tell certain parts.... These maps are not absolute but instead present multiple perspectives—*as do all maps*. While narratives and maps help construct and define worldviews, they are not determined and always open for negotiation.[119]

Perhaps translation should listen to the (re)mappings of linguistic practices that are drawn in any given text, in order to also produce an explicitly deterritorializing, heteroglossic, and fluid assemblage of linguistic resources in translation.

---

[117] James C. Scott, *Seeing Like a State: How Certain Schemes to Improve the Human Condition Have Failed* (New Haven: Yale University Press, 1998).

[118] Goeman describes the practice of (re)mapping as "the labor Native authors and the communities they write within and about undertake in the simultaneously metaphoric and material capacities of map making, to generate new possibilities" beyond imperial and colonial geographies, which enforce state borders, asset control over populations, and overdetermine action and contestation. As quoted in Eve Tuck and Marcia McKenzie, *Place in Research: Theory, Methodology, and Methods* (London/New York: Routledge, 2015), 134–7.

[119] Mishuana Goeman, *Mark My Words: Native Women Mapping Our Nations* (Minneapolis: University of Minnesota Press, 2013), 25.

It is to a series of postnational, decolonial, deterritorialized, queer linguistic mappings that we now turn in order to explore the cartographies of language that are drawn, contested, and imagined in contemporary literary works published in Canada between 2005 and 2020 and written by voices that are marginalized within Canada's linguistic regime. These texts illustrate that linguistic purity is an abjection-based, discriminatory process; that what Madeleine Stratford calls "the cult of the norm"[120] is yet another exclusionary mechanism to delegitimize and exclude people who prefer and choose, to a certain extent, to use particular ways of speaking and writing; and that the prescriptive directionality of translation is just another way to gatekeep and maintain control over resources, linguistic and otherwise, on the basis of ethnolinguistic belonging. These texts have also produced new linguistic assemblages, ones that are not sanctioned, recognized, or valued under the current Canadian bilingual regime. They ask us to approach them, read them, and eventually translate them through a postlingual lens, that is, without following the lines drawn elsewhere on imperial linguistic maps but instead by being attentive to the original and fluid lines that they themselves trace, regardless of dominant linguistic categorizations.

---

[120] Stratford, "Au tour de Babel," 465.

2

Against Standardization

Gregory Scofield and France Daigle Talk Back

Axiom 1: Translation can only take place between standard languages.

This chapter focuses on the idea of standard languages, and specifically on the idea that translation can only take place between standard languages, by looking at the ways in which the boundary between standard and nonstandard forms is constructed and mobilized in the works of Métis poet Gregory Scofield and Acadian novelist France Daigle. As the chapter will show, the border thematized in Scofield's and Daigle's works is not a linguistic boundary separating "one" unitary language from another unitary language but a boundary that creates a distinction between a standard, abstract, monoglossic language (English and French, respectively) and a set of heteroglossic, disorderly linguistic practices—in other words, between an idealized norm and a minoritized usage that always inevitably exceeds the norm. Ultimately, both writers' heterogeneous aesthetics resist standardization, embracing the fluidity and unfixity of linguistic practices instead.

As was demonstrated in the first chapter, most twentieth-century translation theory has focused solely on the written form of standardized languages, relegating the literary representation and expression of oral practices—"vernaculars," "dialects"—to the realm of the untranslatable. As activities that too often uncritically subscribe to "the belief that a 'language' must exist in some authoritative, invariant form,"[1] contemporary translation practice and theory have focused almost exclusively on standard languages, labeling nonstandard forms as a *problem* for translators. Working with the uncritical and unquestioned notion of standard language has obscured, in translation and literary studies, for instance, the fact that a standard language is not an empirically observable reality but a social construct, created and

[1] Milroy, "The Consequences," 17.

maintained through a now well-documented process of standardization. This in turn obscures the fact that "the social construction of [a standard language] involves setting up a powerful language *ideology* as the backbone of the 'legitimate language,'"[2] and so what often seems to be a simple, relatively straightforward question of language turns out to be, essentially, an ideological and political question.

As shown in the first chapter, linguistic standardization was organized in order to eradicate linguistic variation within the nation and to create and implement one "common language" that would unite the national community. Standardization through written form has radically transformed what we understand language to be: by drawing a distinction between language and speech, standardization ultimately broke the equation of language with speech, equating it instead exclusively with the written, standardized, form. Taken to its extreme, this understanding positions nonstandard forms as being somehow *outside* of language altogether, as being "languageless," showing the extent of "the powerfully entrenched nature of the relationship between ideologies of standardization and languagelessness."[3] This chapter turns to the work of Scofield and Daigle, who stage the notion of the standard in their respective works through a critical and informed perspective which points to both the ideological foundations and the social consequences of that notion. Both writers explicitly draw a line between the idea of a norm they are expected to embrace and a selection of social voices that exceed and resist that norm.

Scofield's poetry collections and Daigle's 2011 novel *Pour sûr* textually and formally represent the social tensions that arise between norm and usage. Through a formal separation between a variety of social voices, on the one hand, and a monolithic, manufactured, idealized standard language, on the other, they offer a literary representation of some of the linguistic tensions that arise from a specific language ideology built around the concept of the official, standard language and its opposition to the linguistic practices of minoritized groups. Scofield's heterogeneous poetic voice and the many voices of Daigle's dialogues are presented in opposition to a monolithic and authoritative voice that both authors construct as a powerful, institution-like category, which bears a striking similarity with the standard language ideology described by many sociolinguists.[4] Both writers ultimately present the norm as something that is exogenous, extremely limiting and limited, as well as authoritative in

---

[2] Watts, "The Social Construction," 66. Emphasis added.
[3] Rosa, *Looking Like a Language, Sounding Like a Race*, 143.
[4] For a detailed account of standard language ideology, see Annette Boudreau, *À l'ombre de la langue légitime: L'Acadie dans la francophonie* (Paris: Classiques Garnier, 2016).

nature, always in tension with the heterogeneous, fluid, social nature of oral practices represented in Scofield's poetic voice and Daigle's dialogues. This staging of "different languages"—English, Cree, and Hebrew in Scofield's case; French, English, and Chiac in Daigle's—is only superficially a debate about language; more fundamentally, it is a debate about the *value* we place on different sets of linguistic practices. More specifically, both writers stage some of the tensions that arise between a coercive, legitimate language and the lived experiences of language as embodied, social practice. In these works, the question is not blurring the distinction between standard and nonstandard but rather making it so tangible, so explicit, that it reveals its own artificiality, constructedness, and complicity with hierarchical power.

The linguistic spectrum Scofield and Daigle construct and reveal is that of linguistic legitimacy: on one side, the monolingual and standard norm and, on the other, delegitimized linguistic practices. For Scofield, the English language was and is forced on the many Indigenous communities in Western Canada, most notably through the residential school system, which sought to erase linguistic variability and assimilate Indigenous children into mainstream English, and through missionaries and the process of conversion before that. As for Daigle, not only are French speakers politically and socially minoritized in relation to English speakers in the Eastern Canadian province of New Brunswick, but also Acadians often have strong feelings of linguistic insecurity in relation to standard French.[5] In their work, both Scofield and Daigle explore the gap between their minoritized linguistic practices and the respective norms to which they are expected to adhere. This also entails an exploration of the relationship between orality and writing and the kind of translation qua standardization that is typically taken up to transcribe the former into the latter. Through the interplay of norm and usage, Scofield and Daigle show what is lost in translation when translation is practiced as homogeneous standardization, suggesting that the price that must be paid for the translation of heteroglossia into monoglossia is too high. Through their heteroglossic writing, they dig minoritized linguistic practices out of standard "English" and "French," showing that another kind of writing is possible outside of standardized forms. Their work suggests that the goal is not to adapt minoritized linguistic practices so that they conform to the expectations of the national standard, nor to create and standardize, to whatever extent, a new, alternative legitimate language out of these practices, but rather to "contest hegemonically positioned subjects' modes

---

[5] Annette Boudreau has studied extensively the concept of linguistic insecurity and dispossession in Acadian communities, most notably in *À l'ombre de la langue légitime*.

of perception" of their practices as illegitimate⁶ or, in other words, to free linguistic performance from the notion of legitimacy altogether.

Ultimately, both writers reveal the ways in which they experience the pressures of the standard and the constant measurement of their own practices against that standard. On the one hand, Scofield displays a nostalgic desire for heteroglossia and longs for the retrieval of minoritized Indigenous languages suppressed through the historical processes of translation qua assimilation into normative, mainstream English. On the other, Daigle's approach is fundamentally playful, approaching "standard French" as a game she might not have signed up for but that she nevertheless volunteers to play. If translation into a normative, standardized, monoglossic tongue is an expectation or a game—a rigged one, to be sure, since "for various racialized groups, neither the use of a particular 'national' language nor the standardized variety of that language alone can ensure societal inclusion"⁷— both writers partially refuse to play the game, as Scofield's poetic voice and Daigle's dialogues resist translation into a standardized, official, monoglossic language. Nevertheless, as the following pages will show, it is also a game that Scofield and Daigle agree to participate in, albeit partially, by translating the heteroglossia of the former's poetic voice and the latter's dialogues into an idealized and abstracted voice that appears as the powerful norm. What this chapter will suggest, however, is that they agree to perform the chore of standardization only so as to expose what is lost in the process.

Belonging and Language in the Poetry of Gregory Scofield

In his 1999 memoir *Thunder Through My Veins* (reedited in 2019), Scofield identifies as "a Red River Métis of Cree, Scottish and European descent whose ancestry can be traced back to the fur trade and Métis community of Kinosota, Manitoba."⁸ His grandfather, who denied his own Indigenous ancestry throughout his lifetime, was a Métis born in Kinosota who relocated to Prince Albert, Saskatchewan, and, later, to the outskirts of Vancouver. Scofield was born in Maple Ridge, British Columbia, and his Métis identity and Indigenous ancestry were for the most part hidden from him throughout

---

⁶ Rosa, *Looking Like a Language, Sounding Like a Race*, 6.
⁷ Ibid., 141.
⁸ Gregory Scofield, *Thunder Through My Veins* (Toronto: Penguin Random House/Anchor Canada, Kindle edition, [1999] 2019), 397.

his childhood and teenage years. He was partly raised by a Cree neighbor, who taught him Cree[9]—within Métis communities, there is a continuum of language use encompassing Cree, Michif, Métis French, and standard French, as well as, to a lesser extent, English, Gaelic, Anishinaabemowin, and other Indigenous languages depending on the region, community, time period, and so on.

Scofield's poetry thus explores the Métis experience in Canada, an environment that largely produces the racial, ethnic, and cultural identities "white" and "Indigenous" in mutually exclusive ways. The Métis people originated in the 1700s when French and Scottish fur traders married Indigenous women, such as the Cree and the Anishinaabe. The term "Métis" refers to their descendants, who have since communally formed a distinct culture, collective consciousness, and nationhood in present-day Manitoba, most notably in the Red River Settlement. It is not to be confused with "métis," a French qualifier sometimes used as a blanket term to identify individuals who are of mixed European and (often distant) Indigenous ancestry but have no ties to contemporary Métis communities, nor with the more general "métissage."[10] In the following pages, the term Métis thus refers to the people who have continued ties to a historical Métis community and are accepted by that community in the present. Nevertheless, the Métis identity, as it stems historically from the intermarriage of white European settlers and Native

---

[9] For Scofield's account of his upbringing, which describes in detail his lineage, familial ties, Indigenous relations, search for identity, and personal sense of belonging, see his memoir *Thunder Through My Veins*, especially the second chapter, titled "New Beginnings, Old Worlds Forgotten." In the 2019 reedition, Scofield explains: "My understanding of myself as Métis has evolved and changed since I first wrote this book [in 1999].... However, one thing has remained consistent, which I believed is shared by many of us with mixed ancestry. And that is the question 'Where do I belong?' I've since come to realize, however, that I belong to who I claim, and more importantly to who claims me. And although I belong to many countries and to many ancestors, I belong at my Aunty Georgie's table, the same table where she taught me Cree and the stories that have accompanied me thus far. I belong to my grandfather's community, to Kinosota, where my great grandmother lies buried. I belong to the generations of Scottish and Cree halfbreeds, who worked for the Hudson's Bay Company. I belong to the buffalo hunters, and to the medicine makers. I belong to the nôhkomak, the grandmothers, who came from this land. I belong to them, to nitâniskôwâhkômâkanak, my ancestors" (Scofield, *Thunder*, 17).

[10] Some European-descended people with no ties or connections to contemporary Indigenous communities discover a distant Indigenous ancestor through genealogy and use that ancestor as the sole basis for an eventual shift into an "Indigenous" or "métis" identity, in order to access "special rights" (such as hunting rights) afforded to Indigenous communities under Canadian law. See Darryl Leroux, *Distorted Descent: White Claims to Indigenous Identity* (Winnipeg: University of Manitoba Press, 2019), for a critical discussion of race shifting and claims to Indigeneity through mixed ancestry in present-day Canada.

individuals, is still widely thought of in terms of hybridity. For instance, the use of the (now reclaimed) slur "half-breed" by the Canadian government throughout the late nineteenth and early twentieth centuries when referring to the Métis people shows that the Métis were considered an inferior, bastardized people by settler society, which resulted in past and ongoing discrimination, neglect, and stigmatization on the part of the Canadian authorities.[11]

Scofield's Articulation of Métis Identity and Language

In interviews and in his poetry, Scofield has spoken at length about his sense of belonging in two places, "yet at the same time not belonging to either of those places."[12] Many of his poems tackle the experience of people of Métis ancestry like himself who are "trying very hard to belong," as in "This Is Not a Manifesto":

> split my guts   I will never be brown enough
> white enough to simply
>
> be[13]

The split Scofield is referring to here is a recurring idea in his poetry: the reclaimed figure of the "half-breed" and the idea of being trapped in a condition of in-betweenness recur constantly in *Singing Home the Bones* (2005), *kipocihkân* (2009), and *Witness, I Am* (2016). According to Sophie McCall, the poet navigates "the deep divides not only between White and Native worlds, but also between the colonial labels of half-breed, status, non-status, off-reserve, on-reserve, urban, rural, etc., that continue to shape Native communities."[14]

In this excerpt from "This Is Not a Manifesto," Scofield laments the constant work and effort that are required of him if he wants to fit into

---

[11] For an account of Métis history, identity, and experience, see Maria Campbell's groundbreaking memoir originally published in 1973, *Halfbreed* (Toronto: Penguin Random House, [1973] 2019).

[12] Gregory Scofield, "On Poetry as Testimony, Interview with Shelagh Rogers," CBC Radio, *The Next Chapter*, December 20, 2016, https://www.cbc.ca/radio/thenextchapter/gregory-scofield-noah-richler-and-the-year-s-best-thrillers-1.3886040/gregory-scofield-on-poetry-as-testimony-1.3886101.

[13] Gregory Scofield, *Witness, I Am* (Gibsons: Nightwood Editions, 2016), 81.

[14] Sophie McCall, "Diaspora and Nation in Métis Writing," in *Cultural Grammars of Nation, Diaspora, and Indigeneity in Canada*, ed. Sophie McCall, Christine Kim, and Melina Baum Singer (Waterloo: Wilfrid Laurier University Press, 2012), 27.

either of the categories that are available to him; neither allows him to exist unmarked, that is, without being asked to place himself in categories to which he cannot belong. "Split guts" are not an intrinsic or essential Métis quality but the product of what Jonathan Rosa calls a "spectrum-based racial logics" anchored in "white supremacist colonial management schemas that homogenize and differentiate populations in varying ways."[15] The feeling of being "split" is caused by the fact that the notion of "mixed" ancestry requires the differential construct of race and the notion of "pure," nonmixed ancestry—after all, all people, simply by being human, are necessarily of mixed ancestry. Indeed, "split guts" in Scofield's sense is the inevitable result of the pulling of two rigid poles (Indigenous/white), the result of socially constructed strictly bounded entities which position him in the impossible space of either/or. In that sense, hybridity is also revealed to be the painful product of monoglossia, as what is implied by "hybridity" is the mixing of two "pure" ancestors, cultures, or languages one can never fully reclaim, and the positioning of "hybrid" or "mixed" lineage is always opposed to "pure" lineage, which in reality does not exist, be it white or Indigenous.

As a matter of fact, the ways in which Indigeneity and whiteness are defined and assessed in *Singing* and *Witness* often appear as protocolary and institutionalized, always implying an external authority that has control over the normative definitions of idealized, "pure" identities qua categories: in "Facebook Powwow," the narrator is "too white for the judges";[16] in "Since When" he wonders if he is "detectable by the check of the Census";[17] in "Dangerous Sound" he states his aunty was "not brown enough to testify, ... to be counted, to be reimbursed, to be indemnified";[18] in "This is Not a Manifesto" he says, "I'm not your quantum of pure blood," and warns, "you can swing your axe of authenticity";[19] in "This Is My Blanket" he says of his mother, "Each month she cashed her cheque / because she was federally licensed to";[20] and so on. The assessment of his and his family's identity and belonging is depicted as entirely external to the Métis speaker, following colonial categories of identity and identification, such as blood quantum or legal definitions. The recurrent idea of being "never good enough"[21] for any given category throughout the collection signals both an incapacity and a refusal to subscribe to these normative categories:

---

[15] Rosa, *Looking Like a Language, Sounding Like a Race*, 3.
[16] Scofield, *Witness, I Am*, 83.
[17] Ibid., 84.
[18] Ibid., 73–4.
[19] Ibid., 80.
[20] Gregory Scofield, *Kipocikhân* (Gibsons: Nightwood Editions, 2009), 143.
[21] Scofield, *Witness, I Am*, 80.

I will not split you my blood, I said—
Hookah, I was not sewn for this competition.

I was not made for your approval.[22]

In his poetry, responding to institutional and normative definitions or labels, and perhaps in an attempt to escape them, Scofield traces his own articulation of Métis identity, where he does not subscribe uncritically to a hybridity that would depend on pure white and Native identities. According to Qwo-Li Driskill, Scofield's poetry "maintain[s] a sovereign mixedblood identity," which "claims Métis identity as sovereign from both 'fullblood' and white contexts."[23] The poems highlight the artificiality of hybridity, since it relies precisely on predetermined categories that are also artificial (in this case, colonial labels). While he recognizes these categories as socially real, the poet clearly experiences them as violent in their noncorrespondence with his own Métis subjectivity, which he sees as an active and contingent gesture of identification with available forms, rather than as a static mix between two predetermined identities.

Resisting at once both poles and a "hybrid" blend of the two, Scofield counters with his own articulation of a fluid Métis subjectivity, which does not correspond to a fixed identity but to his own positioning both within and outside preestablished normative categories. In doing so, the poet reveals the shortcomings of the externally predefined categories of Indigeneity and whiteness, as well as the impossibility of uniting the two into a new hybrid whole, which always necessarily implies the blending of two separate entities that function as opposite poles according to a spectrum-based racial logic. This perspective informs the following analysis of Scofield's language, which draws primarily from both the Cree and English linguistic landscapes.

From a linguistic standpoint, scholars have referred to Scofield's mixing of English and Cree as an example of code-switching, understood as the practice of moving back and forth between two languages or "dialects."[24] Not only is this perspective deeply rooted in a structural understanding that conceives

---

[22] Ibid., 83.
[23] Qwo-Li Driskill in McCall, "Diaspora and Nation in Métis Writing," 31. Scofield's own use of the word "katipâmsôchik," which he translates as "the people who own themselves," to refer to Métis people, echoes this rupture from predefined identities. As quoted in Jane Scudeler, "'The Song I Am Singing': Gregory Scofield's Interweaving of Métis, Gay and Jewish Selfhoods," *Studies in Canadian Literatures* 31, no. 1 (2006): 134.
[24] See Jennifer Andrews, "Irony, Métis Style: Reading the Poetry of Marilyn Dumont and Gregory Scofield," *Canadian Poetry* 50 (2002): 6–31; Shelley Stigter, "The Dialectics and Dialogics of Code-Switching in the Poetry of Gregory Scofield and Louise Halfe," *American Indian Quarterly* 30, no. 1 (2006): 49–60; McCall, "Diaspora and Nation in Métis Writing."

of each language as a bounded system, but it also goes precisely against Scofield's efforts in articulating his own Métis subjectivity, as argued earlier. Approaching the poems with caution and seeing the boundaries between Cree and English as ultimately constructed and artificial (but nonetheless socially meaningful, just like the Indigenous/white categories Scofield navigates), it becomes possible to analyze this interweaving of "different languages" as a heteroglossic writing strategy or, as José Del Valle and Luis Gabriel-Stheeman put it, as a "constant process of choosing from a wide linguistic repertoire and not as the simple interaction of two grammars."[25] As Rosa suggests in relation to Latinx identities,

> we must continually attend to the ways in which these forms of coloniality shape perceptions of Latinx bodies in relation to an imagined phenotypic spectrum from Blackness to Whiteness, and Latinx communicative practices in relation to an imagined linguistic spectrum from Spanish to English. Indeed, these spectra ... should be interrogated as racialized colonial logics rather than empirical rubrics within which bodies and linguistic practices can be objectively situated.[26]

Hence, deconstructing the binary colonial logics surrounding race and language (Black/White, Indigenous/Settler, Cree/English) allows for an understanding of Latinx (or Métis) expression as drawing from "a broader assemblage—note, not a spectrum!—of racial categories and language varieties."[27] This implies that Scofield writes in this way not to represent or portray his "Cree self" and his "English self" side by side and to have them "dialogue" with one another, as others have argued, but rather to point to the different social voices and affiliations that make up his own voice, subjectivity, and identity, which are not necessarily limited to predetermined linguistic categories. Reading Scofield's poetry as it appears on the page requires that we acknowledge that the boundary between English and Cree is artificial and that the two are not necessarily distinct; in other words, that these categories are culturally and socially real but not preexistent, tangible, or even observable in the poet's voice. In the same way that Métis identity is about being both white and Indigenous—as imposed labels that one has no choice but to respond to in everyday life—but also about being neither— in the sense that no individual can ever fit perfectly in any given category that is constructed, let alone to two ethnic or linguistic categories that are

---

[25] Del Valle and Gabriel-Stheeman, "Nationalism," 10.
[26] Rosa, *Looking Like a Language, Sounding Like a Race*, 4.
[27] Ibid.

so opposed—Scofield writes in both English and Cree at the same time that he writes in neither. Hence, perhaps the uneasiness Scofield expresses about fitting into both or either "white" and/or "Indigenous" should also extend to the normative differentiating of Cree and English that most scholars have applied to his work thus far.

Heteroglossia and Translation in Scofield's Poetry

In scholarly literature, Scofield is known for his regular use of what is categorized as Cree in his collections, which are otherwise marketed and published as English poetry. The formatting and presentation that accompany this writing device are consistent in the three collections analyzed here: *Singing Home the Bones* (2005), *kipocihkân* (2009), and *Witness, I am* (2016). Across all three collections the Cree elements are always directly included in the body of the poetry, without any typographic emphasis (no italics, no quotation marks), and every word or expression is translated into English at least once. The English translations of Cree words always appear in italics and in the margins, separated from the poems by a large, blank space, and usually consist in relatively formal and plain translations or explanations of the Cree. The excerpt that follows, from the poem "I'll Teach You Cree," provides a representative example of the layout used in all three collections:

with the tip of my spring tongue, ayîki	*frog*
your mouth will be the web	
catching apihkêsis words,	*spider*
a crawling-out ceremony	
that cannot be translated.	
hâw, pîkiskwê!	*Now, speak!*
I'll Teach You Cree, nêhiyawêwin	*the Cree language*
that is the taste	
of pimiy êkwa saskatômina	*fat and saskatoon berries*
Your mouth will be the branches	
I am picking clean,	
a summer heat ceremony	
that cannot be translated.	
hâw, pîkiskwê!	*Now, speak!*[28]

[28] Scofield, *Kipocihkân*, 141–2.

What we see in "I'll Teach You Cree" is, on the left side of the page, a blending of Cree words, expressions, and interjections in the verses which otherwise appear to be in English. As mentioned earlier, Scofield's poetry is published by English publishing houses and marketed as English poetry. From a structural linguistics perspective, Scofield's poetry follows an English syntax, while Cree additions are mostly nouns and do not radically alter the syntax. In terms of the material presence of both languages in the poetic voice, English is also predominant, while Cree elements are less numerous. This kind of linguistic analysis, where one compares quantitatively and structurally two languages in a given text, has been suggested by many scholars with regard to both Scofield and other writers more generally. The reading suggested here, rather than replicating this kind of structural analysis, sees the poetic voice as comprising selections from a wide range of communicative and expressive resources, which are constructed, after the fact, by external forces, as belonging to either Cree or English.

Indeed, the cohabitation of Cree and English takes place within the iteration of the poetic voice on the left. The Cree elements are not presented as foreign or othered through the use of italics or quotation marks. They form part of the poetic voice just as much as the English words do; why, then, should we separate and contrast them in the gesture of criticism? Cree and English are even at times intertwined together on the same line, such as "catching apihkêsis words," jumping from one language to the other with no indication of differentiation, creating meaningful combinations and utterances as one would do within a "single language." In the poetic voice on the left, then, there is no indication that distinct languages intersect. In this way, if we agree that no boundary ontologically separates the Cree and the English languages, it follows that seeing certain elements and words as pertaining to one or the other is an ideological reading and interpretation that we impose on Scofield's poetry.

Much as Brian Lennon has argued that world literature is not a set of existing relationships between systems, which research must discover and expose but that research rather generates these relationships and therefore constructs the illusion of a preexisting system,[29] I suggest that "exposing" certain elements as belonging to the Cree language in Scofield's poetry follows the same kind of fraught methodology Lennon criticizes. Tackling the "return to system" in recent studies of world literature, Lennon argues against the idea that literature lives in systems (including in a cultural world-system) on the basis that the notion of system refers to "a complex, bounded unity [and]

---

[29] Brian Lennon, *In Babel's Shadow: Multilingual Literatures, Monolingual States* (Minneapolis: University of Minnesota Press, 2010), xvii.

implies our discovery, rather than creation, of its schema of organization."³⁰ In the same way, approaching Scofield's poetry with the preconceived idea that Cree and English are two naturally distinct languages might actually obscure his own relationship to language and identity. As Jennifer Adese points out, "[p]lacing Métis at the center of our analyses also recognizes that the tendency of literary critics to try to delineate which aspects of the literature represent the 'Cree influence' and which parts mark the 'French influence' emerges because of the persistence of race-based thought (whether explicitly or implicitly marked)."³¹ As a result, it would be more appropriate to analyze Scofield's poetic voice on the left not as a dualistic use of language but as one fluid and complex set of semiotic and communicative resources which contains socially marked voices through the juxtaposition of what we *are taught to recognize* as different languages, registers, accents, and so on. Thus, if we consider solely the left column of the poetic voice, before translation, there is no boundary that is mobilized, reproduced, or staged by Scofield himself between both languages: the poetic voice on the left draws from linguistic resources that we may perceive as belonging to two different linguistic systems, but it treats these systems as interchangeable or, indeed, indistinguishable.

However, the set of linguistic resources found on the left side of the page in Scofield's poetry is followed to the right by a blank space, on the other side of which are featured what appear to be English translations. Through the partial translations offered in the margins of the poem, a boundary is created, both between non-English and English and between the poet's voice as represented to the left and a certain kind of English, or more precisely a specific idea of English as supposedly objective, disembodied category. In other words, certain elements that appear in the left column are mapped outside of English through their translation into English, in the column to the right.

In "I'll Teach You Cree," it is therefore the gesture of translation and the product of that gesture in the column to the right that stage linguistic difference, and this holds true throughout Scofield's poems: only certain elements are translated, pointing to their non-Englishness or other-than-Englishness. In other words, prior to translation, such difference is not necessarily acknowledged or constructed. The English translations appear in the column to the right as something that materially and temporally comes *after* the iteration of each line. They occupy their own place on the page, away

---

³⁰ Ibid., xvi.
³¹ Jennifer Adese, "The New People: Reading for Peoplehood in Métis Literatures," *Studies in American Indian Literatures* 28, no. 4 (2016): 65.

from the main voice, and further distanced from it by the othering effect of italics. Between the poetic voice and the English translations stands a relatively large blank space, which operates as the space where translation happens, in other words as the border zone between non-English and English. On the left side of the page the poet speaks in his multifaceted voice, regardless of the linguistic border that would separate English from Cree; as to the English translations that appear on the other side of the blank space, they can be interpreted as symbolizing the English language qua normative institution or category or what Sarah Dowling has called "settler monolingualism."[32] Indeed, most, if not all, translations in Scofield's poetry are done in a very formal, normative, almost instructional English. The English translations function as glosses, which mark the Cree words as either "nonstandard" forms or, alternatively, technical terms. In both cases, the English translations imply that lack of knowledge of Cree represents, in a way, a failing on the part of the reader, or at least a gap in the reader's knowledge, one that the poet is offering to remedy.

Examples of translations range from "because I love you a lot" to "the Cree language," "Yes," "I am grateful," "white person," "It rained," and so on. The English translations often read as dictionary-like descriptions: interjections such as "iya" and "êy-êy!" are translated as "exclamation of great pleasure"[33] and "exclamation of humility,"[34] while "awiyâ!" is rendered as "slang for ouch, it hurts!"[35] Other words are translated with more than one synonym, such as "sly or sneaky" for "kîmoc,"[36] "half-sons or half-breed" for "âpihtaw-kosisân,"[37] and "it is foolish or surprising" for "mâmaskâc!";[38] and there is the occasional encyclopedic description, such as "a spinning top used at Chanukah"[39] and "a dog's rear end."[40] Analyzed together, the English translations form a surprisingly unitary whole: the tone is neutral, the translations are mostly referential and explanatory, and the register is uniform, creating a language

---

[32] Dowling describes the notion of settler monolingualism as follows: "My term *settler monolingualism* . . . highlights the ways in which English is understood as the most natural and appropriate way to . . . participate in the mainstream society of Anglophone Canada." According to Dowling, settler monolingualism is a key component of neoliberal multiculturalism as it exists in Canada and the United States, as it creates a linguistic common ground enriched with a sprinkling of tongues that, unlike English, are coded as "immigrant." Dowling, *Translingual Poetics*, 3–4.
[33] Scofield, *kipocihkân*, 127.
[34] Scofield, *Witness, I Am*, 31.
[35] Scofield, *kipocihkân*, 126.
[36] Ibid., 136.
[37] Gregory Scofield, *Singing Home the Bones* (Vancouver: Raincoast Books, 2005), 25.
[38] Ibid., 12.
[39] Scofield, *kipocihkân*, 138.
[40] Scofield, *Singing Home the Bones*, 16.

that is quite unitary and indeed monologic, where "monologic" refers to an abstractly idealized consistency of style.

Such an approach suggests that Scofield posits normative, monologic English in opposition to his own heteroglossic voice, putting them side by side on the page, creating a border not merely between English and Cree but also, more generally, between heteroglossia and monoglossia. This staging of monoglossic translation points to a historicizing argument, one that acknowledges the historical imposition of a monoglossic (colonial) order on a heteroglossic linguistic and expressive landscape. In other words, on one side the poet writes in fluid and heteroglossic ways, and on the other he portrays the idea of standard, monologic English as a category he can only fit into partially, through the process of translation, a process that requires the suppression of his heteroglossia, most importantly of his Indigeneity and his Jewish roots. The heterogeneity offered in the left column can thus be understood to symbolize the actual geographical landscape which came to be conquered and dominated by the homogenizing structure that is colonialism: where there was once not only linguistic heterogeneity but also a rich cultural and political diversity is now governed by a totalizing colonial system. Between the two columns stands an incommensurable gap, where the violence of normative English qua institutional and social category articulated outside of the poetic voice tames the "realities of heteroglossia" expressed through it.[41]

By opposing his own, pre-translation poetic voice and subjectivity and the constructed category of normative, post-translation English, Scofield depicts some of the tensions that arise between a heteroglossic expression that has been and continues to be suppressed by a powerful monoglossic ideal. Even though Scofield's own heteroglossia, which includes forms associated with English, is an effect of colonialism, heteroglossia which draws on colonial, standardized languages is still inherently contrary to monoglossia. Keeping in mind that Scofield writes this in the aftermath of the ongoing colonial cultural and linguistic assimilation of Indigenous peoples in Canada, translation as it is portrayed here is perhaps another word for cultural and linguistic silencing and erasing:

> if I take ki-tâpiskanikan   *your jawbone*
>
> place it scolding on Portage and Main
> will all the dead Indians
> rise up from the cracks, spit bullets
> that made silent our talk?[42]

---

[41] Bakhtin, *The Dialogic Imagination*, 270.
[42] Scofield, *Singing Home the Bones*, 11.

Mistrust of Translation in Scofield's Work

In Scofield's work, translation toward this unitary brand of English seems to operate as a prerequisite for fitting into dominant categories; the poet, who cannot "simply be," has to translate himself in order to fit into English and whiteness, an activity which implies the assimilation of anything that is considered to reside outside these two categories. In *Singing Home the Bones*, *kipocihkân*, and *Witness, I Am*, translation happens exclusively in one direction, toward English, the language that has the most capital, dominance, and power (symbolic and otherwise) in the space where Scofield grew up and still lives, in so-called Western Canada. It should be noted here that languages other than Cree also appear in Scofield's work, for instance Hebrew in the few poems that specifically tackle his newly discovered Jewish heritage on his father's side. In "The Man Who Forgot to Claim His Son," from *kipocihkân*, Hebrew and Yiddish forms are translated in the exact same way as Cree elements elsewhere; the translation and formatting strategies remain the same for this other(ed) language. Since English as a normative and authoritative linguistic institution is the most powerful in Canadian society, it is to be expected that translation in Scofield's work is done in asymmetric, nonreciprocal ways, whatever the minoritized language mobilized by the poetic voice. As the dominant category, English is the language that exerts the most pressure on Scofield, who is expected to mute not only his Cree but also his heteroglossia and voice as a whole, to conform to editorial conventions or reader expectations.

Translation, when it operates in this way, appears to have a destructive and flattening effect on language: what is left in the right column of the poems is a collection of bland, colorless descriptions of elements that clearly have a highly affective and colorful potential in the body of the poems to the left. Repetitions are erased—"miyo-acîmo, âh, miyo-âcimo" becomes "He tells a good story"[43]—affective names for family members and ancestors are rendered into less affective forms—"ni-mâmâ" becomes "my mother,"[44] "Babi" becomes "grandmother"[45]—and compound words are simplified in translation—"manitowimasinahikan" becomes "bible."[46] Creative and

---

[43] Scofield, *Witness, I Am*, 53.
[44] Scofield, *Singing Home the Bones*, 56.
[45] Scofield, *kipocihkân*, 138.
[46] Scofield, *Singing Home the Bones*, 29.

affective uses of language, which underlie the poet's relationships, his own identity, and his voice, are deliberately "lost in translation." Once stripped of all its affective and imaginative aspects, forced into the monologic category that standard English represents, language becomes a characterless and lifeless thing.

This is supplemented by the suspicious attitude Scofield cultivates toward translation in some of his poems. In "I'll Teach You Cree," for instance, the poet mentions several ceremonies that "cannot be translated":

> I will make my camp there
> ê-kohk mistahi ê-sâkihitan   *because I love you a lot*
>
> This cannot be translated.
>
> hâw, pîkiskwê!   *Now, speak!*[47]

Now this emphasis on the impossibility or refusal of translation—the line "that cannot be translated" appears in each stanza, for a total of four times—is placed alongside the very fact of translation; this cannot be translated, yet it is. The juxtaposition of actual translations on the page with Scofield's warning that translation cannot take place reads as a reminder that the translations provided on the page, far from transparent, should perhaps not be trusted. A reader who is only familiar with English is forced to rely on the translations, yet the poet warns about the very impossibility (or refusal) of translation, thereby casting doubt on the English translation's ability to be a legitimate substitute for the (visibly) heteroglossic complexity of the poetic voice.

Translation and its refusal also appear as a theme in "Prayer Song for the Returning of Names and Sons," in which Scofield performs a "renaming song" in an attempt to recall his women ancestors' traditional names. In a note at the end of the collection, he explains: "I am certain my châpan [ancestor] Sarah, my kayâs ochi nikâwi, . . . came to my ancestor/grandfather carrying a name too sacred for him to pronounce."[48] This particular poem is inspired by what he describes as a sacred ceremony that cannot be recorded and is the only poem in the three collections that does not include English translations for some of the Cree elements. The poem ends as follows:

> I've thrown back
> your names;

---

[47] Scofield, *kipocihkân*, 142.
[48] Scofield, *Singing Home the Bones*, 106.

nâmoya kîyawaw	*you are not*
Charlotte, Sarah, Mary	
ekwa Christina.	*and*
nâmoya kîyawaw môniyaskwewak	*you are not white women*

â-haw, ni-châpanak
kayâs ochi nikâwimahk

nâtohta
my song, nikamowin

this prayer song
I am singing.

êy-hey![49]

Previously in the poem, Scofield renames his grandmothers, refusing to call them by their white names. Translating these English names "back," Scofield seeks to reclaim the lost identities of his ancestors, who were forced to relegate their own fluid and complex identities and markers in order to participate in colonial society. But the poet does not translate the English names— Charlotte, Sarah, Mary, and Christina—as one would expect, into Cree, that is, according to the fixed linguistic boundary that translation would generally cross or according to an essentialist view of language that equates Indigenous identities with fixed Indigenous languages; rather, the names Scofield "gives back" to his ancestors are indeed presented in what is generally recognized as English: "Tattooed From The Lip To The Chin Woman," "She Paints Her Face With Red Ochre," and "Charm Woman Who Is Good To Make A Nation." These translations point to a different kind of translation than the one usually displayed in Scofield's poetry. What is recovered or reclaimed here is not "the Cree language" as an essential or original identity but textured, affective, imaginative ways to relate to his ancestors—which can, this suggests, be achieved in any "language" provided it is flexible enough—far away from the bulldozer-like baptisms that erased the poet's grandmothers' specificities and gave them generic, whitewashed English names instead. Furthermore, the end of the poem, quoted earlier, shows a series of Cree words and expressions left untranslated, signaling a gradual move toward the refusal of translation altogether, perhaps to protect the sacredness of these lines from the kind of translation the poet's ancestors' names went through.

---

[49] Ibid., 32–3.

"I'll Teach You Cree": Scofield's Invitation to Join Him in Heteroglossia

Perhaps we should read Scofield's invitation to learn Cree in "I'll Teach You Cree" as an invitation not to learn the Cree language as a whole, bounded, and normative system but as an invitation to participate in a less authoritative, more inclusive heteroglossia which, importantly, should draw on the specificity of denied languages, particularly Indigenous languages. Keeping in mind that "Cree" is just as much a construct as any other named language, but that, unlike many others, it is commonly recognized as variable since it has not yet been standardized as one unitary language,[50] Scofield's invocation of "Cree" can be interpreted as the invocation of the plurality, variation, and difference that "Cree" supposes, in contradistinction to the fixity and unicity that standard English aims for. We might therefore be inclined to receive Scofield's call as an invitation to step away from English and whiteness as monologic, authoritative, erasing categories—as an invitation to move away from the monologic translations on the right (representing standardization and, more generally, colonialism) and to join him instead in the complexity of the voice on the left, a move toward the decentering of anglophone dominance that allows to see, name, and interact with the same world differently. In the poem, the narrator promises the interlocutor: "your mouth will be the web / catching apihkêsis words," "your mouth will be the branches / I am picking clean," "You will have the mouth of a beaver, / thick and luminescent."[51]

The learning of Cree will, Scofield suggests, open many new possibilities as to how to engage with the world around us. This mirrors his own relationship to Cree: brought up in English by his mother who at the time hid and denied her Métis heritage, Scofield was taught Cree around the age of eight by a kind and loving neighbor whom he calls Auntie. As told in his memoir *Thunder Through My Veins*, it is because of this woman that Scofield discovered, explored, and came to embrace Indigenous ways of life, partly through the teaching of Cree. As Daniel Heath Justice observes about Scofield's poetry, "Cree language is woven through the poems, . . . offering other ways to understand these connections, unravellings, and realignments."[52] In

---

[50] See Jean Okimāsis and Arok Wolvengrey, "How to Spell It in Cree: The Standard Roman Orthography," 2008, http://resources.atlas-ling.ca/media/How_To_Spell_It_In_Cree-Standard_Orthography-Plains-Cree.pdf, for a description of the many attempts to write the Cree language using the Roman alphabet and of the difficulties and challenges met by standardization efforts.

[51] Scofield, *kipocihkân*, 142.

[52] Daniel Heath Justice, *Why Indigenous Literatures Matter* (Waterloo: Wilfrid Laurier University Press, 2018), 68.

Scofield's poetry, Cree is not represented as *the only* way to apprehend the world; it is an invitation to always learn and be open to new, different, and ever-changing ways to relate. It represents an alternative to the normative and colonial English/whiteness of the column to the right; an invitation to the inclusive and decolonial heteroglossia of the column to the left. Scofield longs for words, languages, voices outside of monologic English, for the Cree that cannot be translated: "my mouth hungry / The words like a feast."[53] The problem, it seems, is not so much with the linguistic aspect of "English" per se but with its social and political monopoly, its dominance, and its erasure of multiplicity at the social level. Perhaps to be Métis, for Scofield, is first and foremost to refuse the pull of monoglossia.

In summary, the boundary between English and Cree (and other linguistic forms, such as Hebrew) in Scofield's work is only made visible in/through the translations to the right, pointing to the historical process of differentiation and erasure of Indigenous and other minoritized languages. Something has happened in the blank space separating the two columns; the poet's voice has been divided, fragmented, and differentiated according to different language boundaries, ultimately translating any element that is said to belong outside of English. What Scofield invites us to do is to turn around and to move in the opposite direction, from the idea (and ideal) of monologic English and toward more fluid, prismatic ways of belonging, speaking, and living; to travel back across the blank space and to return to a place where linguistic boundaries do not serve the work of homogenization, standardization, and assimilation.

Of course, Scofield's heteroglossia is rooted in decolonial practice, which means the specificity of Indigenous languages and their revitalization are central to the heteroglossia he is putting forward. The idea is not to subsume the specificity of Indigenous languages into an indistinct and uncritical heteroglossia that would satisfy itself with sprinkling a few Indigenous words into English. In other words, dominant language speakers should not read the poet's invitation to "learn Cree," as open and fluid as it may be, as a way out of having to make space for (and perhaps even *learn*) denied languages in the fullness of their difference and opacity. In the Canadian context, simply writing or living in a less bounded English that can accept more linguistic variation does not actually provide a way to address the ongoing destruction of Indigenous languages. To counter colonial monoglossia, Indigenous languages and expression need to be at the forefront of linguistic resistance. Scofield's heteroglossia and invitation to join him there, then, are perhaps

---

[53] Scofield, *Witness, I Am*, 69.

best understood not as an end in themselves but as a step away from English monolingualism on our way to more radical, decolonial linguistic lives.

In Praise of Chiac: Language Ideologies Clash in France Daigle's *Pour sûr*

Switching our focus to the eastern parts of Canada brings us to France Daigle, who helped put Chiac—the name of the "dialect" or "variety" spoken in Moncton, New Brunswick, and its surroundings—on the map of Canada's literary scene with her 2011 novel *Pour sûr*. The Maritime Provinces of Canada—comprised of New Brunswick, Nova Scotia, and Prince Edward Island—while mostly English-speaking, host a significant number of francophone communities. The Acadians are descendants of the French who settled in these territories in the seventeenth and eighteenth centuries before being deported en masse by the English, mostly to British American colonies. Some eventually returned to the Maritimes, mostly to present-day New Brunswick, and developed a history and culture distinct from that of other French groups in Canada, notably those in Quebec. Today, they constitute approximately 32 percent of New Brunswick's population, concentrated in the northern and southeastern parts of the province. Even though the Official Languages Act made the province officially bilingual in 1969, following decades of activism for the recognition of French speakers' linguistic rights, English remains the dominant language in many spheres, and Acadians' linguistic rights are still precarious. Importantly for this section, Acadians living in the southeast of New Brunswick speak what is typically considered a French vernacular, called Chiac, a well-documented variety that is stigmatized because of its deviance from the norm of "standard French," particularly in its incorporation of English words and pronunciations as well as lexical items that are considered archaic in other forms of French.[54]

Born in Moncton, New Brunswick, in 1953, Daigle published her first book in 1983 but only began to experience commercial success and critical appraisal toward the end of the 1990s, with the publication of her Moncton-based trilogy of novels *Pas pire* (1998), *Un fin passage* (2001), and *Petites difficultés d'existence* (2002). If *Pour Sûr* is best known for the significant amount of Chiac it contains, Daigle's early works hardly included any. Indeed, Raoul Boudreau

---

[54] See Spencer Trerice and Catherine Léger, "*Pour sûr* de France Daigle : un miroir des représentations linguistiques à l'égard du chiac," *Revue de l'Université de Moncton* 50, no. 1–2 (2019): 175.

and Catherine Leclerc have observed that, over time, Daigle has moved from a total absence of Acadian references, in her first publications, to a growing and more assertive presence of Acadian speech and cultural references, in her more recent works.[55] *Pour sûr* represents a high point in this trajectory: the novel gives a very prominent role to Chiac. In this narrative, which chronicles the daily lives of a handful of Moncton characters, the readers are reunited with Terry and Carmen, the protagonists of Daigle's earlier trilogy. But while the first three books have little Chiac in them and use typographic devices for linguistic differentiation such as the italicization of English words, *Pour sûr* introduces a new protagonist, sans italics: language itself, particularly Chiac, which the narrator defines as a "hotdge-podge of seventeenth century and modern French, of English words pronounced in an English accent, English words pronounced in a French accent, and a syntactical mix drawn from both languages" and as the "lingua franca of the Acadians of southeastern New Brunswick."[56] Chiac has elsewhere been defined as "[a] mix of French and English" where (old) French acts as the matrix but is nevertheless transformed by the inclusion of English.[57] Linguist Marie-Ève Perrot explains that Chiac is a "mixed code" where French remains dominant not only quantitatively and structurally but also symbolically: according to Perrot, Chiac connotes, from a sociological perspective, an affirmation of francophone identity.[58]

In *Pour sûr*, Daigle tests the limits of this equation of, or affiliation between, Chiac and French. The following pages will argue that Daigle represents both French and Chiac as conflicting ideological forces, thereby complicating the links between the Chiac vernacular and francophone identity.[59] *Pour sûr*'s experimental and highly formalized dual linguistic construction represents, on the one hand, the standard French language as an exogenous, normative institution and, on the other hand, Chiac as a set of embodied and fluid social practices, ultimately highlighting the

---

[55] See Raoul Boudreau, "Le rapport à la langue dans les romans de France Daigle: du refoulement à l'ironie," *Voix et Images* 29, no. 3 (2004): 31–45; Catherine Leclerc, "Hiérarchies et inhibitions francophones: quelques exemples empruntés à France Daigle et à Jacques Poulin," *Zizanie* 1, no. 1 (2017): 26–47.

[56] France Daigle, *For Sure*, trans. Robert Majzels (Toronto: House of Anansi, 2013), 39. In Daigle's own words: "Salmigondis de français du XVIIe siècle et de français moderne, de mots anglais prononcés à l'anglaise, de mots anglais francisés et d'un mélange syntaxique empruntant aux deux langues" (Daigle, *Pour sûr*, 24).

[57] Catherine Leclerc, "Between French and English, Between Ethnography and Assimilation: Strategies for Translating Moncton's Acadian Vernacular," *TTR* 18, no. 2 (2005): 161–2.

[58] Ibid.

[59] While she does not personally challenge these links, Leclerc acknowledges that "[d]espite its strong affiliation both to the French language and to a francophone identity, whether Chiac can belong to French is far from obvious when ideology is taken into account" (Leclerc, "Between French and English," 163).

incommensurability of the normativity of linguistic standardization and the diversity of linguistic practices.

What is at play in *Pour sûr* is not a purely linguistic clash between a standard language and one of its "dialects" or "varieties" but a clash between what Annette Boudreau has referred to as "the ideology of the standard" and the "ideology of the dialect."[60] The ideology of the standard refers to the social and political positioning of the so-called standard form of any given language as its most legitimate, rational, and universal form. This ideology posits language as an essence, implying that it is natural to speak a standard language and that this language should be spoken in more or less the same way everywhere at once. This creates linguistic insecurity within speakers who feel excluded because the language they speak does not align with the (imagined) standard. The ideology of the dialect emerges in response to this linguistic insecurity, seeing linguistic variation—be it geographical, class based, or otherwise—as an important emblem of group identity and as a source of pride and authenticity. Boudreau observes both approaches in Acadia—the collective term for Acadian communities—where some speakers will try to erase all regional markers in order to be perceived as a legitimate speaker of the standard language in certain settings, while they will insist on the differential character of their vernacular, as an important distinguishing component of their identity, in others. As the following analysis will show, both approaches are apparent in Daigle's novel, which explores the attitudes the speakers-characters entertain toward their linguistic practices and those of others.

The Diglossic Distribution of Language in *Pour sûr*

Speaking about why she gradually began incorporating Chiac into her writing over the years, France Daigle observes of her early works that "the reality is, my characters were not speaking in any of my books! I was writing books with no dialogue."[61] Associated with orality, Chiac appears in Daigle's works when she starts including increasing amounts of dialogue. Nearly half of her *Pour sûr*, published in 2011, is comprised of dialogues, which take place for the most part in Chiac, while standard French remains the language of narration. As an example, this excerpt intertwines both the narrative voice in standard French and a dialogue in Chiac:

---

[60] Boudreau, *À l'ombre de la langue légitime*, 165.
[61] In Marie Cadieux, *Éloge du chiac: Partie 2* (Office national du film du Canada, 2009), 37:00.

En fin de compte, pensant que cela pourrait lui servir, un des clients du Babar se mit à déchirer l'entrefilet faisant état du sondage sur la couleur des voyelles.
— Quoisse tu fais là ?
L'interpellé se sentit pris en flagrant délit :
— Euh… je voulais garder l'article pour…
— Es-tu un de ceuses-là qui déchiront des pages dans les mãgazines des bureaux de dentistes pis ça ? Ouelle, ça, ça me dōpe![62]

The narration is written in an unusually formal register for contemporary postmodernist Canadian literature, using the demonstrative pronoun "cela" instead of its colloquial short form "ça"; the formal, literary past tense, the "passé simple"; and grandiloquent words and turns of phrases such as "entrefilet," "interpellé," and "faisant état du sondage." The characters' direct discourse, however, appears to be in a different variety or dialect, in comparison with the narrative voice, precisely because it is *not standard*. The dialogue is populated with what could be seen as "errors" or "mistakes" from a normative perspective: the unusual spelling "quoisse" instead of "qu'est-ce," the third-person plural conjugation of verbs in the present tense with an ending in *-ont* ("déchiront" instead of the standard "déchirent"), and anglicisms, from Gallicized English words ("ouelle" for "well") to English pronunciations made visible by the presence of tildes ("mãgazines," "dōpe"). In other words, the dialogues are recognizable as Chiac only because they are recognizable as deviant from the norm, here standard French. In the novel's own words, "as grammatically logical as it is, Chiac is more often than not denounced as the supreme example of mediocrity, as a monumental deviation from normative French, which is a supposedly superior linguistic form."[63] In turn, it is precisely the presence of Chiac that reveals the presence of standard French in the narration and stages it as such, in the sense that when one reads a novel entirely written in a "standard register," one is unlikely to even notice it. In other words, Daigle's novel reveals that standard French and Chiac are co-constitutive.

This linguistic duality between narration and dialogue enacts a kind of literary diglossia, where the narrative voice in a standard language is associated with a universal, prestigious, neutral, objective, public-sphere voice, and the dialogues represent local, ordinary, everyday, subjective, private-sphere voices. Literary scholar Lise Gauvin has written at length about this kind of linguistic duality—using standard French for the narrative voice

[62] Daigle, *Pour sûr*, 77.
[63] Ibid., 240.

and dialect for the dialogues—in twentieth-century Québécois novels, where the formal narrative voice subordinates the oral dialogues, consequently framing and subsuming vernacular speech as secondary and inferior.[64] According to Gauvin, this kind of literary diglossia enables the narrator to become a kind of ethnographer, displaying a snobbish and elitist attitude toward the various registers and varieties featured in the dialogue, ultimately showcasing the author/narrator's linguistic skillfulness as distinct from the characters' provincial modes of speech. This gap between the narration and the dialogue becomes problematic, as it presents orality and vernaculars as a representable reality while the narration does the representation; in other words, the standard language maintains its implicitly superior, universal, and objective position of authority over the vernacular. As Leclerc, drawing on Bakhtin, points out, "too much linguistic differentiation, especially when it is inscribed between a character and the main narrative voice, creates a distance between said character and the narration, which risks reinforcing the narrative voice's semantic authority."[65]

In the case of *Pour sûr*, it seems as if Daigle takes Bakhtin's warning as a challenge. One could argue that Daigle is aware precisely of the dynamics implied in the narration/dialogue linguistic configuration that Gauvin criticizes in some Québécois realist narratives, as she pushes the configuration almost to the point of absurdity in an attempt, perhaps, to criticize and deconstruct linguistic normativity and the impact it has on Acadians. If at first glance the novel is written in a way that subscribes to the potentially fraught linguistic dichotomy between narration and dialogues flagged by Gauvin, Daigle's novel does so in an extremely deliberate and exaggerated way, which suggests a caricature of what Gauvin criticizes. While the narration indeed circumscribes the dialogues, the dialogues also talk back, so to speak, revealing standard French as a normative, powerful, institutionalized ideal only to then question its legitimacy. Gauvin as well as Leclerc have suggested that breaking this literary diglossia requires that the narration take on a plurality of voices and languages. This is certainly an option. But Daigle, instead of subverting the hierarchy by erasing or blurring it, invests in it in inventive and ironic ways, exaggerating both the narrative voice's self-anointed authority and prestige and the characters' linguistic insecurities. Ultimately, *Pour sûr* constructs two conflicting representations of language—standard metropolitan French as unquestioned normative institution and system and Acadian Chiac as a set of changing,

---

[64] Lise Gauvin, *Les langues du roman: Du plurilinguisme comme stratégie textuelle* (Montréal: Presses de l'Université de Montréal, 1999), 55.
[65] Leclerc, *Des langues en partage*, 81.

constantly questioned lived social practices—ultimately highlighting the incommensurability between the two, as one cannot exist in its bounded form without the other.

French as Normative Institution in *Pour sûr*

In her novel, Daigle uses irony to represent the French language as a deeply authoritative, institutionalized, normative system in three main ways:[66] by taking the language of the narration to an almost farcical level of abstraction and purification, by engaging the theme of institutionalization both in cultural references and metadiscursive remarks, and by constructing an exaggerated (self-)ethnographic gaze directed toward Chiac users.

In terms of the first of these, the narration is written in a hyperformalized, polished, and elegant style, reminiscent of grammar textbooks or nineteenth-century French prose:

> Il allongea à cette page l'étroit ruban blanc rattaché à la tranchefile du volume, qu'il referma et posa sur le coin du comptoir avec l'intention d'y revenir le lendemain. Puis il amorça les procédures de fermeture du commerce puisque Ludmilla, à qui incombait cette tâche d'habitude, avait pris congé plus tôt pour se rendre chez le dentiste.[67]

Oddly specific words such as "tranchefile" ("binding," instead of the more generic "reliure"), the literary positioning of verbs before their subject (in the earlier excerpt, "incombait cette tâche"), and convoluted nominal series like "les procédures de fermeture du commerce" (literally "the procedures for the closing of the [store/business]"; common usage would tend to prefer a simpler verbal construction, such as "fermer le commerce," in place of "fermeture du commerce") proliferate in the narration of *Pour sûr*. Other literary devices, such as the "passé simple" tense ("il amorça"), the positioning of adjectives before nouns, and the abundant use of long adverbs, give the narrative voice an almost absurdly classicist, belles-lettrist style. This creates a highly distanced voice, contrasted with the deeply accented, localized vernacular of the dialogues. Such a process of abstraction can be seen as a deliberate attempt to produce a purified language and decouple the narrative voice from

---

[66] For a discussion of irony in France Daigle's works, see Boudreau, "Le rapport à la langue."
[67] Daigle, *Pour sûr*, 83.

social reality; outside of books, no one *speaks* this brand of pure standard French.[68]

By using this perfectly refined, "universal" standard language, the narration is detached from the specificity of oral practices. For instance, when describing several scenes where a group of characters starts to cultivate a communal garden, the narration consistently refers to the garden as a "potager," whereas the characters themselves never use that word, instead using the more generic "jardin" common in Canadian usage. This phenomenon is repeated throughout the book: everywhere the narration and the characters use different words to refer to the same things—"réfrigérateur" and "frĩdge," "pommes de terre" and "patates," "grand-mère" and "mémére," "entrefilet" and "article," and so on. The narrative voice in the novel systematically resorts to words unmarked in French dictionaries, while the characters tend to use regional, colloquial, or informal, more generic, or English synonyms. Even the voice of the narrator—which we learn midway through the novel is an author named France Daigle, who is writing a novel called *Pour sûr*—undergoes drastic changes when she appears as a character within the narrative to meet with her characters over coffee. In the excerpt that follows, France Daigle the narrator tries to reassure her character Josse, who confronts her about spreading rumors and not being nice enough to her characters:

J'essayai de la rassurer:
— Ãnyways, c'est rien de grave. Une petite rumeur, whõ cãres, vraiment?
— En tout cas, je trouve pas que t'es fãir de piquer sus zeux de même. C'est à cause de zeux que le monte aime sitant tes livres. C'est zeux qui te faisont vivre!
De toute évidence, Josse oubliait que c'était d'abord moi qui les faisais vivre, eux, et elle aussi tant qu'à y être. Mais c'était secondaire.
— Si j'écris pas quoisse que je veux, ça vaut pas la peine d'écrire.

---

[68] Speaking of the movement for the standardization of English, Michael North reminds us: "[t]he standard is not standard, that is to say, but rather the very opposite. Critics willing to play with numbers speculate that perhaps 3 to 4 percent of the population of England speaks standard English, but the truth is that no one speaks standard English because that language is simply whatever shapeless thing is left when all the most common errors are removed." See Michael North, *The Dialect of Modernism* (Oxford: Oxford University Press, 1998), 24.

— Des fois les artistes me drĩvont. Y croyont qui pouvont toutte faire, aller contre le bon sens, être contre toutte. Comme si toutte ça qu'y faisont était si grĕat que ça !
...
— **Les artistes te frustront, c'est ça ?**[69]

Here, the first-person pronoun that appears both in the narrative voice and in the utterances highlighted in bold refer to the same person: France Daigle the author/narrator. Once she steps into a social situation, once she *speaks* outside the confines of the narrative voice, "nonstandard" elements emerge: anglicisms, conjugations in "-ont," "quoisse," phonetic transcriptions, and so on. The distinct constraints that shape the narration and the dialogue thus demand different linguistic performances from Daigle, according to her two roles as authoritative narrator and embodied character in a social setting—in other words according to the written/spoken dichotomy. As much as the narration needs to be standard to be "literary"—that is, to be recognized by the narration's interlocutor, understood here as the reader of French books—the narrator needs to speak Chiac in order to relate to her peers within the book. The narrator seeks a different kind of recognition in the dialogue, where the articulation of a distinct, local voice is crucial if she wants to be seen as a peer, as a community member. Daigle the narrator-character is obviously perfectly capable of writing in both "standard" and "vernacular" forms; both approaches thus depend on whom she decides to address in the book and on what their expectations are with regard to her linguistic performance.

Standard French is also constructed as normative category, system, and institution in *Pour sûr* through the theme of standardization and institutionalization. The narration is populated with regular references to linguistic institutions, with an emphasis on the prescriptive and authoritative nature of dictionaries and language "rules." Countless remarks on the game of Scrabble appear in the first third of the novel: the narrator observes that "*L'Officiel du jeu Scrabble*®, the Larousse dictionary for francophone Scrabble, always capitalizes the name of the game and follows it with the registered trademark symbol®."[70] Out-of-context dictionary definitions populate the narrative, such as "Cited without permission from *Webster's Third New International Dictionary* ©: PLAGIARIST *n*: (lat. plagiarus, from the gr.).

---

[69] Daigle, *Pour sûr*, 652–3, emphasis mine.
[70] Daigle, *For Sure*, 18. In Daigle's own words: "L'Officiel du jeu Scrabble® de Larousse écrit toujours le nom du jeu avec une majuscule et le fait toujours suivre du symbole de la marque déposée ®" (Daigle, *Pour sûr*, 15).

one who plagiarizes: one guilty of literary or artistic theft."[71] The characters constantly look up words in the dictionary, often for prescriptive purposes, condemning a spelling or an English etymology. Prestigious French literary or cultural institutions are also repeatedly mentioned, such as La Pléiade, a Parisian publisher, and *La Bibliothèque idéale*, a compilation of the most important authors and fundamental texts one "should" read. The overly formal and elitist, almost arrogant undertones of these examples and the way they are mobilized in the novel—mostly through encyclopedic and didactic observations in the narration—signal an ironic stance toward the linguistic and cultural practices they represent. The narrator appears to be obsessed with formalities, conventions, and etiquette: from trademark symbols to official statistics to lists of words that are and are not acceptable in Scrabble, norms appear as an underlying thematic thread throughout the novel, most particularly in the narration, where they are (ironically) venerated[72]—"ironically," because the narrator does not shy away from inventing her own normative institutions, such as the "Fictionary," a fictional dictionary with entries such as "SLANGOTHERAPY: n. — 2005. 1. Treatment of mental problems via re-education in linguistic deviance"[73] and the GIRAFE, the "Grand Institution of Rastafarian-Acadia for French Eventually."[74] In the narration, Daigle overcommits to playing by the rules of the standard, creating a sort of caricature of idealized, standard French.

Finally, the narration's overly refined and normative tone is supplemented by the construction of an exaggerated ethnographic gaze directed at the Chiac-speaking characters and at Acadians in general. The narrator, whom we now know is in fact a Chiac-speaking Monctoner, completely detaches herself from the practices of her linguistic community in a series of descriptive narrative remarks, such as the following:

> In Acadian, words ending in *o-i-r* are more often pronounced "*ouère*" or "ware" rather than "*oué*" or "way." The word *miroir*, for example, is

---

[71] Daigle, *For Sure*, 33. In Daigle's own words: "Tiré du Petit Larousse© Larousse-Bordas 1998: PLAGIAIRE. n (lat. plagiarus, du gr.). Personne qui plagie les œuvres des autres; démarqueur" (Daigle, *Pour sûr*, 22).

[72] It should also be mentioned that these institutions and conventions are often evoked because of their inherent exclusion of Acadian references: the narrator highlights the fact that only one Acadian author is included in the Pléiade's catalogue, observes that the Scrabble rules don't include Acadian nouns, and invokes dictionaries to "rectify" the characters' choices of words.

[73] Daigle, *For Sure*, 402–3. In Daigle's own words: "argothérapie : n. f.—2005; 1. Traitement de troubles mentaux par rééducation à la déviance linguistique" (Daigle, *Pour sûr*, 179).

[74] Daigle, *For Sure*, 241. In Daigle's own words: "la Grande instance rastafarienne-acadienne pour un français éventuel" (Daigle, *Pour sûr*, 93).

occasionally pronounced as "*miroué*" or "meerway," but more often "*mirouère*" or "meerware." In this context, the *w* (double *u*) could easily replace the sound "*ou*." Many Acadian pronunciations follow neither the spelling nor the sound dictated by what is commonly referred to as standard French.[75]

The ethnographic gaze Gauvin warns against is pushed to almost the point of absurdity throughout the novel: rather than trying to blend the narrative voice with the character's voices in order to undermine the narration's authority, as Gauvin would have it, Daigle invests in precisely this authority and creates an insurmountable gap between the novel's social voices and the normative standard of the narration. Two poles are thus deliberately created in *Pour sûr* between (written) monoglossia and (oral) heteroglossia, respectively, represented in/by the narration and the dialogues and both performed by the same narrator-character. Ultimately, the three observable devices analyzed earlier—the narration's abstracted language and highly formal register; the theme and language of institutions; and the deliberate construction of an overstated, pseudo-ethnographic relation to the characters' linguistic practices—together signal an authoritative and prescriptive force in tension with what is presented as its opposite, at the other pole: dialogues in Chiac.

Chiac as Social Practice, and Its Relation to Standard French

On the other side of the spectrum, then, lies the dialogue in Chiac. Throughout the novel, Chiac is associated with social life and specific historical and cultural conditions, appearing exclusively in the speech of Acadian characters in the city of Moncton and its surroundings. To reformulate Daigle's words, Chiac appears in *Pour sûr* when some characters *speak*. Chiac is also presented as first and foremost an oral and social phenomenon: as an unidentified character says, "A body has to grow wid it, it's not sometin' you can learn in a

---

[75] Daigle, *For Sure*, 241. In Daigle's own words: "En acadien, la prononciation *ouère* est nettement plus répandue que *oué* en ce qui concerne les mots se terminant en *oir*. Le mot *miroir*, par exemple, donne parfois *miroué*, mais surtout *mirouère*. Dans ce contexte, le *w* (double *v*) pourrait facilement remplacer le son *ou*. Un très grand nombre de prononciations acadiennes ne reproduisent ni l'orthographe ni les sons dictés par le français dit standard" (Daigle, *Pour sûr*, 110).

book, or *pickér* up just like dat."⁷⁶ Consequently, the linguistic heterogeneity of the dialogues is an important characteristic of the novel: certain characters speak with a heavier Chiac than others, the most notable example being the differences in speech between Terry and Carmen, the novel's protagonists. While Terry's use of Chiac is perhaps the most heavy of the novel, his wife Carmen often displays feelings of disapproval toward Chiac; even though she speaks Chiac herself, hers is a more diluted variety, influenced by an explicit desire to speak a more "correct" French. The examples that follow illustrate Terry's deep attachment to Chiac as well as Carmen's corrective impulses alongside her own use of Chiac elements:

> [Terry]—Quelqu'un pourrait dire de quoi comme *Le rēferee cawle un pēnalty quand c'est que les plāyers levont leu' stĭck trop haut.*
> Ludmilla finit par comprendre.
> — Carmen m'aurait tué si j'avais dit ça de même devant Étienne pis Marianne, bȳ thē wāy.⁷⁷
>
> [Carmen] — En tout cas, un hēaring, c'est un procès, pis une jāil, c'est une prison, bȳ thē wāy.
> Terry ne le prit pas mal :
> — Je sais. Ça montre juste comment fort que c'est quante le chiac de Dieppe coule dans tes veines.⁷⁸

In *Pour sûr*, each character has their own relationship to Chiac: French immigrants Ludmilla and Zablonski speak in a way that more closely resembles the narration than Terry's speech, even though they incorporate tiny bits of newly learned Chiac into their sentences; toddler Marianne mumbles her first words in baby talk; Élizabeth, a doctor from Montreal, and Simone, a biologist, speak a variety closer to generic Québécois French; Chico, a young orphan from an underprivileged background, has a more limited vocabulary and uses more words in English; and so on. Thus, there is a variety of registers, ranges, and degrees of Chiac that create a continuum of social voices in the dialogue, in opposition to the monolithic standard French that comprises the narration throughout. In the Bakhtinian sense, *Pour sûr* is a highly dialogic novel, given the variability of social voices presented—

---

[76] Daigle, *For Sure*, 477. In Daigle's own words: "C'est dequoi qu'y faut que tu grandisses avec, pas dequoi que tu peux apprendre dans les livres ou pĭcker ŭp juste de même" (Daigle, *Pour sûr*, 210).
[77] Daigle, *Pour sûr*, 114.
[78] Ibid., 238.

and, further, given the double-voiced discourse of the parodied monoglossic voice of the narration, which gives the narration a semantic intention directly opposed to what it seemingly does.

Chiac is also used in the novel in order to ironically expose the contradictions inherent to the idea of a pure, standard French as it appears in the narration. In the example that follows, two anonymous characters discuss Molière's rumored poor French, concluding that the only reason he is considered one of the greatest writers in the French language today might be that he was, simply, famous:

> — C'est supposé qu'y en avait du temps de Molière qui trouviont que son français était trop populaire, pas assez raffiné.
> — Denne hōw cōme qu'y disont tout le temps la langue de Molière, comme si qu'y était le kīngpin du français ?
> — Probablement parce qu'y a venu fãmous. C'était peut-être le premier Français à venir fãmous.[79]

This conversation illustrates how fraught the process of assessing linguistic competence can be, as it depends on value judgments and ideological categories such as "too popular" and "not refined enough." Here, Molière is recognized as a legitimate speaker, even model, of French, only because of his fame, highlighting the arbitrariness of deciding who counts as a legitimate speaker, how, and why—not unlike Tony Bex and Richard J. Watts's observation that many influential writers "were granted significance not merely for what they wrote, but also for who they were."[80] In another example, Terry looks up a word in the dictionary, curious to know if his use of "rouf" to refer to a roof on the deck of a boat is legitimate or not:

> When he found the word *rouf* in the dictionary, Terry saw that the sole definition of the term corresponded perfectly with the description provided by Daudet, whose phrase the dictionary actually quoted as an example. The word comes from the Dutch *roef* and means the same thing. Terry then looked up *roof* in an English dictionary, and discovered that it too is derived from the Dutch *roef*, which refers to a small shelter on the bridge of a boat, but which the English also use to refer to the roof of a house, the palate of a mouth, and a mountain summit. Terry felt as though he too had attained a kind of summit:

---

[79] Ibid., 32.
[80] Bex and Watts, Introduction to *Standard English*, 15.

Acadians tink der French is bad when dey say *rouf*. Dey tink dey're saying *roof* with a French accent."[81]

Here, the ideology of the standard is questioned, not through the ideology of the dialect but through a close examination of its own internal fallacies: while in Terry's environment "rouf" is considered today a Gallicized version of the English "roof"—and therefore a dangerous anglicism to be avoided at all costs—it is in fact in both languages a historical loan from the Dutch "roef," which means exactly what Terry is referring to. Challenged here are the alleged purity of any linguistic form and the flawed understanding that upholds the ideology of the standard, according to which some linguistic practices are legitimate and others are not, simply by virtue of an institutionalized and thus widespread notion of what is "correct" and what is not. What Terry realizes is that standard French is not something that exists in a pure form: it is first and foremost an idea, a construction that has become commonplace. The idea of the norm (and the ideology of the standard) is continually questioned, challenged, and deconstructed by the novel's Acadian characters, who are measured against it in their daily lives. What is the norm, and *why* is it the norm? Through their questions, the characters of *Pour sûr* reveal the norm, standard French, for what it is: an artificial concept that not only does not reflect or make room for their own linguistic realities but is also full of contradictions.

In this last example, where Terry corrects his son Étienne's choice of word, the norm appears, again, as an idea full of its own contradictions:

— Papa, la trũnk est pas fermée !
— La *valise*, Étienne, on dit *valise*.
— Beaucoup de monde disont *trũnk*.
— Peut-être, ben nous autres, on dit *valise*. Compris ?[82]

Terry condemns his son's use of the English word "trunk" and tells him to use the "more proper" French "valise," embodying the ideology of the standard's

---

[81] Daigle, *For Sure*, 220–1. In Daigle's own words: "Lorsqu'il trouva le mot *rouf* dans le dictionnaire, Terry remarqua que l'unique définition du terme correspondait en tous points à la description de Daudet, dont on citait d'ailleurs la phrase en exemple. Le mot provient du néerlandais *roef*, et sa signification est la même. Terry chercha ensuite le mot *roof* dans le dictionnaire anglais, découvrit qu'il provenait lui aussi du néerlandais *roef*, qui désigne ce petit abri sur le pont d'un bateau, mais que les Anglais utilisent pour désigner à la fois un toit, le palais de la bouche et un sommet. Terry sentit lui-même qu'il venait d'atteindre un sommet : — Les Acadiens croyont qu'y parlont mal quante qu'y disont *rouf*. Y croyont qu'y disont *roof* à la française" (Daigle, *Pour sûr*, 101).

[82] Daigle, *Pour sûr*, 169.

rectifying impulse. However, little does Terry know that this meaning of "valise" is in fact an exclusively Canadian usage, flagged as "québécisme" and "familiar" in French dictionaries[83] and not recorded in either the French Academy's dictionary *Le Robert* or the *Trésor de la langue française*, a sixteen-volume dictionary of nineteenth- and twentieth-century French. The "correct" word to use here, in "standard French," would be "coffre." Two different norms are at play here: the one dictated in Paris and the one dictated in Montreal, which put Acadian speakers in a position doubly on the periphery. Literary scholar François Paré has written about the institutional processes that led to the construction of a Quebec-centered linguistic norm from 1970 onward: the creation of a set of linguistic normative institutions such as the Office québécois de la langue française claiming a new hegemonic status for Québécois French enacted an "absolutely extraordinary ideological reversal," which partially decoupled it from the metropolitan French norm, at the same time that it was posited as yet another normative standard for linguistic practices associated with French elsewhere in Canada, such as in Acadia.[84] The earlier excerpt underlines, then, the artificiality of norms and their correlation with exogenous power, as well as the socially real pressure they continually impose on speakers. The Chiac of Daigle's characters, as a social practice, always remains in tension, in contradiction, and in relation to the idea of a French standard, whatever form this standard may take. Revealing the standard's flawed logic, its inherent contradictions, and its complicity with hierarchical power, Chiac is presented in the novel as an alternative, not as a fixed dialect or variety that is equally legitimate but as an unfixable, playful, fluid social practice.

The Incommensurability of French and Chiac

As Michael North observes, "[a]s 'broken English,' dialect [is] the opposite without which 'pure English' [can] not exist."[85] Indeed, for the characters' voices to be recognizable as "Chiac," we need the category of standard French, and vice versa—without the idea of a universal standard French, labeling distinct regional dialects such as "Chiac" would not make sense. As linguistic categories (as closed, bounded [co-]systems), standard French and Chiac each need the other to exist, and the point of *Pour sûr* is that they are, for that very reason, incompatible. In their nature as hegemonic, standardized, normalizing system and embodied, localized,

---

[83] See, for instance, the entry in the Antidote Dictionary, which is developed in Canada.
[84] François Paré, *Les littératures de l'exiguïté* (Ottawa: Le Nordir, 1992), 42.
[85] North, *The Dialect of Modernism*, 33.

fluid, diverse, social practices, respectively, French and Chiac are presented as incommensurable categories—each occupying its own jurisdiction in *Pour sûr*. The ideology of the standard and its corollary, the ideology of the dialect, while they need each other to remain relevant or useful, are thus caught in a never-ending, unsolvable tension. As opposite categories, Chiac as dialect (identity and difference) and French as standard language (homogeneity and sameness) are merely two sides of the same coin—understanding language as a closed, delimited system. Further, if Chiac can somehow claim a linguistic affiliation with French, because it "contains" French or "comes from" French, the opposite is unthinkable, since standard French requires Chiac and other "dialectal varieties" to be external to itself in order for it to define itself oppositionally.

To attend to Daigle's entire oeuvre is to notice a general move away from the norm's rigidity and toward the fluidity of linguistic practices that culminates with *Pour sûr* in 2011, if only in the dialogue. That being said, standard French as institution/norm never disappears from her work—after all, it does not disappear from the lived realities of Acadians either—but it *is* formally separated from the novel's linguistic and social *practices* and explicitly constructed as an external, authoritative ideological force. Over the years the author has clearly shown a growing suspicion of the standard, pushing its reach and its prestige to an absurd and ironic point and deconstructing its logic through the increased use of Chiac as a social practice that resists the pull of standardization. In this way, my reading here goes against the ones suggested by Raoul Boudreau and Catherine Leclerc before the publication of *Pour sûr*, who claim that "Daigle's writing insists on the compatibility of Acadian French with other varieties of French."[86] Leclerc distinguishes two possibilities for Chiac: "firstly, as part of a wider French repertoire and secondly, as a mixed code in the process of replacing French," and argues that in her works (before *Pour sûr*), Daigle favors the former possibility over the latter.[87] I would argue that not only does this analysis rely on an uncritical view of language as system—seeing Chiac as residing either *inside* or *outside* French—but also that this hypothesis does not hold with the formal linguistic duality of *Pour sûr*.

What is at play in Daigle's most recent novel is not the legitimation of Chiac in relation to French—in other words, the ideology of the dialect—but the deconstruction of both the ideas of standard French and of French

---

[86] Leclerc, "Between French and English," 172. See also Raoul Boudreau, "Les français de Pas pire de France Daigle," in *La création littéraire dans le contexte de l'exiguïté*, ed. Robert Viau (Montréal: Publications MNH, 2000), 62.
[87] Leclerc, "Between French and English," 172.

subdialects. Daigle sheds light on the French norm's flaws and fraught power structure through Chiac, seen not as a fixed, more authentic dialect but as a fluid, more inclusive, less policing social practice. This is only possible because Chiac, being first and foremost an oral phenomenon, is not standardized and, as such, is not rigidly delineated. As the narrator states:

> But where does a language begin, where does it end? When does a language become a different language? Isn't all speech an interpretation of reality, hence a kind of translation, a fleeting attempt of language, a lalanguage? And whether French is old or contemporary or standard or hybrid, isn't language, like life, nothing more than a long processs [*sic*] of uninterrupted hybridization?[88]

In *Pour sûr*, (standard) French and Chiac are incommensurable not as essentially distinct languages or varieties but because of the ideas we formulate about the former and the predominance we assume it has over the latter: the first, an almighty, purified, fixed system we collectively impose on speakers, and the second, a fluid phenomenon which takes place in given sociohistorical communicative settings. Chiac and standard French are incommensurable because the former is defined by an inherent heterogeneity and variation, while the latter has homogeneity as its end goal—similar to the interplay between the left and right columns observed in Scofield's poetry earlier. Indeed, in the same way that Scofield's mixed ancestry requires the fraught notion of "nonmixed ancestors," Daigle's Chiac, as long as it is framed as a "hybrid" language, that is, as a brand of French contaminated by English, requires the impossible notion of nonmixed languages (French and English), which are always seen as superior even though they do not exist. In this sense, the only way Chiac could ever become "compatible" or aligned with French would be to entirely empty it of English, which is to say that it would have to let go of what makes it Chiac.

Of course, in representing certain oral practices in written form, what Daigle is also doing is, to some extent, "fixing" these forms, in the same way that standardization makes a specific set of rules *the only set of rules*. However, Daigle's individual attempt at writing down (observable or imagined) oral practices should not be equated with state-instituted standardizing and homogenizing projects but rather understood as a subjective and creative

---

[88] Daigle, *For Sure*, 1137. In Daigle's own words: "Mais où commence, où finit une langue ? Quand une langue devient-elle une autre langue ? Toute parole n'est-elle pas qu'une interprétation de la réalité, donc une sorte de traduction, de tentative fugace de langage, une lalangue ? Et puis, que le français soit ancien ou actuel ou standard ou hybride, la langue, comme la vie, n'est-elle pas qu'un long processus d'hybridation ininterrompu ?" (Daigle, *Pour sûr*, 504).

exploration of and experimentation with what Chiac might look like on the page for *her*. The idea of a standard Chiac and the movement for the standardization of Chiac is in fact critically contemplated in the novel through several dialogues, most notably in the following excerpt, where two unnamed and unconvinced characters discuss the idea:

> — Yer a writer, wot does you tink?
> — Dat would be a pinch . . . to decide once'n fer all wot our language is, wot's in and wot's out. Fer instance, would de old French words automatically be alright? An' any English words automatically bad? Some powerful smart folks would have to tink long an' hard on it, folks dat could make real sense of it all, and den explain it all so we could see the sense of it.
> — Explain it! Bin twenty-five years dey been explainin' how pollution's after killing de planet. Has folks changed? Not a whole lot.[89]

Rather than arguing for the standardization of Chiac, Daigle merely shows that other kinds of writing are feasible: that it is possible to write in nonstandardized, nonfixed, heteroglossic ways; that it is possible to play a myriad of other linguistic games. Social practices tend to resist prescriptive, reformist movements anyway; as Milroy states, "the principles of linguistic correctness and uniformity [fail] to influence actual usage very deeply."[90]

As an idea and as a project, standardization is revealed to be a kind of translation, one that seeks to translate a variety of different practices into sameness. Thus, the will, or impulse, to standardize anything that is not already standardized or organized as a system, in an attempt to create a legitimate language out of it, can only erase its inherent heterogeneity and create more strata on the ladder of linguistic norms. What Daigle does in *Pour sûr* is not singlehandedly legitimizing, fixing, and standardizing Chiac as a normative system; rather, she deconstructs standard French as a normative

---

[89] Daigle, *For Sure*, 473–4. In Daigle's own words: "—Toi, un écrivain, quesse t'en penses ?

—Ça serait une moyenne affaire . . . Décider une fois pour toutes de ça qu'est notre langue, quoisse qui passe pis quoisse qui passe pas. Comme, le vieux français serait-y automatiquement bon ? Pis l'anglais automatiquement mauvais ? Faudrait que du monde smarte pense à toutte ça, du monde qui pourrait voir le bon sens pis nous donner des explications.

—Des explications ! Ça fait vingt-cinq ans qui nous expliquont que la pollution va tuer la planète. Le monde a-t-y changé ? Pas thât much" (Daigle, *Pour sûr*, 208).

[90] Milroy, "The Consequence," 20.

system and reframes both standard French and Chiac as potential linguistic practices or performances.

In fact, what the insistence on Scrabble, crosswords, and other games throughout the novel points to is that Daigle approaches language, especially "standard French," as a game. It should be noted here that *Pour sûr* is also striking for its ludic quality: for instance, the novel is made up of 12 × 12 topics, each of which is divided into twelve brief passages, carefully numbered and indexed but scattered through the book. The index suggests that the text could be pulled apart and read in another order altogether; in other words, the narrative resembles a Scrabble game. In the narration, Daigle delights in the artificiality and the arbitrariness of the rules of "standard French," willingly playing the game and playing it very well. She does not suggest the artificial standard should be rejected in favor of the "natural," more "authentic" vernacular. The difference between standard French and Chiac, for Daigle, is that with Chiac, she gets to create her own rules, her own game. This interpretation echoes Julien Lefort-Favreau's review of *Pour sûr* in 2013, in which he argues:

> Daigle's writing is terrorist and inclusive at once. She does not take on a victimizing posture, where the illegitimate tongue should be the only one to exist, but neither does she ask, ashamed, permission to use "the proper language." She allows herself to use both Chiac and normative French at the same time, rightfully considering nothing to be forbidden. Her plea for a heterogeneous aesthetics does not only benefit Chiac, but all discourses.[91]

In short, Daigle does not seek to replace (standard) French with Chiac as the legitimate language but to make room for a plethora of liberated and playful voices and practices, which requires the undoing of the norm, not the creation of yet another one. Elevating Chiac to the status or legitimacy of French would amount to trying to climb closer to the top of the linguistic hierarchy, buying into the market of linguistic value. As Bourdieu points out, "it is impossible to save the value afforded to competence without saving the market, in other words without saving the set of political and social conditions that allow for the reproduction of the market, on which the social value afforded to linguistic competence, and its ability to function as linguistic capital, depend."[92] Daigle knows this and, in *Pour sûr*, does the opposite: she mobilizes usage—its fluid, changing, and heteroglossic nature—in order to subvert the market and to counter the idea of linguistic legitimacy, that is, the idea that there is any right way to write.

---

[91] As quoted in Trerice and Léger, "*Pour sûr* de France Daigle," 175–6.
[92] Quoted in Rodrigue Landry, "Légitimité et devenir en situation linguistique minoritaire," *Linguistic Minorities and Society* 5 (2015): 63.

Translation as Social Practice, Translation as Counter-Standardization

In distinct yet similar ways, both Scofield and Daigle construct a tension between norm and usage (whatever forms they may take in different contexts), creating a spectrum with the opposite poles of hetero- and monoglossia. Their works establish a dialectical relationship between the concept of a monologic standard and a number of practices that overflow, displace, and contest the norm, revealing the homogenizing, translative work of standardization as well as the standardizing work of translation. Both authors, rather than trying to elevate social voices to the status of legitimate languages, deconstruct the idea of the standard as they reveal (and, in Daigle's case, revel in) its artificiality. What is interesting in the works analyzed here is precisely that the boundary delimiting the standard and nonstandard forms is revealed as ideological and political (and, in Scofield's case, colonial) rather than as simply linguistic. Recognized as a powerful force that seeks to homogenize and delegitimize actual practices, the idea of the standard becomes, in Scofield's and Daigle's works, something against which heteroglossic poetic and fictional voices consistently push back.

The texts explored in this chapter are a testament to the variable nature of language in use and to the fact that, despite widespread standardization, linguistic diversity is thriving and inevitable, because language is first and foremost a practice, a performance—both in oral and written forms and otherwise. As such, it is not only social but also fundamentally political. The question, then, is not how to treat both standard and nonstandard forms in the same way in translation—as we have seen, they are precisely not treated in the same way in Scofield's and Daigle's texts—but rather how to treat them as different social forces, resources, and practices that stand in opposition and in relation to each other. In critiquing the legitimacy of the monologic and standard form, Scofield and Daigle also champion something else: a multiplicity of forms, a heterogeneity of social voices that, by their very nature, reside outside of the established norm. Scofield's poetry portrays his own subjective response to the normative labeling(s) in which he could never fit; his heteroglossia is about opening to more fluid ways of being and of speaking, drawing on whatever resources are available to him through his relations, both ancestral and present, to counter colonial homogeneity. Daigle's book is fundamentally about the tensions that arise when an exogenous norm is imposed on a given community and about the artificiality, arbitrariness, and potential playfulness of any linguistic rule—and she shows that one way to defuse power is to make a game out of it.

Both works are about resisting monoglossic, standard hegemony and about talking back to a powerful, institutionalized force that prescribes how to write, speak, and ultimately *be*. The linguistic interplay—between heteroglossia and monoglossia, between practices and abstracted norms— that both writers create, formally and textually, as a central element and theme of their work, forces a partial move away from the idea of standard languages in translation; translating both sides of the dichotomy in a standard, unitary variety would simply make no sense at all. In forcing us to reconsider the untranslatability of nonstandard forms, or their framing as essentially a problem for translation, Daigle and Scofield make visible the dubious grounds on which translation practice and theory lie, at the same time that they point to new possibilities for approaching language in writing.

Reading Scofield and Daigle's texts as a critique of the ideology of the standard in relation to their own minoritized linguistic practices signals that a move away from the notion of the standard in translation is not only desirable but also necessary. Seeing language not as a normative system of standardized rules but as a social practice, comprised of "sets of resources called into play by social actors under [specific] social and historical conditions,"[93] allows us to move beyond the standard/nonstandard dichotomy without denying its social causes, realities, and effects. As we have seen, a structural linguistic approach, because of its connection to standard language ideology, forecloses the possibility of translating nonstandard forms altogether. Seeing language, including writing in what is commonly perceived as standard French or English, as a social practice allows for a much better understanding of how language *actually works*, in what are considered both standard and nonstandard forms, that is, not according to fixed lines between different languages, varieties, and dialects but rather according to the intersections of particular social, cultural, political, and historical processes that partially predetermine linguistic practices—although individual agency also inevitably plays an important role. Recognizing the sociohistorical processes that lead to the delimitation of standard and nonstandard is the first step to a better understanding of the linguistic elements of the social, cultural, and political positionality that these writers are portraying, with regard to norms, or rules, that are always exogenous. In short, translating both Scofield's and Daigle's works with an approach that uncritically relies on standard language ideology would be contrary to precisely what these texts contest and completely miss the mark in terms of what these texts are actually about—exposing the pressure of a monoglossic, standard ideology on individual and collective linguistic

---

[93] Heller, "Bilingualism as Ideology and Practice," 15.

practices. I conclude here by exploring some possible avenues for translating Scofield's and Daigle's texts that would take into account the tensions, conflicts, and struggles portrayed in these texts and described throughout this chapter.

In the case of Scofield's poetic voice, keeping both its heteroglossia and the formal contrast with a monologic, standard national language in the right column should be at the center of a critical translation project. By mobilizing different linguistic practices, Scofield mobilizes different (often silenced) stories and histories: he gives voice to his mother and aunt and their voiceless generation, allowing different histories of silencing and discrimination to intersect, and interweaves different subject positions in order to create one for himself, on his own terms. The title of his 2009 collection *kipocihkân* is, according to the publisher's website, Cree slang for someone who is mute or unable to speak.[94] Scofield's work charts his own journey out of an imposed silence, learning to embrace a variety of languages, registers, and voices in the process, apparently the only way for him to overcome the authoritative, normative, and silencing monolithic structure of hegemonic English qua whiteness.

One possibility for the translation of Scofield's poetry would be to find another standard, national, hegemonic language that functions elsewhere in similar ways to English in Western Canada: French in Quebec, for instance, or Spanish in Latin America. Other socially meaningful voices could then be presented in tension with, and as an alternative to, the monolithic and normative product of imperial translation/assimilation now represented as, say, French. The Cree and Hebrew elements could perhaps also be translated into other languages that occupy a similar position with regard to the new imperial, hegemonic language that replaces English, rather than mechanically importing the Cree and Hebrew elements into the French translation, as would usually be done in this case.[95] In the case of a French translation in

---

[94] Harbour Publishing, "kipocihkân: Poems New and Selected," https://harbourpublishing.com/products/9780889712287.

[95] This obviously displaces the work from its original authorial location, detaching it from its original context of production, but I would argue that these are already displaced through the translation of the English elements into French. Translation creates, by its very definition, a fundamental and radical displacement of a given text; to believe that it is possible to keep Scofield's identity (or parts of it) intact in French would be a fiction. This is why I prefer to speak of a text's *positionality and relationality* rather than of a text's supposed *identity* in translation: the goal is, in my view, to produce a translated text which occupies or presents a discursive position similar to the one(s) occupied by or presented in the source text. Keeping the Cree and Hebrew elements intact in translation, if these languages and the subject positions they represent (in Canada, with regard to English) do not have any social, cultural, or political relationship to the language that will translate the English elements, requires us to ask whether considering other heteroglossic configurations that would be more meaningful in this regard could help to produce a newly meaningful text for a different audience within a different cultural and linguistic landscape.

Quebec, for instance, Cree could occupy a similar position with regard to the official language, but it could be a different Cree than the one Scofield writes in, since the Cree communities in this territory have their own unique ways of speaking. Hebrew could also work, or perhaps even Yiddish, which has a specific history as a minoritized language in Montreal. If translated elsewhere, in Mexico for instance, an Indigenous language from that territory could potentially translate the Cree elements in Scofield's poetry. In short, if we translate the English elements into another language—already displacing the poet's identity and positionality to a new place and time where a completely different set of cultural, social, and political inequalities and struggles take place—why not consider other intersecting, heteroglossic, and interwoven possibilities for translation in a new linguistic, which is to say social, configuration? Perhaps some Cree and Hebrew elements could be kept intact, while others could become more meaningful if translated into other languages.

This could also potentially respond to Scofield's invitation to participate in more inclusive, heteroglossic ways of envisioning language: translators could add their own voice to the blend of social voices that compose the original poems, creating an even more heteroglossic, echoed, diverse voice in translation, rather than trying to tame it. What linguistic forms spoken by the translator or the translator's ancestors, friends, or neighbors are erased by the official, public language where they live and work? Translators would also have to literally "learn Cree": instead of copying and pasting the elements that are not in English in the source text; they would have to collaborate with social actors, make new relations, and learn to produce a meaningful text with languages other than the hegemonic one in their culture, and readers would be presented with voices that are meaningful and relevant in their own social and cultural contexts. Participating in the kind of heteroglossia Scofield portrays, envisions, and calls for, and reproducing it in translation, for instance, would require translators to step out of the standard language ideology and to actually *practice* heteroglossia in translation as well, either by drawing on their own linguistic relations or by making new ones. This, in turn, would switch the focus from translators' "mastery" of the "standard language" as the sole or main criteria for practicing translation to recognizing the ability to mobilize a broad and diverse range of linguistic resources as a significant asset for the practice of translation.

As for *Pour sûr*, it has in fact been translated by Canadian novelist, poet, and playwright Robert Majzels and published by House of Anansi Press under the title *For Sure* in 2013. Majzels, who has translated five of Daigle's novels since *1953: Chronicle of a Birth Foretold* in 1997, has changed his approach to translating the author's language from one book to the next, in the same way that Daigle has changed her own approach to including Chiac in her novels.[96] While the scarce presence of Chiac in her previous novels was a relatively easy challenge for Majzels, *Pour sûr* forced him to reconsider his approach and come up with a new solution from scratch. Author and translator alike have discussed the 2013 translation, both process and product, extensively. Daigle has observed that Majzels succeeded in creating "an English that wasn't ordinary," in composing "a type of English that's a bit 'Maritimer,' but not too much, with the verbs conjugated more or less as they are in Chiac."[97] Majzels has explained his own approach for the translation of *Pour sûr* as follows:

> I needed a more rigorous and structured language to translate her Chiac [compared to her previous novels]. But not a standard English, which would conceal the difference operating in the French. I was compelled to invent a non-normative English. In both cases *I was resisting conventional translation practices in refusing to normalize the language.*
>
> . . .
>
> I began to study Newfoundlandese and Cape Breton Industrial accent, which is influenced by Irish. Both of these are stigmatised or minor languages of English. They're also, like Chiac, maritime languages. I listened to tapes of people speaking these languages, and read some literature. I started reading the *Dictionary of Newfoundland English*.
>
> . . .

---

[96] When an interviewer asks her if her thoughts on Chiac have changed over the years, Daigle answers: "Radically. They've changed radically. In fact, I'm faced with a dilemma I haven't necessarily resolved. I was raised, like many others, to think that proper French was 'true' French. As for Chiac, it was an accident, or a product of negligence or laziness or failure. But it was not to be promoted. It was a sub-product of French in this particular context, in this region. So, it was something negative. I wasn't working towards writing in Chiac—not at all—while all around me there were Acadians, less inhibited than I was, using English words or writing in a more spoken style. But I didn't feel I wanted to do that, either. In the end, it took me one, two, three—I don't know how many books; I wrote six or seven without dialogue. I couldn't write dialogue, and I knew it was because I couldn't decide which language to write it in. For me, it didn't make any sense to write dialogue in standard French, except where it might be applicable. But to make people from here speak in proper, standard French was senseless. A while back, I was invited to write plays. I did so and was able to coast along, because, for me, theatre isn't serious. With theatre, you're entertained for a night. So I permitted myself to throw in some Chiac—not necessarily a lot of Chiac—but, little by little, I was able to relax a bit when it came to Chiac. Even the books I wrote prior to *Pour sûr* have some Chiac in them, but nevertheless it's pretty benign." In Andrea Cabajsky, "The Vivid Feeling of Creating: An Interview with France Daigle," *Studies in Canadian Literature* 39, no. 2 (2014): 262–3.

[97] In Cabajsky, "The Vivid Feeling of Creating," 266.

I didn't want to simply translate Chiac into a recognized English minor language, the way for instance Tremblay has been translated into Scottish. I couldn't allow the reader to forget that this was Chiac the characters were speaking. Because that's what this book is about, the culture and language of Acadia. Because the readers, if there were going to be any, would be Anglophones, and the book had to be seen in the context of the relationship of English to French in North America, and Canada in particular. But it also had to point to stigmatized versions of English, minor languages such as Newfoundlandese, Irish, Scottish, etc. all of which have the experience of colonial and imperial rule.[98]

Thus, Majzels explicitly draws on a number of sources, not from a supposedly fixed variety, to create a heteroglossic assemblage. Let us see how this translates in Majzels's version. Following is an interaction between two Monctoners, which takes place in Chiac in the original text, marked in the margin as a "Chiac Lesson":

"How is it dat in Chiac dey sometimes puts an apostrophe right before de *n* and udder times dey puts it right after?"
"Must be a new rule, I figures. Dat sometimes you puts it '*n* sometimes you doesn't."
"And does you tink kids should be learning dem rules, as well?"
"Eh boy, what d'ya tink! One ting fer sure, 'twould make learnin' a whole lot easier, on account of 'twould be der real language."
"Well, how soon afore dey gets started?"
"Dey don't know, do dey. Dat's sometin' dey've not decided."[99]

Majzels's dialogues contain similar characteristics to Daigle's representation of Chiac: "faulty" verb conjugations, phonetic transcriptions rather than "correct" spellings, orality markers, contractions, and so on. But Majzels's strategy is not aimed at representing a "real," "existing," "equivalent" "dialect" from, say, Newfoundland in order to translate Daigle's heteroglossic dialogue; as he mentions, he produces an assemblage of several nonnormative, minoritized forms of English, and it is precisely this that produces an effective result, in clear opposition to the monologism of the narration in "standard English."

---

[98] Catherine Leclerc and Robert Majzels, "In Conversation: Catherine Leclerc and Robert Majzels," *Lemon Hound*, 2013, https://lemonhound.com/2013/09/27/in-conversation-catherine-leclerc-robert-majzels/. Emphasis added.
[99] Daigle, *For sure*, 208–9.

Instead of finding a "real," "equivalent" bounded dialect in which to render the characters' speech—at the end of the day, Daigle's renditions of Chiac are also fictional, that is, her own creation—Majzels draws on a multiplicity of sources to create voices that evoke and portray the same thing Chiac does in Daigle's version: orality and heterogeneity, a distinctive, nonstandard grammar/vernacular and thus the belonging to a shared discursive, cultural, practice-based (fictional) community, and the minoritization of this community with regard to a normative, standard English. Such an approach to translation is very much aligned with Scofield and Daigle's call for taking a critical distance from the authority of the standard and embracing a variety of unbounded social practices.

Furthermore, Majzels's translation includes a number of French elements, for instance when he uses "Le Petit Étienne" and "Le Grand Étienne" to distinguish two characters or simply when he inserts French words, as in "It forms the communauté d'agglomération of Pau-Pyrénées with 13 neighbouring communes to carry out local tasks together."[100] He also at times adds his own nod to Daigle's inter- and meta-textuality, such as in the following endnote: "The Yi Jing method of divination serves as the structural framework for France Daigle's *Life's Little Difficulties* (translated from the French by Robert Majzels, House of Anansi Press, 2004)."[101] Where the source text only mentions the French edition of Daigle's novel, Majzels replaces it with his own translation, making his presence and his subjectivity as a translator explicitly felt. In short, Majzels creatively intervenes throughout the translation, even *adding* to the heteroglossia of Daigle's version of *Pour sûr* by making his own voice visible and by adding another linguistic layer with the presence of French forms.

Perhaps Majzels is drawing on his own experience of and fondness for heteroglossia: born in Montreal of Jewish parents, he is known as a novelist and poet for his polyphonic style, most notably for his first novel *Hellman's Scrapbook*. It should also be noted that Majzels's version of *For Sure* made the Governor General's Awards shortlist in the Translation category. It has been called a "tour de force" by the IMPAC Dublin Literary Award, for which it made the longlist in 2015. It would seem, in the end, that exploring the interweaving of voices, even adding to it, instead of centering his practice on the idea of standard languages—even if that meant "resisting conventional translation practices," in other words refusing to play the game of standardized translation—has been fruitful for Majzels in this particular case. Instead of shying away from the translation of Daigle's vernacular, the

[100] Ibid., 219.
[101] Ibid., 275.

translator invested in it, participating in a similar kind of literary language creation, playing an entirely new game of his own making.

To conclude, one of *Pour sûr*'s anonymous characters ask, "So, de real question is dis: should we be talkin' like we write, or writin' like we talk?"[102] While Scofield and Daigle do not provide a fixed, definitive answer, they certainly point to a tentative resolution. In true France Daigle fashion, the answer can in fact be found in the question itself, particularly in the way the question is asked: as social practices, writing (and translating) should reflect the social—fluid, changing, heterogeneous—nature of all language, writing no less than speech, more than it generally does. It is not that we should literally write as we speak but rather that, perhaps, writing and translation practices should leave the normativity of the standard behind and draw instead on the heterogeneity of observable (or imagined) *practices*.

---

[102] Ibid., 468. In Daigle's own words: "Sõ, la vraie question devrait être: faut-y parler comme qu'on écrit ou ben don écrire comme qu'on parle?" (Daigle, *Pour sûr*, 206).

3

The Linguistic Abject

The Queering of Language in Kevin Lambert and Joshua Whitehead

Axiom 2: Translation is a rendering from one language to another.

The there of queer utopia cannot simply be that of the faltering yet still influential nation-state.

—José Esteban Muñoz, *Cruising Utopia*

This chapter focuses on the assumption that we necessarily translate *from one language to another*, in other words, that linguistic boundaries correspond to objective rules that scholars and translators need to identify and follow. Thus, the following pages tackle the notion of languages' autonomy, that is, the idea that distinct languages exist as "empirical rubrics within which . . . linguistic practices can be objectively situated,"[1] rather than their being constructed and their differences maintained by metalinguistic acts of differentiation, including that of translation. More specifically, it looks at how two writers, Kevin Lambert and Joshua Whitehead, engage the Québécois and Canadian linguistic order(s) in their books at the same time that they trouble the social and sexual order on other fronts. In their work, these two writers mobilize and thematize the queer abject, and more generally the workings of social abjection, unsettling and challenging heteronormative criteria of social belonging. Strikingly, both writers have a similar relationship to language, in the sense that they write in mostly nonnormative ways and incorporate "foreign" elements, linguistic or otherwise, into their writings, which are nevertheless published and marketed according to the monolingual logic of literary publishing (which, in turn, mirrors Quebec's and Canada's linguistic policies). As will be argued in this chapter, their work asks us to reconsider the conventional linguistic boundaries we are familiar with by

---

[1] Rosa, *Looking Like a Language, Sounding Like a Race*, 4.

drawing alternative, explicitly heteroglossic and self-critical cartographies of language. Since the "conceptualization and representation of sameness and difference, of borders and bordering" is a central concern of both queer theory and translation studies,[2] this chapter looks at how two queer writers challenge traditional articulations of sameness and difference along sexual and linguistic lines at once.

The following pages look at linguistic difference as it typically plays out in translation—understood as transposing an utterance or a text from one language to another—through the lens of abjection. As we will see, the queer abject in Lambert and Whitehead's works reveals the extent to which the construction of linguistic boundaries operates according to a logic of abjection as exclusion. Tracing the linguistic abject can help us not only to deconstruct linguistic boundaries but also to better grasp the political potential of a writing strategy that welcomes linguistic elements that are "out of place" within an established language of publication. As many queer theorists have shown, supposedly sovereign national, social, and sexual identities are normative categories constructed and reproduced through an oppositional and exclusionary logic, and this chapter suggests that we look at language as a category which functions in much the same way. From this perspective, so-called multilingual writing is not the juxtaposition of different, autonomous languages but the incorporation of socially, politically, and historically abjectified forms and practices into what has always been an imagined system; it calls into question the very notion of linguistic autonomy, rather than reaffirming it.

A focus on linguistic abjection allows us to recognize the social and material realities of the structural understanding of language and of the hegemony of dominant, colonial languages in Canada, without reifying these languages as "natural" or "legitimate." This follows Jonathan Rosa's raciolinguistic perspective, which focuses on contesting the categorization, by hegemonically positioned subjects, of minoritized linguistic practices, rather than on the modification of these minoritized practices so that they fit into available hegemonic categories.[3] Furthermore, theorizing linguistic difference through the notion of abjection helps us grasp the political potential of works such as Lambert's and Whitehead's on the linguistic level, recognizing the "threat" that such writing poses for the dominant linguistic order, its categories, and its differentiated hierarchies. On the one hand, a focus on linguistic abjection reveals that linguistic categories are never "fixed"

---

[2] Brian James Baer, *Queer Theory and Translation Studies: Language, Politics, Desire* (New York: Routledge, 2020), 3.
[3] Rosa, *Looking Like a Language, Sounding Like a Race*.

and rely on active and ever-changing exclusionary mechanisms that vary through time and space, depending on who gets to impose and police "their language" over a given political territory. On the other hand, embracing the linguistic abject functions as an inclusionary gesture that is capable of caring for abjected, minoritized experiences.

Linguistic Abjection and the Political Potential of the Abject

The presence of linguistic forms that are seen as belonging *outside* of a language's boundaries—as "matter out of place," as Mary Douglas puts it[4]— produces textual results that highlight the linguistic abject. The notions of matter out of place and abjection imply two conditions: first, a set of ordered relations—here understood as English Canada's and Quebec's linguistic orders, where one official language subsumes a number of other languages and linguistic practices—and, second, a contravention of that order.[5] The writers analyzed in this chapter contravene the set of linguistic relations that define their respective contexts—in Lambert's case, the monolingual French national model adopted by the province of Quebec, and for Whitehead, the English monolingualism of the Anglo-Canadian literary canon, often referred to as CanLit. They do so by infusing their predetermined languages of publication with elements they usually exclude, creating linguistically "impure," "polluted" forms—and by ultimately excluding, in fact, the standard forms of the languages they are said to write in.

Abjection, that is, the rejection of everything expelled from the body, is, in a physiological sense, a fundamental and inevitable human reaction that serves biological purposes, such as to avoid being poisoned or contracting a disease through contact with bacteria, dirt, decomposition, and so on—in other words to avoid the threat of death. In 1980, Julia Kristeva theorized social and political exclusion through this elementary physiological reaction: abjection within the social realm occurs when certain bodies or practices are excluded from normative categories of identity—and thus from a delimited social body—and denied legitimacy through their discursive association with toxicity, dirtiness, obscenity, and so forth. She states: "Excrement and its equivalents (rot, infection, disease, corpses, etc.) represent danger that

---

[4] Douglas, *Purity and Danger*, 36.
[5] Ibid., 44.

comes from outside one's identity: the self threatened by the not-self, society threatened by its exterior, life threatened by death."[6]

Queer theory has affirmed the abject's political potential by positing that, through its founding repudiation, the abject acts as a "threatening spectre" for the bounded and delineated entity[7]—be it a subject, a community, or indeed a language. As Georges Bataille argues, since abjection is the incapacity to fully accept the imperative act of exclusion—the "sovereign" excludes, but never entirely abolishes or annihilates, because it always depends on the abject to delineate its own identity[8]—the abject always remains a threat to what has excluded it in the first place, "alien and internal" at the same time.[9] For Judith Butler, the abject can be produced as a "troubling return, not only as an *imaginary* contestation that effects a failure in the workings of the inevitable law, but as an enabling disruption, the occasion for a radical rearticulation of the symbolic horizon."[10]

In *No Future*, Lee Edelman argues that contemporary politics are governed by what he calls reproductive futurism: "politics, however radical the means by which specific constituencies attempt to produce a more desirable social order, remains, at its core, conservative insofar as it works to affirm a structure, to authenticate social order, which it then intends to transmit to the future."[11] He locates queerness outside the political consensus surrounding the absolute and unquestionable value of reproductive futurism and social viability: queerness instead comes to represent the liberal order's "death drive." In a similar vein, Jack Halberstam discusses the idea of "queer failure," a failure, that is, to conform to heteronormative ideals:

> Queer studies offer us one method for imagining, not some fantasy of an elsewhere, but existing alternatives to hegemonic systems. What Gramsci terms "common sense" depends heavily on the production of norms, and so the critique of dominant forms of common sense is also, in some sense, a critique of norms. Heteronormative common sense leads to the equation of success with advancement, capital accumulation, family, ethical conduct, and hope. Other subordinate, queer, or counter-hegemonic modes of common sense lead to the

---

[6] Kristeva, *Pouvoirs de l'horreur*, 86.
[7] Butler, *Bodies That Matter*, xiii.
[8] Bataille, *Œuvres complètes*, 220.
[9] Lee Edelman, *No Future: Queer Theory and the Death Drive* (Durham: Duke University Press, 2004), 9.
[10] Butler, *Bodies That Matter*, xxx, italics original.
[11] Edelman, *No Future*, 2.

association of failure with nonconformity, anticapitalist practices, nonreproductive life styles, negativity, and critique. José Muñoz has produced the most elaborate account of queer failure to date and he explains the connection between queers and failure in terms of a utopian "rejection of pragmatism," on the one hand, and an equally utopian refusal of social norms on the other.[12]

For Edelman and Halberstam, the queer is what resists the viability of the social order, as it challenges the very reproduction of its differentiated categories. Much as the "Other" is actually created through its very exclusion, queerness attains its ethical and political value precisely insofar as it accedes to that negative identification. For this reason, Edelman and Halberstam suggest fully embracing negative identifications in order to dismantle the social order altogether, instead of trying to associate queerness with the positive, the normal, the acceptable.

Noting that the theoretical notion of the queer could never constitute an authentic or substantive identity, Edelman argues that queerness is always a structural position, contingent on a specific hierarchy or segmentation of differentiated normative categories:

> By denying our identification with the negativity of this [death] drive, and hence our disidentification from the promise of futurity, those of us inhabiting the place of the queer may be able to cast off that queerness and enter the properly political sphere, but only by shifting the figural burden of queerness to someone else. The structural position of queerness, after all, and the need to fill it remain.[13]

Instead, he suggests that the impossible project of a radical queer resistance to the social order would "oppose itself to the structural determinants of politics as such, which is also to say, that would oppose itself to the logic of opposition," refusing "every substantialization of identity, which is always oppositionally defined."[14] Always changing in form and content, queerness nevertheless inhabits the relational border zone of the abject and, as such, acquires political power as that which constantly threatens the social order. Consequently, embracing the abject, dwelling in its failure to comply, would

---

[12] Jack Halberstam, *The Queer Art of Failure* (Durham: Duke University Press, 2011), 89.
[13] Edelman, *No Future*, 27.
[14] Ibid., 4.

carry more radical political and ethical potential than seeking acceptance within the proper social body and its established rules.[15]

Embracing the abject is precisely what Lambert and Whitehead do, on both the queer and the linguistic fronts, in their works. Both in their twenties, both openly queer, they each published a novel in 2018 that instantly turned them into major literary figures in Quebec and English Canada, respectively: Lambert's *Querelle de Roberval* (which followed his 2017 novel *Tu aimeras ce que tu as tué*) and Whitehead's *Jonny Appleseed* (which followed his 2017 poetry collection, *full-metal indigiqueer*) have garnered tremendous critical approval and commercial success since their publication. In their writing, both Lambert and Whitehead thematically revel in the queer abject. Further, the language they both use is especially striking: while Lambert's work is published, marketed, and labeled as French and Whitehead's as English, both writers use a highly vernacular prose, in both the dialogue and the narration, which they often infuse with linguistically "improper" elements—other languages, spelling "mistakes," swear words, social media slang, unusual or nonstandard typographic elements, and so on. It is no coincidence that these texts, so invested in the figure of the (queer) abject, are written in decidedly nonnormative, iconoclastic, and fragmented languages.

Looking first at Lambert's novel *Querelle de Roberval*, then at Whitehead's poetry collection *full-metal indigiqueer* and novel *Jonny Appleseed*, this chapter will frame Lambert's and Whitehead's writing not as the juxtaposition of discrete linguistic systems (i.e., as "multilingual") but as the injection of abject elements into their (received and normative) languages of publication, which are always imposed from the outset and from the outside. This will reveal how—much as the abject grounds but also undoes, disturbs, and haunts normative categories such as the subject, the nation, and the category of sex—the linguistic abject deconstructs the boundaries between languages more fundamentally than the notion of multilingual

---

[15] For a critique of Edelman's "antirelational thesis," see José Esteban Muñoz, *Cruising Utopia: The Then and There of Queer Futurity* (New York: Columbia University Press, 2009), 11–13, 88–95. Muñoz argues that Edelman's rejection of reproductive futurism is a romance of "the negative, wishful thinking, and investments in deferring various dreams of difference" along the axes of race and gender, for instance. Insisting on a more pragmatic need for queer collectivity, Muñoz argues that queerness is primarily about futurity and hope and puts forward what he calls "critical utopianism." I agree that Edelman's thesis, since it is a strictly ethical one, ignores the material nature and results of political struggle and lacks intersectionality. The invocation of Edelman's thesis here should not be interpreted as an endorsement of the antirelational thesis in queer theory but as a demonstration that the queer abject is always a structural and relational position within a normative order, and that it is precisely this position that gives it its subversive power.

writing does. Whereas multilingual writing is often understood as the more or less neutral juxtaposition of autonomous languages of equal (linguistic) value, the framework of linguistic abjection points to the social presence of a major or dominant language that silences and excludes others around it. Furthermore, what the following readings of Lambert and Whitehead suggest is that perhaps, just like queerness, linguistic practices that refuse the norm—here, a linguistic one—can never define or correspond to a fixed category that extends to a corollary cultural identity; they can only ever disturb one, albeit to different degrees. Through their queer aesthetics that refuse the normative linguistic order, Lambert and Whitehead map future social relations; heteroglossia, much like queerness, "is essentially about the rejection of a here and now and an insistence on potentiality or concrete possibility for another world."[16]

In this chapter I look at how Lambert and Whitehead disturb the linguistic order through their invocation of the linguistic abject. These two writers have different relationships to the predetermined set of linguistic relations in which they inscribe their texts: Lambert is a white Québécois man and thus would usually be recognized as a legitimate speaker of French in Quebec, while Whitehead, as an Indigenous writer, is historically positioned outside the colonial language of English in which he publishes. Put differently, one could say that Lambert engages with linguistic abjection from the privileged position of speaking from *inside* the normative category of French, while Whitehead writes, positionally speaking, from *outside* (or from the margins of) the ethnonationalist category of English. Because of their positionality, and because their linguistic relations draw on different social, historical, and political histories, linguistic abjection takes on different meanings in their works.

In the following pages, we will turn first to Lambert's prose in *Querelle de Roberval* to see how the novel exposes and questions the violence of normativity and abjection, including within the linguistic space of Québécois French. In Lambert's work, Québécois French is understood both as an abjected variety when pitted against the metropolitan norm on a global scale and as a new norm capable (and guilty) of abjection in the colonial context of Quebec—echoing what Dalie Giroux has called the "fluctuation between the figure of the colonizer and that of the colonized specific to the Quebec situation."[17] As for Whitehead, in *full-metal indigiqueer* and *Jonny Appleseed* we will see how the fragmentation of the colonial language through its

---

[16] Muñoz, *Cruising Utopia*, 1.
[17] Dalie Giroux, *Parler en Amérique: Oralité, colonialisme, territoire* (Montreal: Mémoire d'encrier, 2019), 39.

"infection" with "matter out of place" creates an effect of illegibility for an imagined monolingual (English) readership. This illegibility in turn opens up new spaces to imagine language and linguistic practices otherwise, outside of the structural and colonial linguistic assemblage of so-called Canada. Further, this illegibility functions as a heteroglossic address, which in turn serves as an invitation to interact with the text outside of the readily available and supposedly transparent grammar of monolingual settler colonialism. Finally, the chapter concludes with what these two different relationships to linguistic abjection mean for the practice of translation, suggesting that translation should, as these texts do, embrace the linguistic abject. If translation is to participate in the anti-colonial, counter-hegemonic, and anti-racist undoing of normative, imperial, exclusionary categories, then it must learn to map language differently.

Queer, Class, and Cultural Abjection: The Violence of Normativity and the Limits of Québécois French in Kevin Lambert's *Querelle de Roberval*

Readers need not go very far in Kevin Lambert's second novel, *Querelle de Roberval*, to discover the unabashedly violent style that permeates the book: the very first chapter, titled "Shift de nuit" ("Night Shift"), consists of graphic descriptions of the protagonist's sex life. In the first pages, through a vivid vocabulary and associations with incest and church pedophilia, Lambert produces a raw portrayal of homosexuality: "they [the young boys] adore being dominated by men who could be their fathers"; "the hot spunk running down their thighs"; "the long, hard shaft sunk in up to his balls, make the soiled boys come, the scandalous spread-eagled boys, swallowers of his honeyed jism"; and so on.[18] In interviews, Lambert has been clear that his goal was to put the reader's tolerance to the test with regard to queerness and to push the reader's limits in terms of what is considered "acceptable," rejecting the liberal politics of respectability.

Lambert's gamble in *Querelle de Roberval* seems to have paid off; the raw, violent, and explicit narrative modeled on Jean Genet's 1947 *Querelle*

---

[18] Kevin Lambert, *Querelle of Roberval*, trans. Donald Winkler (Windsor: Biblioasis, 2022), 18, 19, 20–1. In Lambert's own words: "ils aiment se faire dominer par des hommes qui pourraient être leur père" (Lambert, *Querelle de Roberval*, 14); "les crachats chauds qui leur coulent le long des cuisses" (15); "sa verge longue et raide qu'il enfonce jusqu'aux couilles [fait] jouir les garçons souillés" (15).

de Brest has become a true book-event in Quebec, where it was a finalist for the major Prix des libraires and the Prix littéraire des collégiens in 2019, and even in France, where it was published in September 2019 and shortlisted for four prestigious prizes: the Prix littéraire du *Monde*, the Wepler, the Médicis, and the Prix Sade, which it won—no small feat for a narrative set in Saguenay-Lac-St-Jean and written by a 26-year-old Québécois writer. *Querelle de Roberval* follows Querelle,[19] a handsome, masculine gay man from Montreal who moves to rural Roberval (in Lac-Saint-Jean, Quebec, about 450 kilometers away from Montreal) to work at a sawmill, where he immediately shakes up the workers' and inhabitants' heteronormative beliefs and ways of life. Shortly after he arrives, the sawmill workers coincidentally go on strike, and the novel follows the escalating anger and frustration of the strike to an extremely violent and ultimately deadly ending. *Querelle de Roberval* is a full-frontal assault on all types of power—the police, governments, unions, bosses, universities, the media, and more—at the same time that it foregrounds the experiences, beliefs, and discourses of people who are marginalized by these powerful institutions for being queer, lower class, far from urban centers, or all the above. The feeling of being cast off and forgotten by governments, the media, and society in general creates in Lambert's rural characters a latent violence, which they eventually translate into a series of cruel and brutal revolts against people considered "other," or different, ultimately misdirecting their violence toward individuals while the social order remains essentially intact.

Abjection is at the center of Lambert's novel, both in the physiological and the social sense. In an interview, the author explicitly positions himself against what he sees as a trend of "positive representation" that makes gay writing and gay characters more digestible for a liberal, straight, and heteronormative audience:

> It's almost as if the only way to be political in literature is to create happy, blissful gay characters, to describe homosexuality according to the criteria of heterosexuality: no anal sex, no disease, only one lover. It's an important issue for literature, this discourse of normalization. I'm not interested in writing blissful characters, what interests me is the abjection of homosexuality. . . . As a gay man, you understand quickly that you're constructed in the abject. You embody a decline of masculinity, in the same way that some embody the decline of the nation. I've tried to espouse the norm for a long while, but failure has

---

[19] The French common noun "querelle" refers to a dispute, a quarrel, a feud. It is not usually, if ever, used as a first name (outside of Genet's and Lambert's works, that is).

become what I am, the position I can occupy. I live in the trimmings, in the failures of masculinity, and I'm very comfortable there.[20]

In the novel, abjection is presented as a simple fact of life for the protagonist: "Querelle opted to seek refuge in his own abjection, on a field of dishonour that matched the shaping of his own desires. In his defilement, he fashioned himself a garment in which, prideless, he clothed himself."[21] However, the theme of queer abjection—in the figures of Querelle and of three unnamed and unruly teenagers—is juxtaposed with the social, political, and economic marginalization of lower-class workers in rural regions. By exposing the often xenophobic and homophobic discourse of white, rural, French-speaking, and economically dispossessed individuals in Quebec, Lambert analyzes and deconstructs the limits of the Québécois (ethnonational) social body, showing how its purported delineation on linguistic grounds hides other forms of social exclusion.

Importantly for the argument of this chapter, the themes of queer and social abjection go hand in hand with a narration that ostentatiously brings a series of "out of place"—vernacular, nonstandard, and English—elements into the novel's language of publication, French. At the same time that it exposes the violence of Roberval's fictional heteronormative order through the presence of abject queer figures, Lambert's novel offers a language that is "queered" by abject elements, exposing both the normativity of standard French and the normativity of the dominant Québécois cultural identity, which is centered on what it considers to be its own specific brand of the French language. Lambert's posture as a queer writer who has experienced queer abjection pushes him to consider how abjection also takes place on cultural and linguistic grounds and to consider the violence of Québécois cultural identity that is built around a more or less rigid conception of the French language.

The Rise and Fall of the Queer Abject in *Querelle de Roberval*

When the novel begins, Querelle, a young homosexual man born and raised in Montreal, has just arrived in Roberval a few weeks earlier. We know very

---

[20] As quoted in Dominic Tardif, "Les nouveaux mâles de la littérature québécoise," *Le Devoir* (Montréal, QC), September 29, 2018, https://www.ledevoir.com/lire/537851/les-nouveaux-males-de-la-litterature-quebecoise.

[21] Lambert, *Querelle of Roberval*, 149. In Lambert's own words: "Querelle a fait le choix de se terrer dans l'abject qui est le sien, dans un scandale qui épouse les formes de son désir. Dans sa souillure, il s'est découpé un manteau qu'il revêt sans fierté" (Lambert, *Querelle de Roberval*, 114).

little about him, other than his handsome and very masculine features and his sexual prowess. The narrator shares virtually no detail about Querelle's past, personality, or aspirations. Everything we know about him comes from hearsay, as if the narrator were merely reporting on rumors running around town about the character:

> Querelle. The name is circulating, is making the rounds. . . . Querelle is Roberval's bogeyman, people place bets on his age—sometimes twenty-five, sometimes fifty—on the colour of his skin and hair, brown, green, black, on the shape of his mouth and eyes. Like that evil creature, he spirits away adolescents, corrupts them, carves them up, devours them; like the fabled monster, no one knows where he comes from: from Montreal, from the Mafia, or from Saudi Arabia, but one thing is certain: he lives in a cave, often roams the beaches, and works side by side with your godchild's girlfriend.[22]

Querelle is less a character whom readers will empathize with or relate to—note how racially indistinct he is in the preceding excerpt, for instance—than an outsider figure whose role is to unsettle the novel's normative setting and trigger a series of disturbing and violent events. The narrative is not at all invested in his character development, and very little importance is accorded to his voice; Querelle appears as a kind of generic figure of homosexuality, a placeholder for queerness. As such, he represents "the figure of the queer, embodying that order's traumatic encounter with its own inescapable failure."[23] This is made clear in part by the fact that his homosexuality and sexual habits are the only things the narrator and other characters talk about and in part by a series of violent reactions that seek to "other" and neutralize him in order to protect a certain kind of heteronormative masculinity and, consequently, Roberval's social hierarchy and stability.

Querelle does not get to control his own narrative, always appearing in the third person, his sexuality presented exclusively through the lens of Roberval's circulating gossip. The description of Querelle's sexual habits

---

[22] Lambert, *Querelle of Roberval*, 108–9. In Lambert's own words: "Querelle, à Roberval, a la phénoménalité d'un Bonhomme Sept Heures, on parie sur son âge — il a tantôt vingt-cinq, tantôt cinquante —, sur la couleur de sa peau et de ses cheveux, bruns, verts, noirs, sur la forme de sa bouche et de ses yeux. Comme la créature malveillante, il enlève les adolescents, les corrompt, les découpe, les dévore ; comme le monstre fabuleux, on ignore d'où il vient, de Montréal, de la mafia ou de l'Arabie saoudite, mais une chose est sûre : il vit dans une caverne, traîne souvent à la plage et travaille avec l'amie de ton filleul. On parle de ce fauteur de trouble, des légendes champignonnent au sujet de ses bagarres et de ses amitiés particulières" (Lambert, *Querelle de Roberval*, 83).
[23] Edelman, *No Future*, 26.

is graphic and raw and tends to mobilize abject forms such as spit, sperm, and blood: "his desire to fill a throat with sperm," "witchcraft set down in kink composed of tears, blood, sperm."[24] Homosexuality is thus constructed and depicted in the book through the bodily abject, echoing a rich tradition of abject representations in French literature (Genet, Bataille, Artaud, Céline). Querelle's homosexuality also functions as a marker of difference throughout the novel, as it is his most defining characteristic—the second most important one being the fact that he is from Montreal—constantly underlined and exacerbated by hearsay and the narrator. As a gay man from elsewhere, Querelle is not only different but also represents a danger, a threat to Roberval's society, the "we" constructed through the collective voice of rumor:

> The youths at the student dorm and the Saint-Félicien college revere this striking *public enemy*, they romance the nights spent in his apartment, laud his impressive member and the words he pours into their ears while he's spearing them. . . . A tenacious rumour of unknown origins contends that it's Querelle who kidnapped little Michaël Bolduc, missing since November, in order to tie him up in his closet and subject him to an array of sexual torments.[25]

The queer abject is also depicted in the novel through the figures of three rebellious teenagers: called simply "the first," "the second," and "the third." They engage in the novel's most appalling and scandalous acts, like setting fire to the homes of the employees on strike on Christmas Eve and having intercourse with a corpse. The three boys live together in the basement of the second's absent mother and spend their time smoking weed and crack and having unprotected sex.

Querelle de Roberval ends in a shocking and violent scene where the sawmill workers and their opponents in the strike engage in a bloody battle on a baseball field, in which Querelle ends up severely hurt, with his throat cut open and his spine broken. When his friend Jézabel comes back to the

---

[24] Lambert, *Querelle of Roberval*, 62, 315. In Lambert's own words: "ses envies de remplir une gorge de sperme" (Lambert, *Querelle de Roberval*, 48); "sorcelleries dessinées d'une encre faite de larmes, de sang, et de sperme" (242).

[25] Lambert, *Querelle of Roberval*, 109. Emphasis added. In Lambert's own words: "Les jeunes de la Cité étudiante et du cégep de Saint-Félicien vénèrent le bel ennemi public, ils romancent les nuits passées dans son trois et demie, vantent sa queue impressionnante et les mots qu'il leur glisse à l'oreille pendant qu'il les emmanche . . . Une rumeur tenace aux origines obscures veut que ce soit Querelle qui ait enlevé le petit Michaël Bolduc, porté disparu depuis novembre, pour l'attacher dans son garde-robe et lui faire subir toutes sortes de tortures sexuelles" (Lambert, *Querelle de Roberval*, 84).

field to recover her coat and sees him lying there all alone, she plants a stake in his heart to end his suffering. Querelle dies and the abject seems to be gone with him—but is not quite. The three boys come across Querelle's body on the baseball field while they are out skateboarding and biking on the streets, high on crack. They sing, dance, and scream around his corpse before exploring the dead body lying in front of them. They peek at his penis, take a look at his buttocks, kiss him on the lips: he is beautiful. At this point in the novel, the reader knows exactly what is about to happen:

> The first tries the bat handle planted in his chest, gently pulls out. No reaction, blood flows from the wound. The third wets his finger, buries it in the cadaver's boiling hot anus. . . . The third continues to masturbate, then spits in his hand, moistens Querelle's hole. The first is having trouble getting hard, he's smoked too much, he asks the second to take the dead man's cock into his mouth, to excite him. The third spreads Querelle's legs, then thrusts his member up his ass. The second does what he's been asked. The first, erect at last, straddles the body, moves down on the gash left by the stake, now removed, and fucks Querelle in his wound.[26]

In spite of the violent and shocking nature of this Bataille-esque scene where Querelle's corpse is defiled, there is also a striking tenderness here. The following paragraph focuses on how the boys honor the dead body, fall in love with him, whisper loving words in his ear: "They pay him their most beautiful tribute, give praise through the skin and the flesh."[27] As Kristeva observes, the human corpse is seen as a source of impurity and must not be touched: "rotting body, without life, now made entirely of excretion, troubling element between the animate and the inorganic: the corpse is the fundamental pollution."[28] Yet, in this scene, Querelle, doubly abject because

---

[26] Lambert, *Querelle of Roberval*, 323–4. In Lambert's own words: "Le premier tâte le manche du batte [de baseball] qu'il a de planté dans le chest, le retire doucement. Aucune réaction, du sang coule par la plaie. Le troisième humecte son doigt, l'enfonce dans le cul bouillant du cadavre . . . Le troisième continue de se branler, puis crache dans sa main, mouille le trou de Querelle. Le premier a de la misère à bander dur, il a trop fumé, il demande au deuxième de prendre dans sa bouche la queue du mort, pour l'exciter. Le troisième déplace les jambes de Querelle, puis lui enfonce son gland dans le cul. Le deuxième fait ce qu'on lui demande. Le premier, qui bande enfin, enjambe le corps, s'approche de la plaie laissée par le pieu retiré et fourre Querelle dans sa blessure" (Lambert, *Querelle de Roberval*, 250).
[27] Lambert, *Querelle of Roberval*, 324. In Lambert's own words: "Ils lui font le plus bel hommage, louange de chair et de peau" (Lambert, *Querelle de Roberval*, 251).
[28] Kristeva, *Pouvoirs de l'horreur*, 127.

of his queerness and his death, is embraced, honored, and loved, in yet another act of revolt on the part of the three teenagers.

In *Querelle de Roberval*, the heteropatriarchal order responds to the death drive of queerness with its own death drive *aimed at* queerness. Throughout the novel, queer figures disturb Roberval's heteronormativity, but in the end the latter is too strong, and within it, it is impossible for queerness to flourish. The three teenagers even end up committing suicide, and their abject traces are soon erased: "their tears, their urine, their sperm were cleaned away with disinfectants."[29] In the end, the novel is not so much about the potentiality of queerness but rather about the repressive conditions in which queerness is shown to exist, that is, the violent forces that seek constantly to neutralize sexual difference. Heteronormativity and patriarchal ideals of masculinity are portrayed as powerful forces which repress their queer abject and, as a result, limit this abject's expression within the social realm. Thus, what Lambert does is, first and foremost, expose the violence of heteronormativity, its emergence from a normative, heteropatriarchal "us" that excludes queerness and seeks to annihilate queer life, which echoes why many queer writers, including Lambert, have stated that they needed to move away from their rural hometown and to the city in order to survive.[30]

The Violence of Normativity: Language in *Querelle de Roberval*

Lambert's prose also exposes a distinct but nonetheless similar kind of normative violence, aimed this time at the *linguistic* abject. Beyond sexuality, there is one other important normative force that he challenges and troubles, this time within the *form* of the narrative: the French language. Lambert mobilizes two main kinds of linguistic abject: first, a geographical abject that opposes the metropolitan standard of French and the linguistic practices in Quebec, and second, a vernacular abject that functions primarily as a class marker. In *Querelle de Roberval*, the queer and the linguistic abject interact with each other as two distinct but related manifestations of the same social violence, which functions to contain multiplicity and difference, be it on sexual or on linguistic grounds. Taking cues from the exposed violence of

---

[29] Lambert, *Querelle of Roberval*, 346. In Lambert's own words: "on nettoya avec des désinfectants leurs larmes, leur urine, leur sperme" (Lambert, *Querelle de Roberval*, 269).

[30] For instance, Gabrielle Boulianne-Tremblay, a trans writer from rural Charlevoix in Quebec, said in an Instagram post dated May 18, 2022: "I first ran away from Charlevoix so as not to die, and now it sees me more alive than ever" (@gabrielle.boulianne.t on Instagram; my translation).

heteronormativity and its tragic consequences for queer bodies throughout the novel, the linguistic abject in *Querelle de Roberval* serves the same function but on the linguistic front: exposing the violence of linguistic normativity as well as revealing its repressive function that seeks to neutralize linguistic difference and exclude those who are thought to not conform.

Throughout the narrative, Lambert mobilizes a highly vernacular prose that often clashes with metropolitan ideals of French, embracing a specific kind of linguistic abject, which the French norm regularly presents as nonstandard, regional, vulgar, and so on. At first sight, this use of a rural, working-class, and Quebec-specific vernacular appears as a positive reclamation, aimed at giving legitimacy to this specific variety or mode of expression within the hierarchy of French(es). This is one way to frame Lambert's writing, but framing the use of what is typically recognized as a Québécois, rural, and working-class vernacular as, rather, heteroglossic allows us to see that giving legitimacy to said vernacular is not an end in itself in *Querelle de Roberval*. Indeed, realizing that this more or less fixed vernacular can quickly become yet another delineated variety which can and will be used to exclude certain speakers from the (always imagined) collective Québécois social body, Lambert's prose also points to the limited political potential of reclaiming, as a white Québécois writer, working-class Québécois vernacular. What the following analysis reveals is the dual and changing structural position(s) of French in Quebec, as a variety that is both delegitimized and normative, depending on which standpoint we adopt.

First, let us consider the power relations between different "varieties" of French on a global scale. French as an imperial and global language is usually understood and defined according to the norms and canons of metropolitan French, which arises out of France's political center, Paris. On a global scale, French as it is spoken (and, to a lesser extent, as it is written) in Quebec is understood as different, if not deviant, from the standard, metropolitan French of the Académie française.[31] *Querelle de Roberval* is written in what is typically perceived as a vernacular and extremely local brand of French, which frequently transgresses the rules of standard French by incorporating elements that, from a structuralist perspective, would be located at its margins. Various nonstandard elements inspired by oral practices populate both the narration and dialogue, most notably English lexical items, local expressions

---

[31] Dalie Giroux asserts that "the gap between American oral French and Metropolitan French, and more generally the gap between the former and normative French, is frequently considered as a sign of backwardness, as the result of an unfortunate isolation, rather than as the fact of a culturally and territorially distinct experience." Giroux, *Parler en Amérique*, 41.

or "québécismes," and profanity. Take the following passage, which provides a representative example of both narration and dialogue throughout the book:

> Querelle s'en vient chaudaille, il s'en aperçoit en se levant pour aller pisser. Il croise Christian qui est après partir, on se voit demain. Au moins, on peut s'amocher, ça demande pas trop de concentration, tenir une crisse de pancarte ! Jézabel a l'air top shape, pourtant elle se torche autant que lui. Elle sourit au client qu'elle est en train de servir, place une joke et rit de l'histoire qu'il vient de lui conter. Elle tolère bien la boisson, est pas tuable, mais tu sais qu'elle est chaude comme un pâté quand elle danse toute seule derrière le bar ou bien qu'elle se met à être smatte avec les bonhommes, qu'elle les traite pas comme des attardés. L'alcool la désinhibe, elle parle fort, s'ostine. « Ah pis les astie de Français qui savent pas qu'au Lac, les serveuses travaillent pas pour des pinottes, j'les encule toutes ! » En regardant Querelle : « Woups, scusez. Cheers ! » Jézabel aussi aurait besoin d'une soirée off. Elle aligne deux bouteilles de rouge sur le comptoir, on va-tu boire ça ailleurs?[32]

Recognizable here is a more or less generic rural Québécois orality, of which various key elements populate Lambert's tongue. When discussing the subaltern nature of Canadian French(es), Dalie Giroux stresses the following dimensions: "the gap with metropolitan French; . . . the relationship (of shame or pride) to English; . . . street language; . . . vulgar speech, creolity and swear words; images, analogies and metaphors of spoken language," which are all observable in Lambert's novel.[33]

For example, several lexical items, such as "flos," "smatte," "chaudaille," "se torcher," "s'amocher," and "s'ostiner," are neither found in the Académie française's dictionary nor in Le Petit Robert—"flos," "smatte," and "ostiner" are recorded in the Antidote Dictionary, a software developed in Montreal, but only with the labels "Quebec, colloquial." The text uses typical Québécois profanities,[34] or "sacres": "crisse," "tabarnac," "astie," and so on. Contractions and expressions are decidedly regional as well: "chaude comme un pâté" (literally, "hot/drunk as a pâté/pot pie") has two double meanings due to regional usage, "chaude" meaning "hot" but also "drunk" (the second meaning only observed in Canadian usage) and "pâté" meaning not only a fatty and savory spread usually made from chopped fish or meat and typically

---

[32] Lambert, *Querelle de Roberval*, 70.
[33] Giroux, *Parler en Amérique*, 64.
[34] They even have their own Wikipedia page: https://fr.wikipedia.org/wiki/Sacre_qu%C3%A9b%C3%A9cois.

consumed *cold* but also, in its Québécois usage, referring to a deep-dish meat pie made with flaky pastry, consumed *hot*—in other words, this phrase is only comprehensible with reference to the local meanings of these words. "Travailler pour des pinottes" is a famous French-Canadian expression borrowed from the English expression "working for peanuts," with "pinottes" being the French spelling of "peanuts." Finally, the excerpt contains syntactical specificities, like the elision of the third-person singular pronoun "elle" ("est pas tuable," a phonetic transcription of Québécois speech) and the addition of the postposed interrogative particle "-tu," as in "on va-tu." It also contains words traceable to English, or "anglicismes," which appear in the text without any typographic indication: on page 69 and 70 alone, we find "imbibée de cigarettes cheaps et de shots de Jack," "[des] anciennes dates," "le rack à vaisselle," "soirée off," "Jézabel a l'air top shape," and "une joke." Words such as "la job," "le shift," "le boss," "le dude," "la shop," "cute," and "cheap" appear repeatedly throughout the novel. Words of English origin are also often spelled and inflected according to French morphology, in ways which show how they have been integrated into French grammar and (though not textually represented) phonology: "C'est crowdé," "slaquer la cadence," "slammer," "un coup dans le vadge," and so on.

These elements are listed earlier merely to show the extent to which they populate Lambert's language. The frequency of so-called anglicismes, québécismes, and other nonmetropolitan linguistic elements in *Querelle de Roberval* is such that the novel was *adapted* for its publication in Europe by a French publisher in 2019. Indeed, the version published in France has been rewritten in a more standard, metropolitan French (though it keeps some of its vernacular aspects, adapted to a European context); as reviewer Catherine Lalonde notes, references that were deemed too Québécois have been replaced by French "equivalents"—a term usually reserved for translation between "different languages"—and the title character lost his local specificity by becoming just *Querelle*. In other words, it had to be cleared—or cleaned—of a series of linguistic elements that were deemed too foreign, not "French" enough, for it to be supposedly more acceptable and digestible to metropolitan readers. The editor of the European edition, Benoit Virôt, has made the following comment on the process of rewriting Lambert's book: "In order to preserve the flow and the energy of the orality, we had to minimize certain obstacles: whether that meant anglicisms, quebecisms, spoken phrasings *for you but not for us*, or what looked too much like an archaism."[35]

---

[35] In Catherine Lalonde, "Littérature : Querelle de Paris," *Le Devoir* (Montréal, QC), September 14, 2019, https://www.ledevoir.com/lire/562617/litterature-querelle-de-paris. Emphasis added.

Striking here is the delineation of a "we" and a "you" that operate according to a linguistic qua geographical boundary that separates the French of France and the French of Quebec and posits the two as *not the same*. Of course, this differentiation happens unilaterally and never in the opposite direction.[36] There is a certain kind of speaker (or readership) that requires translation and another that does not, because the latter is considered to have a broader range of linguistic resources.

For instance, where the edition published in Quebec reads, "Les plus game de la gang (c'était souvent les plus fifs, même s'ils essayaient de le cacher) allaient jusqu'à bouffer de la graine," the French edition reads as follows: "Les plus prêts à tout (c'était souvent les plus efféminés, même s'ils essayaient de le cacher) allaient jusqu'à bouffer de la queue." In this sentence only, four lexical items—"game," "gang," "fifs," and "graine," the first two anglicisms and the second two labeled "Québec, familier" in the Antidote Dictionary—have been replaced by more "standard" elements[37]—"prêts à tout" and "efféminés," the latter representing a sanitization of the original "fifs"—and one vulgar, but metropolitan, word, "queue." The distance from the norm observed in Lambert's original sentence, in other words "the gap with metropolitan French" that Giroux describes as an important dimension of subaltern varieties of French, is completely erased. Consequently, the language of Lambert's novel as published in France does not occupy the same structural position in relation to the normativity of the French language on a global scale; it has been moved up the hierarchy of the linguistic order, purified of its regional markers so as to come closer to a "standard," that is, metropolitan, level. This linguistic hierarchy and the abjection that supports it, of course, exist prior to and outside of the writing of the Québécois version of *Querelle de Roberval*, but we see here a dramatic illustration of how real-life linguistic abjection and differentiation between "varieties" or between "standard" and "regional" shape the reading of Lambert's language as linguistically abject, here along mostly imperial and geographical lines, in opposition to a metropolitan, more "standard" French, as illustrated by its "adaptation" in France.

If the queer abject is mobilized in Lambert's novel to expose the social violence of heteropatriarchal normativity, his use of the linguistic abject can

---

[36] A similar example is that of Québécois movies, for instance Xavier Dolan's works, which are subtitled in standard French for European audiences, while French movies are never subtitled for Québécois audiences. As for books, such as we see with Lambert's adaptation for France, I do not know of a single literary work first published in France that had to be adapted for "different" francophone audiences.

[37] This is not to imply that metropolitan speakers do not have a vernacular way of saying things but, rather, that their vernacular composes and informs the standard.

also be interpreted as exposing a similar violence but on linguistic grounds. In the context of Lambert's broader interrogation of the workings of power, the queer and the linguistic abject can be seen as corollary effects of the same social violence, that of the monolingual and heterosexual modern nation-state. Both heteronormativity and linguistic normativity dictate how bodies should appear, what they should do, and what they should sound like. And so, as Roberval's heteropatriarchal order represses, and literally kills, queerness, could it not be said that the French normative order does the same thing with regard to the "queered" or abject linguistic practices it erases, such as Franglais and working-class vernaculars? Is not the adapted version of *Querelle* in metropolitan French perhaps the linguistic equivalent to Querelle's corpse?

Reclaiming Rural, Working-Class Speech: The Limits of Writing in a Québécois Vernacular

In *Querelle de Roberval*, the linguistic abject also operates along class lines in the Québécois context. Much as the queer abject is a fact of life for Querelle and the three teenagers, Lambert's vernacular is also a fact of life for the working-class characters in Roberval and, as such, functions as a class marker that signals economic and political marginalization throughout the narrative. The language that Lambert mobilizes points to the "subaltern language that is American French, the language of the habitants, the travelers, and the early interpreters, the factory workers, the lumberjacks, the peasants, the mothers, and their children, the language of the countryside, the language of the street," in other words, the language of the dispossessed.[38] Chapters taking place in lower-class and working-class settings—the local dive bar, the sawmill, the picket line, the teenagers' basement—such as "Lumpenprolétariat" and "Division du travail" are the ones written with the most anglicisms, for instance. The more dispossessed the character or the setting, the more transgressive the language, and vice versa. At other times, *Querelle de Roberval*'s narrator will in fact adopt a very sophisticated, standard language, reminiscent of Daigle's grandiloquent narration, especially when referring to some kind of intellectual, financial, or political elite *as opposed to* the working-class strikers, as in the following passage:

> Pendant les saisons de récolte, des mers entières aux remous de pointes noires sont transformées en abattis par des dinosaures aux tendons

[38] Giroux, *Parler en Amérique*, 63.

hydrauliques, avant que les reboiseurs débarquent des cégeps et des universités armés de leurs cassettes pour couvrir ces déserts d'un fragile tapis de pinceaux verts. Parfois, dans leurs conquêtes impériales, les contractants doivent contourner ne serait-ce qu'un lieu de frai, qu'une sépulture ancestrale, qu'une zone de cueillette de plantes médicinales, qu'un campement ou qu'un passage d'orignaux sur les vastes espaces qu'occupent depuis toujours les familles autochtones qu'Évolu a la générosité de piller à large profit en échange de stimulations économiques et de création d'emplois, rejouant infiniment la comédie des réserves et des pensionnats pour gonfler ses bourses. Les calculateurs de la possibilité forestière, ingénieurs, aménagistes, ministres et donneurs de contrats se réunissent autour d'une table élégante sur laquelle ils font valser un dé en or, une relique utilisée depuis l'époque de François Paradis, pipée depuis les mêmes grands froids, qu'ils lancent pour déterminer à combien de millions de mètres cubes sera fixé cette année le volume de résineux bûchés; ils le relancent discrètement si par malheur le hasard se fait trop pingre.[39]

The placement of verbs before their subjects ("qu'*occupent* les familles autochtones," "*sera* fixé le volume") and of adjectives and nouns ("fragile tapis," "vastes espaces," "résineux bûchés"), the presence of the "ne de négation" (including in the very formal "ne serait-ce"), standard words where elsewhere in the novel an anglicism is used to refer to the same concept (e.g., "emplois" instead of "jobs"), choices of words reminiscent of metropolitan French ("pingre," "pipés"), and lyrical sentences ("entire seas with whirlpools of black peaks" to describe a forest and the poetic and caricatural "to cover these deserts with a fragile rug of green paintbrushes" to describe tree planting) create a profoundly (and exaggeratedly) literary and standard tone that could not be more different from the rest of the chapter in which this passage occurs. Both before and after this passage, the narrator describes a workday in the life of Jézabel with a much less "proper" French: "cette job-là," "un autre truck," "une couple de jokes," "la ligne du canter," "containers," and so on. There is thus an interplay of registers that come to represent and index different group identities, mostly in terms of class, throughout the narrative: different registers also signal different spaces, from the dive bar where Jézabel works to an elegant table where important men meet to discuss important matters.

---

[39] Lambert, *Querelle de Roberval*, 134–5.

On the subject of class markers, the presence of English (beyond Franglais) in the novel deserves some attention. English appears mostly in passages discussing the decision by Brian Ferland, the workers' rich and despotic boss, to raise his children in English:

> Mamie Chantal casse son anglais en annonçant le prochain cadeau. Elle s'est déjà ostinée là-dessus avec Brian, elle a jamais compris pourquoi, à la maison, il tient tant à ce qu'on parle juste en anglais aux enfants, mais elle a fini par se fermer la trappe et écouter son fils, pour lui faire plaisir. Après tout, peut-être qu'il a raison, peut-être que ça va leur donner plus de chances dans la vie, qu'ils vont pouvoir voyager et travailler pour des grosses compagnies. Elizabeth is getting quite angry because her brother just opened a brand new Xbox while she hasn't received any big present yet, that's unfair, she only have des petits kits Playmobil roses with princess dresses, roses aussi. The next gift is going to . . . Elizabeth! Elle déchire le papier et shouts with joy when she sees la boîte d'un beau Xbox pour elle aussi, the pink version, avec des jeux de princesse à part de ça. Est contente, la petite torvisse, even if she prefers war games. Elle saute dans les bras de papa et maman, thank you, thank you, thank you.[40]

It is no coincidence that the workers' boss has an English given name and wants his children to grow up speaking English: this is an obvious nod to the historical economic subjugation of French Canadians by an Anglophone elite minority up until the 1970s. High forms of French being associated with the intellectual and political elite and English being associated with the financial elite and the employers point to both historical linguistic realities and literary tropes surrounding linguistic insecurity in Quebec. English and normative, formal French are usually associated with financial success, intellectual merit, and so on, whereas the mix of the two has historically been associated with "the state of being colonized (anglicization), the feeling of being culturally behind (archaism), the lack of instruction (ignorance of syntax, of French vocabulary), an absence of sophistication (vulgarity), cultural isolation (being unintelligible for strangers)."[41] Here, Lambert's use of English and "high" forms of French is undoubtedly critical and sarcastic: grandiloquent speech is ridiculed and presented as elitist and so is the tentative English of Mamie

---

[40] Ibid., 102–3.
[41] Chantal Bouchard quoted in Boudreau, À l'ombre de la langue légitime, 207. This is clear in Christian Rioux's columns, where he discredits the use of Franglais by observing that "joual" is a mix of French and English historically associated with the poorest neighborhoods in Montreal, equating the level of "bastardization" of French to the level of poverty and implying that both are to be avoided like the plague.

Chantal. Normative French and English come to represent certain kinds of socioeconomical power, while "abject" ways of speaking are associated with working-class characters.

Lambert's language appears to subscribe to what Benoît Melançon describes as "an unabashed position when it comes to debates around language, uninhibited in relation to the French norm and uninhibited in relation to Quebec's novelistic tradition"—a position Melançon observes in more than forty novels published in Quebec since 2000.[42] Lambert recognizes his language as abject in relation to the metropolitan norm and chooses to revel in this abjection. He embraces the linguistic abject—anglicisms, québécisms, spelling "mistakes," and so on—precisely because of its negative valuation, both historical and contemporary. Writing from the border zone of the abject is what gives the language of *Querelle de Roberval* a violent and transgressive effect within the global linguistic order of French and the classist and elitist normative expectations of the Québécois literary scene or intellectual milieu.

However, Lambert's goal is not to rehabilitate the working-class and rural Québécois vernacular as a "legitimate"—and so by extension powerful and dominant—language, understanding that this language would, in turn, further exclude and abject other modes of expression that do not fall within it. This understanding is revealed through the allegorical figure of strike leader Jacques Fauteux, through whom Lambert explores the violent exclusions that inherently come with the enunciation of a descriptive, identitarian collective "us"—here, the collective Québécois social body, "le peuple québécois," of which the French language is one of the main pillars, if not the main pillar.

As discussed earlier, abjection in Lambert's novel also takes the form of socioeconomic marginalization and dispossession. This mobilization of abjection is perhaps closer to Georges Bataille's understanding of the concept than Kristeva's psychoanalytic analysis; indeed, Bataille roots abjection in the sociopolitical sphere, where it accounts for the dynamic of rejection and exclusion of dispossessed groups, primarily the working class, by the nation-state. It is interesting, then, that Lambert chooses a labor strike as the immediate backdrop for his novel, much as Genet chose the working-class, criminal, and dirty world of sailors for his own *Querelle* in 1947. Financial insecurity and dispossession represent an underlying thread in Lambert's novel and are what pushed Jacques Fauteux, the sawmill union leader, to take his own life. He leaves behind, as a suicide note, the political speech he was scheduled to deliver in front of a handful of journalists, following the announcement of a lockout at the sawmill:

---

[42] Benoît Melançon, "Un roman, ses langues. Prolégomènes," *Études françaises* 52, no. 2 (2016): 115.

We have decided to set everything in motion so that the region's workers may take their lives into their own hands. We want complete independence for the working world, we want all workers to unite in a free society purged forever of its clique of hungry sharks, the "big boss" owners and the foreigners who have made all of Lac Saint-Jean a preserve of cheap labour and unscrupulous exploitation.[43]

In the first half of the letter, Fauteux attempts to draw solidarity with workers everywhere in the province, emphasizing the working class's dispossession and lack of power and appearing to blame those who are in power, that is, the financial and political elite. While he appears at first as a true socialist revolutionary and hero of workers' rights, the "reasons" behind his and his peers' dispossession that he is hinting at are in fact extremely troubling: he ends up blaming immigrants, women, and the queer community for the depravation of society and the stealing of jobs. The end of Fauteux's speech-cum-suicide letter contains blatant hate speech and is quite violent in content:

We are living in a society of terrorized, effeminate, social-slaves. In a world where values have vanished, it's got to the point where women tell us what to do at work, and where men take themselves for women. The faggots have taken over television and the government, and now we have to hire armless sweepers, imbeciles on hockey teams, deaf people to answer the telephone, foreigners to teach us French, and at night, when you turn on the news, it's the fatties telling us how to eat healthy![44]

---

[43] Lambert, *Querelle of Roberval*, 263–4. Winkler's translation erases here the traces of linguistically abject forms present in the original, which reads: "On est décidés à tout mettre en œuvre pour que les travailleurs et travailleuses de la région prennent en main leur destin. On veut l'indépendance totale du monde du travail, que tous les ouvriers se réunissent dans une société libre et purgée à jamais de sa clique de requins voraces, des «big boss» patroneux et des étrangers qui ont fait du Lac-Saint-Jean au grand complet une chasse gardée du cheap labor et de l'exploitation sans scrupules" (Lambert, *Querelle de Roberval*, 203).

[44] Lambert, *Querelle of Roberval*, 267–8. In Lambert's own words: "Nous vivons dans une société d'esclaves terrorisés, d'efféminés et de parvenus, dans un monde où les valeurs disparaissent. C'est rendu que des femmes nous disent quoi faire à l'ouvrage et que des hommes se prennent pour des femmes. Les tapettes ont pris le contrôle de la télévision et du Parlement, c'est rendu qu'on nous force à engager des manchots pour passer le balai, des légumes dans les équipes de hockey, des sourds pour répondre au téléphone, des aveugles pour conduire les autobus de nos enfants, des importés pour leur apprendre le français, pis le soir, quand on ouvre le canal nouvelles, c'est des grosses qui nous disent quoi manger pour être en santé !" (Lambert, *Querelle de Roberval*, 206).

While he seems at first to revolt against the ruling class responsible for his dispossession—judges, MPs, employers—Fauteux's reaction to his socioeconomic powerlessness is to cling to the other kinds of power he holds—sexual, racial, cultural, linguistic—and to assert his superiority over groups of people he deems different and threatening, not on a socioeconomic level but on a sexual and cultural level. The blame quickly shifts to women, queer people, the disabled community, and racialized and religious minorities, revealing Fauteux's insecurities regarding his own gender and cultural identity. As socially abjectified individuals, immigrants—especially racialized ones such as "Mexicans, Arabs and other Tamils of the Third World"[45]—queer people, fat people, and so on are presented as yet another kind of threat to Fauteux's masculinist view of his identity, the strikers' struggle, and Roberval's social order.

Fauteux's speech, which is supposed to respond to the announcement of a lockout and defend workers' rights and conditions, thus quickly turns into a xenophobic and homophobic call to action to protect other, unrelated things that he believes to be under threat but that have no direct link to his working conditions: heteronormativity and masculinity and Québécois cultural identity. In his final sentences, he calls for the prohibition of contact with certain groups of "Others," almost exclusively on cultural and linguistic grounds: "Banish the immigrants from your home! Refuse to answer to people who don't speak French! Who hide their faces behind veils!"[46] In other words, he discursively demarcates the limits of what he thinks is the collective Québécois social body, excluding in the same gesture a series of religious, cultural, and linguistic features, in order to secure what little access to institutionalized power and resources (jobs, salaries, etc.) he has. What Lambert is doing, in seeking to understand the ways that language becomes an emblem of group identity, is considering the role that race and related categories of difference play in shaping perceptions of language use.

In his distress as a dispossessed worker and out of his deep sense of violation by city people and the financial elite, Fauteux overwrites his class struggle with his cultural identity struggle: at the very end of his speech, he states, "Nous sommes des ouvriers *québécois* et nous irons jusqu'au bout"[47] (note that the more gender-inclusive "travailleurs et travailleuses" at the beginning of his letter has become "ouvriers" in the masculine). His focus has

---

[45] Lambert, *Querelle of Roberval*, 205.
[46] Ibid., 268–9. In Lambert's own words: "Chassez les immigrants de chez vous! Refusez de répondre au monde qui parlent pas français ! À celles qui se cachent la face avec des foulards!" (Lambert, *Querelle de Roberval*, 207).
[47] Lambert, *Querelle de Roberval*, 207. Translated by Donald Winkler as: "We are the workers of Quebec and we will forge on to the end" (Lambert, *Querelle of Roberval*, 269).

shifted to sexually, socially, and culturally abject elements in opposition to a masculinist and ethnonationalist perception of Québécois identity, instead of focusing on the similarities between himself and these groups and the fact that they are all subjected to the same kind of socioeconomic dispossession under late capitalism and neoliberalism. We see several different forces of abjection—sexual, class based, and cultural/linguistic—intersecting in Fauteux's discourse, where he positions himself as a victim of a certain kind of abjection but actively participates in reproducing other kinds of abjection, discrimination, and oppression. Abjection appears as something we all participate in; we simply draw the lines differently.

If we are to take our cue from Lambert as to what happens during the normative delineation of any social or cultural category, we can apply this cautionary tale to the legitimization, in Quebec, of the so-called Québécois variety of French. To put it differently, Lambert realizes that he, too, might be addressing a certain kind of imagined readership in the Québécois vernacular, for whom his writing will be more or less transparent and relatable. To whom is this vernacular legible, and to whom is it less so? Who is included and who is not, in the collective voice of hearsay, in this collectively "owned" vernacular? If there is a certain transgressive potential to writing in nonnormative ways in French on a global scale, that is, in relation to metropolitan and imperial norms, from the more localized standpoint of Quebec, this writing strategy suddenly appears as less subversive and perhaps even as hegemonic, given the institutional status of French in Quebec as well as Lambert's own positionality there. Through the figure of Jacques Fauteux, Lambert is hinting at the dangers inherent in perceiving a Québécois (rural, working-class, white) "variety" as precisely that: a variety that can be distinguished from the other modes of speaking it excludes in order to constitute itself. In other words, one should not mistake the politics of recognition and respectability for emancipation: arguing that the abject should become subject, without destroying the system that constructs the subject in relation to abject others, is not liberatory but reproductive.

As such, it is possible to see beyond the idea that the Québécois vernacular in Lambert's novel is an end in itself. Rather, we can see in his exploration of multiple registers, tones, and voices—framed as the mobilization of different forms of the linguistic abject—a perhaps incomplete dissection of power through the technology of language. On the one hand, Lambert exposes and undermines the violence of metropolitan French normative ideals by calling upon an abjected *geographical* variation, that of Québécois French. On the other hand, a more local perspective on *Querelle de Roberval* points to an understanding that, in the political context of Quebec, Québécois French as a variety constructed as a symbol of territorial nationalism is precisely *not* abject. On the contrary, it abjects in its own right linguistic practices and forms deemed "different," reproducing a system that simply privileges "Québécois French" over other modes of expression. Hence, Lambert points to the realization that changing the structural position of a given "variety" or a given "language" in relation to a sedimented hierarchy does not change anything about the fact that the hierarchy exists in the first place: the structure remains, and with it, the violence necessary for its maintenance, now simply directed elsewhere.

The very explicit and physical violence that breaks out at the end of the novel is simply a translation of the latent violence that permeated the narrative all along, that violence which normative categories impose on individuals and bodies that inhabit their edges, as seen in the xenophobic, homophobic, and sexist discourses of certain dispossessed characters. *Querelle de Roberval* highlights the violence of any kind of normativity that underlies "sovereign" identity categories, be they sexual or cultural, because they rely on a founding exclusion that is inherently oppressive. Any language as normative category then also carries with it the violence of abjection that Bataille, Butler, Lambert, and others condemn in the social realm. Much as he challenges the limits of the proper social body by mobilizing its queer and working-class abject, Lambert challenges the limits of proper French by infusing it with its abject, thus queering it with what it usually rejects. In *Querelle de Roberval*, English words and other abject linguistic elements therefore violate the normativity of French, becoming a violence against the language—and a violent language—through their threatening nature as abject things; that these very things were removed for the novel's publication in Paris, that is, the center of French linguistic normativity, emphasizes this point. This violation of French, in turn, reveals the violence behind the idea of any "variety" of French as a discrete, or sovereign, system, making its founding exclusions visible. Finally, through the figure of Jacques Fauteux, Lambert offers a cautionary tale to writers and translators who could be tempted to resort to a "variety" of any given "language"—perceived as more or less fixed and emblematic of national communities understood as racially or culturally distinct from the linguistic center—that they think they own. As Deleuze and Guattari remind us, "the [French] Canadian singer can also perform the most reactionary reterritorialization, the most Oedipean Oh mama, Oh my country."[48] Perhaps turning to any kind of recognizable variety, no matter how subaltern or minoritized on a global scale, is not so subversive after all.

---

[48] Deleuze and Guattari, *Kafka: Pour une littérature mineure*, 45.

"i am virus to the system": Indigiqueer Abjection and the Queering of Language in Joshua Whitehead's *full-metal indigiqueer* and *Jonny Appleseed*

Joshua Whitehead stands at the forefront of contemporary "Indigiqueer" literary expression in North America, having greatly contributed to the popularization of the term with the publication of his first poetry collection in 2017. Whitehead's collection and his subsequent novel are populated by speakers, narrators, and characters that embody Indigenous queerness (or, queer Indigeneity), that is, what it means to be both Indigenous and queer. While *full-metal indigiqueer* is an experimental poetry collection about a cyber, Indigiqueer, virus-like character named Zoa, the novel *Jonny Appleseed* follows Jonny, a Two-Spirit[49] Oji-Cree boy, on his journey to heartbreak and self-love in a world that does not love him back. Whitehead has spoken at length about the tensions that arise when one is both Indigenous and Queer, testifying to how both identities have for the most part been articulated as mutually exclusive. For Whitehead, currently dominant articulations of Indigenous authenticity and identity do not make room for queerness, and dominant articulations of queer identity are centered around white, cis, gay men.[50]

While significant work has been done to "queer" Indigenous Studies and to "Indigenize" queer theory,[51] younger Indigiqueer writers still emphasize

---

[49] For an exhaustive and critical account of what the Two-Spirit identity stands for, see Jenny L. Davis, "More than Just 'Gay Indians': Intersecting Articulations of Two-Spirit Gender, Sexuality, and Indigenousness," in *Queer Excursions: Retheorizing Binaries in Language, Gender, and Sexuality*, ed. Jenny L. Davis, Lil Zimman, and Joshua Raclaw (Oxford: Oxford University Press, 2014), 62–80.

[50] In Rosanna Deerchild, "Poet Joshua Whitehead Redefines Two-Spirit Identity in *full-metal indigiqueer*," CBC Radio, *Unreserved*, 2017, https://www.cbc.ca/radio/unreserved/from-dystopian-futures-to-secret-pasts-check-out-these-indigenous-storytellers-over-the-holidays-1.4443312/poet-joshua-whitehead-redefines-two-spirit-identity-in-full-metal-indigiqueer-1.4447321.

[51] See Qwo-Li Driskill, Chris Finley, Brian Joseph Gilley, and Scott Lauria Morgensen, Introduction to *Queer Indigenous Studies: Critical Interventions in Theory, Politics, and Literature* (Tucson: University of Arizona Press, 2011), 1–28; Daniel Heath Justice, Bethany Schneider, and Mark Rifkin, "Introduction," *GLQ: A Journal of Gay and Lesbian Studies* 16, no. 1–2 (2016): 5–39. According to Daniel Heath Justice, "Efforts within queer studies to critique the presumptive whiteness of much queer work and to address histories and ongoing dynamics of racialization have tended to efface issues of indigeneity and settlement, and as Native feminists have argued, articulations of Native nationhood can normalize the heteropatriarchal dynamics of settler governance." See also Billy-Ray Belcourt, "Can the Other of Native Studies Speak?" *Decolonization: Indigeneity, Education, Society* (2016), https://decolonization.wordpress.com/2016/02/01/can-the-other-of-native-studies-speak/, for the question of queer exclusion within Indigenous Studies.

the disconnect between dominant articulations of queerness and Indigeneity, within and outside of academia. Cree scholar and poet Billy-Ray Belcourt states, for instance, that queer Natives have no institutional home, and that a turn to interdisciplinarity only "obfuscates Native Studies' hetero- and cisnormative foundations."[52] Leanne Betasamosake Simpson has also written at length on the topic of heteropatriarchal domination within Indigenous communities and ceremonies, most notably in *As We Have Always Done*, where she suggests that narrow and singular interpretations of Indigenous knowledge systems have led to the marginalization of queerness within Indigenous thinking as well as to a "'tradition' stepped in dogma, exclusion, erasure, and violence" of and against queer bodies and practices.[53] In Whitehead's work, the public performance of both identities often presents them as being mutually exclusive; as Jonny, the narrator and protagonist of *Jonny Appleseed*, plainly states on page 6, "Hell, I played straight on the rez in order to be NDN and here [in the city of Winnipeg] I played white in order to be queer."[54] Further, Whitehead has observed that, throughout his life, his queerness has led to "situations of isolation, of fear and sometimes even removal from certain [Indigenous] spaces; bingo halls, or sometimes family dinners or even from ceremony and tradition itself."[55] As is the case with all heteronormative spaces and communities, the queer body is excluded and cast out, securing the boundaries of these spaces and communities as their threatening (yet constitutive) outside.

This exclusion, as both Indigenous and non-Indigenous scholars have argued, is, of course, a result of the settler colonial project, which relies on the "violent reordering of Native genders and sexualities."[56] For Kanien'kehá:ka scholar Audra Simpson, for instance, recognizing that the Canadian colonial project is not only raced but also gendered is key: "The state that I seek to name has a character, it has a male character, it is more than likely white, or aspiring to an unmarked center of whiteness, and definitely heteropatriarchal."[57] Bethany Schneider has argued that the "'civilization' imposed by settler ideologies on Native cultures is explicitly bound up in heteronormative structures of family and labor."[58] Both Simpson and Schneider thus contend

---

[52] Belcourt, "Can the Other of Native Studies Speak?"
[53] Leanne Betasamosake Simpson, *As We Have Always Done: Indigenous Freedom through Radical Resistance* (Minneapolis: University of Minnesota Press, 2017), 129–30.
[54] Joshua Whitehead, *Jonny Appleseed* (Vancouver: Arsenal Pulp Press, 2018), 44.
[55] In Deerchild, "Poet Joshua Whitehead."
[56] Justice et al., "Introduction," 20.
[57] Audra Simpson, "The State Is a Man: Theresa Spence, Loretta Saunders and the Gender of Settler Sovereignty," *Theory & Event* 19, no. 4 (2016), https://muse.jhu.edu/article/633280/.
[58] In Justice et al., "Introduction," 15.

that settler heteronormative structures are a central component of Indigenous dispossession. Gendered violence and race-based violence—anti-Indigenous racism, assimilation policies, cultural genocide, and so on—are revealed as two sides of the same coin, as different but related manifestations of the same settler, colonial, heterosexual, monolingual nation-state project. It is in that sense that Daniel Heath Justice (Cherokee) suggests that "Native and queer studies have, together and separately, worked to theorize and defend various kinds of diversity as well as individual and collective self-representation in the face of totalizing state legalities and ideologies."[59] In this section, I look to Whitehead's Indigiqueer expression for its "potential to disrupt colonial projects and to rebalance Indigenous communities" in relation to queer genders and sexualities[60] as well as in relation to nonnormative linguistic forms and practices.

Whitehead centers queer abjection in his writing, not only by including the queer body in his narratives but also by focusing on the fullness of its abjection and rawness. He also works with another kind of abjection, that of the Indigenous body, which undergoes a similar exclusion and dehumanization under the racial hierarchy underlying the Canadian white settler state. Rather than making queerness and Indigeneity palatable to straight and non-Indigenous audiences by toning them down, Whitehead revels in negative stereotypes—poverty, addiction, trauma, disease, and so on—and turns them on their heads by embracing them, in line with Edelman's suggestion that "[r]ather than rejecting, with liberal discourse, this ascription of negativity to the queer, we might, as I argue, do better to consider accepting and even embracing it."[61] To show that "Two-Spirit and queer Indigenous folx are not a 'was,'"[62] Whitehead creates an Indigiqueer poetics profoundly invested in both queer and Indigenous abjection, in the sense that it recognizes the experiences that have been excluded from dominant articulations of both Indigeneity and queerness—a process of exclusion on which these dominant articulations depend to retain their presumed sovereignty through an opposition to what they are *not*. Whitehead writes from and about this intersectional space of queerness and Indigeneity, in order to "[bring] these taboo topics, sex-positivity, the vivacity and the viciousness of two-spiritness or indigiqueerness to the table."[63] In both *full-metal indigiqueer* and *Jonny Appleseed*, the abject parts of Indigiqueer life are

---

[59] Ibid., 5–6.
[60] Driskill et al., Introduction to *Queer Indigenous Studies*, 18.
[61] Edelman, *No Future*, 4.
[62] Whitehead, *Jonny Appleseed*, 221.
[63] In Deerchild, "Poet Joshua Whitehead."

presented in a highly positive, playful, and unabashed fashion, from teenage masturbation to dreams of bestiality and anal sex, suggesting that the abject is a space of resilience and playfulness in which one can thrive and that the reclaiming of terms and practices that have been used as grounds to abject certain groups can become a "site of resistance, the possibility of an enabling social and political resignification."[64]

The remainder of this chapter looks at certain passages and scenes from *full-metal indigiqueer* and *Jonny Appleseed* that explicitly and thematically play with the notion of Indigiqueer abjection, before looking closely at the types of languages and registers these books mobilize, particularly in sections where such abjection is foregrounded. Standard English, for Whitehead, seems unsuited to express the abject, be it queer or Indigenous. Indeed, he usually resorts to several different linguistic registers—Prairie slang, online vernacular, Ojibway and Cree, and so on—to describe queer sex and decolonial intimacy.[65] Whitehead's language, analyzed in the light of his dwelling in Indigiqueer abjection, suggests that, much like the heteronormative notions of sex and gender, the notion of English as system is constituted by and depends on an outside that it actively rejects for its own sake, creating illegitimate bodies and practices in its wake. From this perspective, what is usually known as multilingual writing can be conceived of as a kind of writing that disrupts the sovereignty of the so-called English linguistic system by infusing it with abjectified and othered elements, operating a similar "reterritorialization" of the linguistic and cultural abject. Indeed, while queer performativity works by "resignifying the abjection of homosexuality into defiance and legitimacy,"[66] my reading of Whitehead suggests that performing multiple languages and registers can work in the same way with regard to minoritized and delegitimized languages and vernaculars. Whitehead's writing, both in content through his mobilization of the queer abject and in form through the mobilization of the linguistic abject, thus challenges the notion of the autonomy of linguistic systems.

---

[64] Butler, *Bodies That Matter*, 176.
[65] Decoloniality is understood here as a way to learn and explore the knowledge, the relations, and the intimacies what have been and are still discredited and erased by the forces of settler colonialism, including that of normative imperial linguistic categories. Whereas "anti-colonial" signals a response to colonialism, "decolonial" characterizes knowledge and ways of being in relation with the world that are not designed as a deliberate response to colonialism, in other words that do not address colonialism directly. In the context of Indigenous writing, I encountered the concept for the first time in Leanne Betasamosake Simpson's 2013 collection *Islands of Decolonial Love*. For Simpson, decolonial love is a kind of love that is not governed by colonial scripts, and that can be found outside of colonial structures, hierarchies, and categorizations.
[66] Butler, *Bodies That Matter*, xxviii.

Language, in *full-metal indigiqueer* and *Jonny Appleseed*, presents itself much like the queer body: porous, transgressive, and drawing power to destabilize the social order from the abject.

Urine, Blood, Semen, Feces: The Lexicon of Abjection in *full-metal indigiqueer* and *Jonny Appleseed*

In *full-metal indigiqueer* and *Jonny Appleseed*, Whitehead invokes urine, blood, semen, and feces throughout his narratives to discuss situations of social exclusion and humiliation. Not one to shy away from bodily fluids and waste, he celebrates these elementary abject forms, first in *full-metal indigiqueer*, where he creates a kind of viral cyber character who counterattacks colonialism by infecting its structures, and later in *Jonny Appleseed*, where bodily fluids play a more affective and tender role in the context of radical and decolonial intimacy and self-love.

full-metal indigiqueer is full of references to bodily fluids and waste, to disease and death, always in relation to the avatar-protagonist, Zoa: from "mucosa jiggling jello" to "cells diseased with germ," "prehistoric carcass / lizards, beasts, ndn bones / oozing from the wounds," "black blood money / organic fleshy cheques," and "our latest bowel movement," abjection proliferates.[67] Zoa has clearly been wounded and infected by the heteropatriarchal and capitalist structure of settler colonialism that casts them out and wants to see Indigiqueer people disappear altogether. But abjection is also embraced, both as a predetermined condition and a potential weapon against colonialism. Indeed, there is a kind of pride in being abject and infectious throughout the collection—a reversal of the semantic capital of rejection inscribed in the abject, which suggests that one should take pride in rejecting the colonial norm. For instance, in "The Fa—(Ted) Queene, An Ipic P.M." Zoa states, in an erudite language reminiscent of Early Modern English, a variety usually associated with canonical, British authors: "i am the indigenous bogeyman / you should fear me / i am the most lothsom, filthie, foule / & full of vile disdaine."[68] Later in the collection, Zoa claims, almost as if posing a challenge, "i am toxic and disease / kiss me & catch a cold of shame."[69] In *full-metal*, Zoa, in all their Indigeneity and queerness, is

---

[67] Joshua Whitehead, *full-metal indigiqueer* (Vancouver: Talonbooks, 2017), 31, 34, 38. Nonstandard spacing in original.
[68] The title is an allusion to Edmund Spenser's Early Modern epic *The Faerie Queene*, and the last verse is a direct quotation from Book One, which refers to the monster called Errour. Whitehead, *full-metal indigiqueer*, 44.
[69] Ibid., 76.

a "virus to the system" of colonialism,[70] representing all that is abject, that is, unabashedly queer and Indigenous, and producing it "as a troubling return, not only as an imaginary contestation that effects a failure in the workings of [colonialism's] inevitable law, but as an enabling disruption."[71] Excluded as colonialism's Indigenous and queer abject, Zoa becomes a virus that threatens to infect colonialism through their very presence and survival, enacting a sort of vengeful biological warfare. Further, when the abject appears in other characters, Zoa seems to welcome it:

> you vomit in your mouth
> bols colours it blue
> spit it out into a redsolocup
> i think: its kind of pretty
> tell you: "kiss me anyways"
> i dont really care
> the acid in your mouth
> match the words in mine[72]

Here, Zoa seeks others like them, creating through queer sex and intimacy an army of abject beings. In *full-metal indigiqueer*, the abject is the weapon par excellence for fighting colonialism, infecting it with what it constantly rejects, with its own waste, thus making it impossible for it to stay orderly and proper: "this ndn too, fights back / semtex semen syntax."[73] Here, the juxtaposition of an explosive device, sperm, and language represents the different ways in which Zoa fights back—direct action, queer performativity, and poetics/cultural resurgence—all of which disrupt the exclusionary matrix of colonialism.

In *Jonny Appleseed*, the abject is mobilized in a radically different way. Here, the protagonist is less invested in fighting colonialism than in finding decolonial intimacies and connections that will allow him to love and be loved. In contrast to the weaponization of the abject in *full-metal*, here the abject becomes something to care for, to love. At the very end of the novel, Jonny has an internal conversation with his deceased grandmother, in which he imagines her saying, "*humility is just a humiliation you loved so much it transformed*";[74] and in the acknowledgments at the end of the

---

[70] Ibid., 35.
[71] Butler, *Bodies That Matter*, xxx.
[72] Whitehead, *full-metal indigiqueer*, 84.
[73] Ibid., 34.
[74] Whitehead, *Jonny Appleseed*, 216, italics original.

book, Whitehead shares something he learned while writing the book: "if we animate our pain, it becomes something we can make love to."[75] The abject, imposed from the outside and causing humiliation, pain, and trauma, is nevertheless something we can learn to love. Nowhere is this more eloquently illustrated than in the golden shower scene of chapter XXIII, where Jonny goes on his first catfish date with Tias, who will go on to become his best friend and lover. On their way back home, Jonny and Tias are met by Logan and his gang of bullies, who start calling the two young friends "faggots" and "gayboys," telling them they have "H-I-V and A-I-D," associating them with a life-threatening virus contracted through blood. Then, in an act of ultimate abjection, the bullies urinate on Jonny: "And then each boy pulled out their floppy penises and urinated all over me. My clothes were soaked and my hair was shiny with piss."[76] They then prompt Tias to do the same, and he complies, to avoid being abjectified or excluded himself:

> Tias was still crouching behind me, his eyes closed. Logan and his posse, waiting for Tias to join in on their golden shower, crossed their arms and waited. One of Logan's friends slapped his fist against his palm. Tias opened his eyes and I held his gaze as he slowly stood up. His hands were shaking as he slowly undid his zipper. I closed my eyes and nodded. The warmth of his urine splashing on my shirt startled me. When I opened my eyes, he was crying. His limp penis hung and the last few drops of piss leaked from his fingers. His eyes were sunk deep in his head and his arms were wrapped around his waist. His entire body read regret, but even then, I thought, no boy has ever looked so goddamned precious.[77]

Here, Whitehead represents queer abjection and social exclusion through one of the most elementary abject forms: Logan and the others associate Jonny with urine, covering him in abjection and stripping him of his dignity and humanity. But while this scene is certainly tainted with humiliation, pain, and trauma, it is also filled with hope and beauty, and Jonny decides to embrace it, as he explicitly nods and agrees to Tias urinating on him. In the end, in spite of the troubling and humiliating nature of this moment, Jonny focuses on its silver linings: the startling and reassuring warmth of Tias's urine and the thought that "no boy has ever looked so goddamned precious."

In *Jonny Appleseed*, abjection is simply a fact of life for the protagonist: "Our bodies were made of cells that were braided together, and particles of blood,

---

[75] Ibid., 221.
[76] Ibid., 92.
[77] Ibid., 92–3.

semen, and shit that leaked and oozed out from us—bits of discharge that were both living and dying."[78] The novel is more about caring for those abjectified parts and experiences than it is about revolting against the exclusionary matrix that requires and produces the domain of abject beings in which he finds himself. For Jonny, urine, semen, and blood are sources of both pain and joy, and he is interested in finding pleasure and solace in his abjectified body and experiences. For instance, in the fourth grade, he goes to a Halloween dance at school dressed as Minnie Mouse and dances with another boy. When he gets home, his stepfather Roger is furious and beats Jonny with his belt: "The sound of his leather belt slapping against the bare skin of my ass crackled throughout the house. . . . My flesh reddened and began to split. Roger had broken the skin and I could feel a tiny dabble of blood trickling between my cheeks."[79] When Jonny finally runs to his room, he inspects the marks on his buttocks in the mirror: "They were tender and throbbing. It hurt, but I had to admit, a part of me was excited too."[80] Then, he takes off his pants and lies down on the carpet, on his stomach, and masturbates for the very first time, experimenting with the sensations his body can produce and feel:

> Not only was that my first encounter with Roger's mean streak, but it was also the awakening of my queer body. The trickle of blood, the splitting of skin, the pain on my ass cheeks, the full-body pleasure of an ejaculation—I felt as new as those rare trees split wide open after a storm, all tender and wondrously ravaged.[81]

There are several registers of violence at play in that scene, including that of a parental figure aimed at a child. It is striking that in both Lambert and Whitehead's narratives, fathers are mobilized as violent figures who seek to punish, contain, and destroy queerness. The father here can also be seen to symbolize the state, as the head of the national family. This is especially apt in Whitehead's case, considering that Canadian law has long considered Indigenous individuals as "wards of the state," enacting a paternalistic legal relationship that illustrates the historical and imperial notion that Indigenous peoples are children who need to be brought into "civilized" colonial ways of life.[82] Even if Roger, one of the two fatherly figures in *Jonny Appleseed*, is

---

[78] Ibid., 182.
[79] Ibid., 173.
[80] Ibid.
[81] Ibid., 174.
[82] See Justice et al., "Introduction," 17, for a thorough discussion of the historical infantilization of Native nations by the US government, which can arguably be extended to the Canadian context.

Indigenous (the other is Tias's white foster father, who is equally macho), his portrayal in the book heavily points to "the influence and adoption of a sexist, 'macho-warrior' pose that [draws] far more from white stereotypes of Native masculinity than from decidedly more complex and often less hyperaggressive tribal models."[83]

In any case, Roger's mean streak produces an act of queer abjection, but it is through this act, and through the resulting pain, that Jonny discovers his queerness. Symbols of abjection are associated throughout the book with scenes of exclusion and humiliation that nonetheless always end on a hopeful note, on the opening of new possibilities: "that's sometimes the strangest thing about pain, that sites of trauma, when dressed after the gash, can become sites of pleasure."[84] *Jonny Appleseed* is precisely about dressing one's wounds by accepting them, embracing them, performing them, and narrating them. While Zoa's mobilization of the abject can be seen as a project of transgression against colonial structures, Jonny's imperative is, above all, in the border zone of the abject, *survivance*—a term proposed by Gerald Vizenor in place of mere survival. As Vizenor puts it, "Native survivance is an active sense of presence over absence, deracination, and oblivion; survivance is the continuance of stories . . . Survivance stories are renunciations of dominance, detractions, obstructions, the unbearable sentiments of tragedy, and the legacy of victimry."[85]

The Linguistic Abject in Whitehead's Indigiqueer Poetics

Following the previous discussion, which showed that the discursive category of the abject is mobilized, first, in *full-metal indigiqueer* as an act of transgression against the system that produces it to cast it out and, second, in *Jonny Appleseed* as something one can learn to care for, accept, and love despite its rejection by social and discursive forces, I now want to suggest that the presence of languages and registers other than "standard English" in these texts can be seen to function in much the same way.

---

[83] Justice et al., "Introduction," 10.
[84] Whitehead, *Jonny Appleseed*, 179.
[85] Gerald Vizenor, *Survivance: Narratives of Native Presence* (Lincoln: University of Nebraska Press, 2009), 1. In the words of Bethany Schneider: "A queer spin on this word understands that it is not about 'survival' in a necessarily reproductive, future-driven mode. In the face of a slathering, constantly reiterated, pornotropic desire for Native absence, suffering, and disappearance, 'survivance' turns away from a dialectical response that would simply answer death with birth, disappearance with expansion. It is a word about place and presence rather than futures and pasts, and it allows for forgetting and remembering, dying and living, making and destroying, repetition and reiteration" (in Justice et al., "Introduction," 20).

After all, the notion of English (or any imperial, normative, standardized language) also takes the form of what Foucault calls a "regulatory ideal,"[86] which relies on an exclusionary matrix not unlike that of the category of sex that Butler deconstructs. In Canada, Eve Haque and Donna Patrick have shown that language policies have been used as a way to "address state concerns with national unity and control, producing forms of racial exclusion and maintaining a white-settler nation," and that these policies are intended to manage racial difference through "processes of erasure, forced assimilation and exclusion through the technology of language."[87] The residential school system, for example, established in the 1870s, served the assimilationist agenda of eradicating Indigenous languages and enforcing the use by Indigenous children of "civilizing" English and French languages through techniques that included the punishment of Indigenous children for speaking their home language.[88] The processes through which a dominant and normative language such as English establishes and maintains itself, that is, through the active suppression of certain elements it produces as other, thus resemble the ways in which queer bodies have been "foreclosed or banished from the proper domain of 'sex,'"[89] for instance through conversion therapy. Indeed, Heller and McElhinny have shown that

> the shape of the nation goes beyond the association of bodies and territories through shared bounded languages. The form of the language is also important. The most obvious domain has to do with whether linguistic material is understood to properly belong inside a linguistic boundary or on the outside. Most frequently, attention is paid to lexical material (words) in what is now a long tradition of purism. . . . These policing efforts can also extend to prosody, phonology, morphology, and syntax.[90]

In Whitehead's works, different languages and vernacular forms operate in similar ways to his mobilization of queer abject forms: in *full-metal*, as a virus-like force that counters what excludes it in the first place by infecting

---

[86] Michel Foucault as quoted in Butler, *Bodies That Matter*, xi.
[87] Eve Haque and Donna Patrick, "Indigenous Languages and the Racial Hierarchisation of Language Policy in Canada," *Journal of Multilingual and Multicultural Development* 36, no. 1 (2015): 27.
[88] Ibid., 29, 37.
[89] Butler, *Bodies That Matter*, xxx.
[90] Heller and McElhinny, *Language, Capitalism, Colonialism*, 106.

it—in the context of Canadian colonialism, which is not over but ongoing[91]—and, in *Jonny Appleseed*, as something that needs to be cared for—in the context of cultural resurgence and Indigenous survivance.

The language of *full-metal indigiqueer* is striking from the very beginning, its table of contents filled with cryptic titles such as "e/espywithmylittle(i)," "a[u] cla[i]r the l[own]e," "kundera has the answers for nostos-algos ndns," "douwanttoknowwhatmakestheredmenred[questionmark]," and so on. Often difficult to read because of its opacity and undecipherability, the collection contains several passages written in what approximates computer or robotic language, such as this one:

> fa:: :: :: :: ::lcon:: : :: :: ::video: :: :: :::: :downloadingpleasuresoftware: :: :: :: ::::
> :: : :: ::: : :: : :: :: : : ::reconciled:: ::: ::vi:::::deo:::::::in::::stallation:::: ::com: :: :::
> :: plete[me] :: : :: :::: :.[92]

Here, colons are inserted between and within words, subdividing language through their infectious proliferation. This creates a strange rhythm that bears little resemblance to the way one would speak or even read normally, at the same time that it demands a considerable effort to put the syllables back together to create words and meaning. Elsewhere, a similar effect of unreadability is created through the absence of spaces—"wheniscoffthemaam stompsherfootandmymanagerwalksoveraskswhatswrongmaamtellshimthati amrudebeyondbelief"—the substitution of numbers for certain letters—"n4m3: a w0rd or s3t of wor4s b1 wh1ch a p3rs0n, 4nimal, 10lace, or th1n5 is kn03n, 4ddr3s5ed, 01, r3ferr3d to"—and the absence of apostrophes—"shes," "youll," "id."[93] All of the examples listed here would generally be recognized as being written in English, but it is a diseased, infected English, a kind of English that is not "proper," to use Kristeva's word. In *full-metal*, numbers (from long series taken out of grocery receipts and bank card transactions to individual numbers functioning as letters), the unusual use of punctuation (be it the use of several colons, the absence of apostrophes and/or spaces, or the lexical transcription of punctuation signs such as "[period]" and "[questionmark]" throughout the collection), and unusual spellings ("cuzzin," "ndn," etc.) create a language that is both recognizable and unrecognizable as

---

[91] See Glen Sean Coulthard, *Red Skin, White Masks: Rejecting the Colonial Politics of Recognition* (Minneapolis: University of Minnesota Press, 2014), as well as Patrick Wolfe's insistence that settler colonialism is a structure and not (just) an event: Patrick Wolfe, *Settler Colonialism and the Transformation of Anthropology: The Politics and Poetics of an Ethnographic Event* (New York: Cassell, 1999).
[92] Whitehead, *full-metal indigiqueer*, 39.
[93] Ibid., 21, 29, 49, 54, 89.

"English." The following excerpt, which again alludes to Spenser, shows all of these devices in play simultaneously:

peyak[period]
1 am the red crosse knight
patr0n of true ho11nesse
thank you: :: spenser: :::
for m0u1ng me to western sh[or]e
whom to auenge, you ask[questionmark]
una had from far compeld
i am here to reuenge[94]

Here, the underlying structure of English as a system is disturbed and infected by numbers, a series of colons, brackets, obsolete spellings, and a Cree word. Normative linguistic institutions such as dictionaries and grammars tend to expel, reject, and deny old spellings and lexical items, defining them as other in space or in time, meaning that what is considered "inside" a language at a given time can come to belong "outside" the same language over time. Importantly, what the infected English of *full-metal* suggests is that the "outside" of English "is not an absolute 'outside' [nor] an ontological thereness that exceeds or counters the boundaries of discourse; as a constitutive 'outside,' it is that which can only be thought—when it can—in relation to that discourse, at and as its most tenuous borders."[95] By bringing numbers, other languages, obsolete spellings, and so forth on the page, Whitehead confronts the idea of the English language as linguistic system with both its purported inside and its "constitutive outside," thus making its fictional nature visible. The result, not easily unified into a readable and recognizable whole, is a challenging one for the reader, revealing above all the sedimentation of our reading habits over time. The earlier excerpt raises questions as to what does and does not count as English: is punctuation English, and is English still English without punctuation? Are (Arabic) numbers linguistic? What is the difference between Cree and English? By injecting "out-of-place" items into the "English" poems, and by making meaning out of, and from, the border zone of what we know as English, the language of *full-metal* blurs the distinction between English and its constitutive outside, thus disturbing its system, its order, and its presumed sovereignty as a linguistic body.

[94] Ibid., 43.
[95] Butler, *Bodies That Matter*, xvii.

In *Jonny Appleseed*, meanwhile, Indigenous languages and certain vernaculars are mobilized in affective ways. The first-person narrative is written in a conversational and vernacular prose, making no distinction in terms of register between the narration and the dialogues. The novel is mostly written in what most would consider English, though it is a profoundly subjective and embodied English—characterized at times by a "rez accent," at other times by drag queen slang, Snapchat and Grindr expressions, and so on—but Indigenous languages, namely Ojibway and Cree, also make several appearances. Throughout the novel, Cree words hold particularly affective connotations: they are mostly used to refer to loved ones, such as Jonny's kokum, mushom, and nikâwiy, and the Cree for "I love you," "kisâkihitin," appears twelve times in total. Whitehead also uses Cree for emotionally charged dialogues between Jonny and his best friend and lover, Tias; the last words they exchange after they break up are "'Kihtwâm?' he asked. 'Ekosi,' I replied"—*ekosi* meaning "goodbye forever" or "adieu."⁹⁶ Most, if not all, instances of Cree in the novel signal tenderness, love, and care, as if Jonny is trying to find spaces for decolonial love and intimacy outside of the rigid and oppressive structure of the colonial language. The most striking presence of Indigenous languages, however, is in chapter XVII, where Jonny dreams of maskwa (bear). The scene describes the welding and blending of entities, bodies, and land that happens through intercourse between Jonny and maskwa and is filled with both Ojibway and Cree elements:

> The song of the round dance grows louder in my ears, unaltered by the tongue that scrapes and cleans me—wabanonong manidoo owaabamaan anishinaabek. I can't help but cry—I don't understand the words but my tendons do, my bones react and jig in the skin. The beat doubles, rabbit and beaver thwack in conversation. I feel something hard press against the small of my back—zhaawanong manidoo owaabamaan anishinaabek. He places his paws on top of my hands, they feel like the bottom of my mom's mocs. Then his claws press into the tips of my fingers, piercing them, blood and foam leaking out from my fingertips—ningaabii'anong manidoo owaabamaan anishinaabek. All of the forest is watching maskwa top me as the birds cackle and avert their eyes. A woodpecker sits high in a tree and riddles the trunk with a beat that dubs the round dance—kiiwedinong manidoo owaabamaan anishinaabek. Maskwa unsheathes himself, the baculum

---

⁹⁶ Whitehead, *Jonny Appleseed*, 187.

stiff and ready; he enters me with a hefty breath and it doesn't hurt. I wonder if he's getting ready to eat me. He digs through my body, feels for the bean in me, buzzes against it, looks for the bone that holds my tapwewin. I tell him there's nothing there, but he scrapes from me a seed from when I was kikâwiy, anishinaabek-nehiyaw iskwewayi-napêw. And as he pulls out, he jiggles the bean again, makes me come into the mud, licks the salt from my eyes—all of this treaty land is filled with me. As he leaves, the music fades, my heart-drum-beat lulls to a slow pace, my body relaxes, lets loose its fluids. Kâkike, he huffs, kisâkihitin kâkike.[97]

That both Ojibway and Cree have such a significant presence in this scene, in a novel that embraces the abject, is no coincidence. In Jonny's dream, both languages, long suppressed, resurface, enabling a return of what has been cast out by the colonial logics of monolingualism. The superposition of Ojibway and Cree specifically with the boundary-threatening abject of the scene suggests that Jonny has a similar relationship to these two languages as he does to his queerness; both his queerness and Indigeneity are marginalized, excluded, abjectified, and both intersect in his dream through the figure of maskwa. "I don't understand the words but my tendons do," says Jonny, who does not speak Ojibway and has a limited knowledge of Cree. The marked presence of Ojibway in this excerpt is thus ritual, and it represents something which has been actively abjectified and suppressed by "residential schooling and other assimilationist policies [that] have played a major role in the 'un-learning' of indigenous language and culture,"[98] and which is now being brought back as part of a broader movement of Indigenous cultural resurgence. Here, Indigenous linguistic forms function as an audience delimitation technique: monolingual English speakers find themselves unexpectedly excluded from the language of *Jonny Appleseed*, which opens itself only to people with some knowledge of Cree and/or Ojibway. For monolingual readers, then, the idea is not so much to comprehend or make sense out of these linguistic elements as to create space for them, to welcome their opacity, and to let them flourish on their own. The scene is one of linguistic encounter, of languages touching each other and loosening their boundaries—a scene which, much like the queer body in Whitehead's works, "can acquire political import insofar as it exposes the fiction of self-contained language-systems (historically sedimented as national and colonial), undoes

---

[97] Ibid., 71.
[98] Haque and Patrick, "Indigenous Languages," 37.

them and repurposes them as constitutively interdependent, vulnerable, constantly interpenetrated."[99]

The Queering of Language

The use of non-English elements—not only Cree and Ojibway words but also numbers and other disruptive writing devices—in Whitehead's work can thus be conceived as the linguistic and cultural equivalent of queer abjection, not in relation to a heterosexual exclusionary matrix but to a colonial and cultural one that centers normative English as the legitimate, "civilized" language and that affirms its sovereignty and power through the exclusion of other languages and registers. The linguistic "abject" that appears in both *full-metal indigiqueer* and *Jonny Appleseed* can thus be seen as the formal, linguistic corollary to the themes and symbols of queer abjection that fill both books, representing the "Indigi" in Indigiqueer. Perhaps, for Whitehead, writing in an explicitly heteroglossic and nonnormative manner is the only way to write about Indigiqueer abjection.[100] It figures as a troubling return caused by the "refusal to respect the heavily policed boundaries among languages that so many missionaries, administrators, teachers, linguists, and anthropologists have devoted so much work to producing [and] a similar refusal to respect the conventions of standardized language."[101] If the abjected queer body is one that transgresses the heteronormative order, then the language Whitehead offers us can be seen as a queered language, one that challenges the linguistic order and its normative regime, with hierarchical categories such as "English" and "French" and boundaries that consolidate them. Whitehead's two main approaches to both the queer and the linguistic abject, its weaponization in the fight against colonialism and its preservation and *survivance* through care and love, bear a striking resemblance to Butler's discussion of the need to refigure the queer outside:

> The task is to refigure this necessary "outside" as a future horizon, one in which the violence of exclusion is perpetually in the process of being overcome. *But of equal importance is the preservation of the outside*, the site where discourse meets its limits, where the opacity

---

[99] Elena Basile, "A Scene of Intimate Entanglements, or Reckoning with the 'Fuck' of Translation," in *Queering Translation, Translating the Queer*, ed. Brian Baer James and Klaus Kaindl (New York: Routledge, 2018), 29.
[100] Billy-Ray Belcourt echoes this hypothesis: "NDN literature: to treat language brutally while still writing beautifully." Billy-Ray Belcourt, *A History of My Brief Body* (Toronto: Penguin Random House, 2020), 127.
[101] Heller and McElhinny, *Language, Capitalism, Colonialism*, 21.

of what is not included in a given regime of truth acts as a disruptive site of linguistic impropriety and unrepresentability, illuminating the violent and contingent boundaries of that normative regime precisely through the inability of that regime to represent that which might pose a fundamental threat to its continuity. In this sense, radical and inclusive representability is not precisely the goal: to include, to speak as, to bring in every marginal and excluded position within a given discourse is to claim that a singular discourse meets its limits nowhere, that it can and will domesticate all signs of difference.[102]

However, while queerness and Indigeneity have a great deal in common as structural positions constructed along specific axes of differentiation, they cannot be so easily equated. If queerness is defined solely by heteronormativity, Indigeneity is not solely defined by the Canadian state. Simply put, Cree and Anishinaabe and Innu *people* existed before the arrival of Europeans, whereas queerness (as a concept or identity) did not exist before the emergence and consolidation of heteronormativity. To put it differently, if "the identity of Canadians is tied to the identity of Indigenous people in this country,"[103] the opposite is not entirely true. As an ethnoracial category, Indigeneity is indeed oppositionally constructed according to a certain racial and social order in opposition to other identities such as settler, immigrant, white, and so on. But Indigeneity, for Indigenous peoples themselves, is also a set of specific and place-based practices, a "way of being in the world,"[104] that exist independently of the social order which depends on their ongoing oppression and displacement. Daniel Heath Justice has discussed the problematic nature of ethnic categories for Indigenous peoples: "contemporary identity in Canada . . . is figured in one's ethnic heritage and 'blood' rather than in one's obligations to kin and place."[105] Drawing on the work of Ella Cara Deloria, he asserts that to be Indigenous is rather to engage in learned practices that are the result of a complex and deliberate but entirely learnable process of intergenerational education and exchange. For Justice, Indigenous writers such as Whitehead tell stories to "rebuild, reassert, reclaim, and reestablish connections and relationships that return to ourselves, our lands, and our communities."[106]

---

[102] Butler, *Bodies That Matter*, 25. Emphasis added.
[103] Lee Maracle, *My Conversations with Canadians* (Toronto: Book*hug, 2017), 22.
[104] Justice, *Why Indigenous Literatures Matter*, xix.
[105] Ibid., 58.
[106] Ibid., 65.

There is thus a refusal to engage with or respond to the colonial order altogether, a refusal which allows for "resurgent practices of cultural self-recognition and empowerment" to take place somewhat outside of it.[107] Indigenous scholars such as Glen Coulthard, Audra Simpson, Leanne Betasamosake Simpson, Lee Maracle, and Daniel Heath Justice are in fact less interested in moving the Indigenous ethnic category up the ladder of the Canadian social order than in returning to self-determination and change from within.[108] In this context, then, perhaps Indigeneity does not rest as easily in the abject as queerness does. Structurally, the Indigenous abject does challenge and threaten the Canadian social order, but from within, specific forms and experiences of Indigeneity within particular communities—Deneness, Oji-Creeness, Anishinaabeness, and so on—are not defined according to this order and thus cannot be abject. "Indigenous abjection," while very real in a social and material sense considering the domination, both historical and present, of the Canadian state, only holds up insofar as we take the standpoint of the colonial order. Hence, Whitehead's maskwa scene goes beyond the abject, resembling a decolonial healing ceremony (the offering of tobacco, the drum beat of a round dance song) for Jonny who has "hurt [his] Cree." What this means is that from a certain point of view, the maskwa scene can be seen as abject; but from a different angle, it can also represent a spiritual and cultural act of resurgence from within, a set of practices—communion with the land, relationality with nature, learning new ways to relate to the territory, including through naming practices and language, and so on—that define Indigeneity as anything but abject.

In that case, the queer and the Indigenous "abjects" can also be read as something other than abject, since they refuse to participate in the dualism of the normative and the abject. Whereas in *full-metal*, the linguistic abject is mobilized in direct response to the linguistic structures and order of colonialism (by "infecting" colonial English), in *Jonny Appleseed* linguistic fragmentation and heteroglossia point rather to a decolonial otherwise, outside of, or parallel to, a monolingual and hegemonic configuration of language. The result created by the use of such heteroglossic writing devices is one that is illegible (or abject), but only to a public that reads it with a monolingual and colonial lens, which seeks transparency, clarity, and legibility. As Belcourt puts it, "one of the most vital modalities of decolonial

---

[107] Coulthard, *Red Skin, White Masks*, 23.
[108] See Ibid.; Audra Simpson, *Mohawk Interruptus: Political Life across the Borders of Settler States* (Durham: Duke University Press, 2014); Simpson, *As We Have Always Done*; Maracle, *My Conversations with Canadians*; and Justice, *Why Indigenous Literatures Matter*.

life is that of remaining unaddressable to a settler public."[109] In turn, the space that emerges out of this refusal to address a settler public, to be understood by that settler public, is a space that addresses, and thus creates, a different kind of public. Further, these passages are just as much not addressed to other specific Indigenous communities, for instance to an Innu or a Cherokee public, who are presented with "other" languages in exactly the same way as settlers are. As Belcourt adds: "our indecipherability turns out to be material for a commune of rebellion."[110]

By "refusing to play the game"[111] of colonial monolingualism and legibility, by refusing to translate his heteroglossia into a more palatable language for a settler audience, Whitehead enacts a decolonial politics of refusal. Audra Simpson would describe it as a choice that is about *not* writing in English, holding this linguistic category in a position of doubt: Whitehead's "political posture is, in short, saying *I am not playing with you. You are not the only political or historical [or linguistic] show in town, and I know it.*"[112] The concern is not so much about being included in already available categories and/or legitimate modes of expression; it is about creating worlds outside of these structures by addressing an audience that is called into existence through this very address. Belcourt echoes this when he states: "My concern is not with being included in Native Studies—as if being included was all that we wanted—but with epistemologies that build worlds that can't hold all of us."[113] What Whitehead's Indigiqueer poetics does is precisely that: build a world that can hold both queerness and Indigeneity, not through exhaustive representability but through its permissiveness, its flexibility, and its openness to the abject, including, and perhaps most importantly, on the grounds of language.

This echoes José Esteban Muñoz's thoughts on queer futurity, where queerness is understood as a utopian formation based on refusing the "impoverished and toxic" present and on desiring alternative temporal, spatial, and social relations—what he calls the "then and there" of queerness. For Muñoz, queerness is always in the horizon, which is to say that it cannot ever be contained, fixed, or appropriated in the present. He suggests that "holding queerness in a sort of ontologically humble state, under a conceptual grid in which we do not claim to always already know queerness in the world, potentially staves off the ossifying effects of neoliberal ideology and

---

[109] Belcourt, *A History of My Brief Body*, 96.
[110] Ibid., 107.
[111] Simpson, *Mohawk Interruptus*, 25.
[112] Simpson, "The State Is a Man."
[113] Belcourt, "Can the Other of Native Studies Speak?"

the degradation of politics."[114] Perhaps both the queerness and heteroglossia in Whitehead's works can be conceived of in similar ways, as they refuse to partake in the normative reproduction of sexual and linguistic categories as we know them, insisting instead on the concrete possibility of another world.

Translating the (Indigi)Queer, (Indigi)Queering Translation

The idea of the linguistic system's autonomy is parallel to that of the modern subject: in both cases, more or less fixed, closed boundaries delineate their limits and separate them from a series of objects and elements that could "pollute" them. Deconstructing the contours of the social body and identity (Lambert) and of the human body as subject (Whitehead) has helped deconstruct the idea of language as closed system as well. What the preceding analysis of Lambert's and Whitehead's narratives suggests is that the notion of languages' autonomy, too, is a fiction. In Elena Basile's words, the "linguistic encounters" that the writers analyzed in this chapter stage reveal the fiction of language, much as the sexual encounter undoes the subject:

> Languages and subjects "come undone" in the sexual and in the translative encounter when the materiality of their intermingling passes a threshold of perception, such that they can no longer be governed by the ideational rule of transparent self-identity. To word it somewhat differently: Both in the case of translation and in the case of sex the unruly material entanglement of signifiers and of bodies, which the expression "coming undone" gestures toward, reveals how a language or a subjectivity's ideational existence as discrete and separate entities is a provisional fiction that requires a constant, and always retroactive, policing of boundaries to be kept in place.[115]

Nevertheless, to slightly adapt Butler's words, "if [language] is a fiction, it is one within whose necessities we live."[116] The normative category of language, as much as it is constructed, still heavily structures social beliefs about language, linguistic policies, the publishing industry, scholarship on literature, and so on—in other words, linguistic life. It is not a category

---

[114] Muñoz, *Cruising Utopia*, 22.
[115] Basile, "A Scene of Intimate Entanglements," 30–1.
[116] Butler, *Bodies That Matter*, xv.

anyone can afford to ignore, especially not writers, scholars, and translators. But, following Rusty Barrett, the underlying assumption of a binary such as French/English in translation studies and practice is "a regulatory force that reinstates binary oppositions as a way of maintaining normative assumptions about the range of possibilities" of translation.[117] In other words, translation is content with a present that is "impoverished and toxic" for people who, because of their linguistic backgrounds and practices, do not feel the privilege of majoritarian belonging.[118]

Analyzing these two authors' explicitly heteroglossic writing through the lens of abjection reveals the alternative cartographies of linguistic inclusion/exclusion they draw. Rather than following the hegemonic and conventional boundaries of the languages in which they publish, the contours of their narrator's and character's voices host a variety of fluid linguistic practices, in turn drawing the contours of a collective "us" defined outside of the category of normative French or English. Lambert questions the identitarian collective "us" articulated through a rural Québécois vernacular, whose legitimacy rests on a series of linguistic, cultural, and racial exclusions that need to be acknowledged, problematized, and challenged. As for Whitehead, the collective he is addressing is in the making, not yet fixed, and, as Lambert's cautionary tale seems to suggest, maybe its crystallization is not something we should aim for. To borrow Muñoz's words,

> [t]his "we" does not speak to a merely identitarian logic but instead to a logic of futurity. The "we" speaks to a "we" that is "not yet conscious," the future society that is being invoked and addressed at the same moment. The "we" is not content to describe who the collective is but more nearly describes what the collective and the larger social order could be, what it should be.[119]

All the various heteroglossic devices analyzed in this chapter—the fragmentation of normative language, the mobilization of the linguistic abject, effects of unreadability—should therefore not be understood as ends in themselves but as pointing to a deliberate and never-ending process of unfixing language, in other words to "anticolonial and decolonial possibilities for unsettling normative forms of ... identity and expressivity,"[120] which in turn disrupt any ossified understanding of language.

---

[117] Barrett, "The Emergence," 213.
[118] Muñoz, *Cruising Utopia*, 22.
[119] Ibid., 20.
[120] Rosa, *Looking Like a Language, Sounding Like a Race*, 29.

This is why analyzing nonnormative ways of writing—and speaking—through the lens of abjection is productive: to adapt Kristeva's words, "the abject solicits language as much as it obliterates it."[121] The idea of linguistic abjection helps us understand that "other languages" or subaltern dialects are not ontologically different but are, instead, practices that are constantly rejected and constructed as other, different, and subaltern and that occupy varying structural positions in relation to a normative, dominant, powerful category. Once linguistic boundaries are recognized as being constructed and actively reproduced and maintained, it becomes easier to transgress them, instead of seeing them as an imperative to be obeyed. Furthermore, recognizing the exclusionary logic of a linguistic norm and its social consequences poses ethical and political challenges to dominant definitions of translation, a practice which tends to observe the norm. It opens up new questions about what we can translate and what we should be accountable for, other than the integrity and purity of abstract linguistic systems. For instance, the task of the translator could be to recreate, into a new predetermined language, the gap between the different registers of a text like *Querelle de Roberval*. As Whitehead's language suggests, the double task of the translator could also be to infect a predetermined normative language with what it casts out and to care for the linguistic abject in any given linguistic setting.

Further, the notion of the linguistic abject helps us see the political potential of Lambert's and Whitehead's writing strategies as refusing to participate to the survival of fixed, established, often oppressive linguistic categories—especially dominant and colonial ones. In the words of Dalie Giroux, "the idea is rather to work to the exploration, creation and development of a knowledge and a practice of North America's subaltern languages, as they are—broken, partial, contaminated, disseminated, obscured, mixed."[122]

Nonnormative ways of writing create, to varying extents, an effect of illegibility: they are "practices that refuse both the form and the content of traditional canons [and that] may lead to unbounded forms of speculation, modes of thinking that ally not with rigor and order but with inspiration and unpredictability."[123] This illegibility, especially in Whitehead's work but also in Lambert's in the context of its adaptation in France—the latter a missed opportunity for both translators and readers to engage with and in heteroglossia—is not something that demands to be resolved, whether in

---

[121] Kristeva, *Pouvoirs de l'horreur*, 12.
[122] Giroux, *Parler en Amérique*, 54.
[123] Halberstam, *The Queer Art of Failure*, 10.

the act of reading or in the act of translation. If translation is to participate in these writers' projects, of questioning and deconstructing dominant articulations of language and the articulations of collective cultural identity they support (Lambert) and of addressing/creating new publics outside of the available, colonial linguistic structures of address (Whitehead), it must draw on heteroglossia as much as it can, perhaps even more so than the source texts.

Is translation not, after all, the space par excellence to practice the inclusion of socially and historically abjectified linguistic forms into the hegemonic languages in which we have no choice but to work? Should the goal of translation be the reaffirmation of the linguistic configurations and ideologies that already structure it in the first place, or to trouble that order, regardless of the form of its source material? Rather than following the linguistic boundaries as given, should translation not draw different, always-changing cartographies of language from one text to another? Reflecting on the links between disruptive, postlingual kinds of translation and queerness, Brian James Baer suggests that "[w]hat is also crucial in the context of the modern nation and what aligns translation with queer sexuality is its nonreproductive nature."[124] If the dominant approach to translation does reproduce the linguistic grounds on which the nation-state lies, welcoming the abject in translation and producing heteroglossic translations can in fact be seen as the refusal to reproduce settler monolingualism, and the will to look to another linguistic horizon instead, whether or not source texts do the same—we will explore the possibility of translating monoglossic texts postlingually further in the concluding chapter.

This chapter has shown that Lambert and Whitehead, through their inventive, fluid, abject, transgressive, queer languages, refuse to take part in an exclusionary cultural-nationalistic political project that would rely on a fixed, bounded language. By welcoming the linguistic abject into their respective predetermined, imperial language, they call for the perpetual disruption of any normative language. Much like the queer, for these writers language is "never fully owned, but always and only redeployed, twisted, queered from a prior usage and in the direction of urgent and expanding political purposes."[125] Hence, translating such texts according to normative boundaries would go against everything these texts do and stand for. The reading, studying, and translating of literary texts that deploy the queer and the linguistic abject in transgressive ways—as we have seen

---

[124] Baer, *Queer Theory and Translation Studies*, 6.
[125] Butler, *Bodies That Matter*, 173.

in both Lambert and Whitehead—must answer not to the safekeeping of language as a normative category but rather to their call for the queering of language. Perhaps these works also suggest that language, in its inherent heteroglossia, is always already queer: language, much like queerness, "is not simply a being but a doing for and toward the future. Queerness is essentially about the rejection of a here and now and an insistence on potentiality or concrete possibility for another world."[126]

---

[126] Muñoz, *Cruising Utopia*, 1.

4

Motherless Tongues

The Unfamiliar Writings and Translations of Oana Avasilichioaei and Nathanaël

Axiom 3: The ideal directionality of translation is from one's second language into one's native language.

Building on the previous chapters, which challenged the neutrality and objectivity of the notion of a standard language and exposed the exclusionary mechanisms behind the imperial project of constructing and maintaining languages as distinct, this chapter delves into the third axiom that underlies the practice and theory of translation: the dichotomy of the source language (SL) and the target language (TL), interpreted here as an extension of the concepts of mother tongue and foreign tongues. The following pages tackle the (uni)directionality of translation as a process that transposes an utterance *from* one language *to* another, more specifically from a "foreign tongue" to one's "mother tongue." As the previous chapters demonstrated, a structural conception of language draws a specific kind of linguistic cartography, one that maps languages as distinct and delineated from each other and that distinguishes between "correct" and "improper" ways of speaking and writing in any of those delineated languages. This linguistic mapping is supplemented by its association with certain kinds of speakers and bodies through the ethnonationalist, genealogical notion of "mother tongue."

The aim of this chapter is twofold: first, it seeks to deconstruct the prescriptive idea that one should translate from a "foreign tongue" and into one's "mother tongue," not by arguing for the validity of the opposite direction, as others have convincingly done,[1] but by undoing the very notions of "mother" and "foreign" altogether, drawing on the work of Jacques Derrida. Second, and more generally, it challenges the understanding of translation

---

[1] See, for instance, Pokorn, *Challenging the Traditional Axioms*.

as movement between two languages spatially understood as delineated and relatively fixed territories, a movement conventionally understood as bringing something "foreign" into "one's" language or culture. To do so, we turn to two writers who both appear, for one reason or another, to be "illegitimate" speakers of the language(s) they write and publish in: Oana Avasilichioaei and Nathanaël, who write, to different extents, in a language that would not be considered their "mother tongue." Moreover, they both write in a nonmonolingual fashion, mobilizing a broad set of socially meaningful linguistic forms to signal varying affiliations, locations, and connections across time, space, and language(s). Their heteroglossic works not only complicate the inherent directionality of translation as movement from *one* language to another, as they are not written in one singular, recognizable, unitary language; they also force us to redefine what it means to own a language and to get away from the concepts of "domestic" and "foreign." Whether language is conceived as water and movement (Avasilichioaei) or as a liminal practice between bodies (Nathanaël), it becomes impossible for translation to follow its traditional, prescriptive directionality, conceived as a movement from the Other toward the Self, as the traditional foundations on which this binary rests come undone. What is more, both writers have thematically explored translation in some of their creative works, most notably in Avasilichioaei's *Expeditions of a Chimaera* (cowritten with Erín Moure) and Nathanaël's *Hatred of Translation*, where they each outline a philosophy of translation that challenges the traditional dichotomies of translation studies.

The Depropriation of Language

A seminal work that questions the idea of the natural property of language is, of course, Jacques Derrida's *Le Monolinguisme de l'autre, ou la prothèse d'origine*, published in 1996. In this exploration of his own relationship to the French language as an Algerian Jew, Derrida asks what it means to have a language delegated to us. He explains that, growing up, access to any language other than French—he gives the examples of Arabic or Berber—was prohibited to him, but that even French, the only language he spoke, was also forbidden in some way—in the sense that he could never fully own it. For him, "French was supposedly a mother tongue, but its source, its norms, its rules, its law were situated elsewhere."[2] In other words, his

---

[2] Jacques Derrida, *Le Monolinguisme de l'autre, ou la prothèse d'origine* (Paris: Galilée, 1996), 72.

"monolingualism," the only language he was ever to be identified with, was, as Rey Chow puts it, always "imposed and coerced by the other. 'The other' . . . operating on the foundation of a repressive sovereignty, demands that the colonized adhere to a single language, against which the colonized is always found to be inferior."³ In Derrida's account, the Other represents, of course, the colonizer: "The language of the Metropole was the mother tongue, in fact the substitute for a mother tongue (is it ever any different?) as the language of the other."⁴ Here, Derrida hints that the so-called mother tongue is always a substitute, an ideal—*is it ever any different?*—even for the colonizer who claims ownership of a given imperial language such as French. Indeed, for Derrida, the monolingualism *of* the Other does not evoke ownership or property, but provenance.

Derrida develops an argument about the impossibility of *owning* a language, according to which there is a "universal truth of an essential alienation in language—which is always of the other."⁵ Once it is recognized that language is not, inherently, anyone's property,⁶ claims of ownership of a certain language are unveiled simply as a way to both safeguard unequal access to power and resources and legitimize this inequality on the grounds of language. In this sense, the supposed superiority of "native speakers," otherwise understood as the only individuals who can claim ownership of or belonging to their "mother tongue," has in fact nothing to do with linguistic competence. Language is never truly owned in an ontological sense, but it certainly can be symbolically *appropriated* by various kinds of power. According to Derrida, the colonial situation of the Algerian Jew is exemplary of the larger, universal phenomenon of all subjects' displacement from language, seen here as the inherent foreignness of any language constructed as a delimited, representable entity. In the same vein, Rey Chow suggests that colonial and postcolonial subjects, because they have a direct experience of language as a foreign and imposed object with which they must wrestle to survive, are better positioned to recognize that language is a kind of "impermanent, detachable, and (ex) changeable" prosthesis. According to Chow:

> In this extreme conceptual shift lies a chance of overturning the burden of negativity that tends to attach itself tenaciously to languaging as a

---

[3] Chow, *Not Like a Native Speaker*, 23.
[4] Derrida, *Le Monolinguisme de l'autre*, 74.
[5] Ibid., 113.
[6] "Parce que le maître ne possède pas en propre, *naturellement*, ce qu'il appelle pourtant sa langue; parce que, quoi qu'il veuille ou fasse, il ne peut entretenir avec elle des rapports de propriété ou d'identité naturels, nationaux, congénitaux, ontologiques; . . . parce que la langue n'est pas son bien naturel." Derrida, *Le Monolinguisme de l'autre*, 45.

postcolonial experience. The libidinal or figural logic that accompanies racialized language relations can then, perhaps, proceed beyond the familiar, subjective feelings of loss, insult, injury, and erasure that imbue so much of postcolonial thinking and writing. Rather than being signs of inferiority, for instance, aphasia and double disfigurement can be conceptualized anew as forms of unveiling, as what expose the untenability of "proper" (and proprietary) speech as such.[7]

Following Derrida and Chow, it becomes clear that the notion of "mother tongue" is simply an untenable colonial *narrative* used to distinguish between a legitimate caste of subjects or citizens and the rest. As they suggest, our so-called mother tongue—"la langue *dite* maternelle"[8]—was never ours in the first place; it is always located elsewhere, imposed from the outside.

The idea that the identification of language with race or ancestry is purely ideological is, of course, not new. As Eva C. Karpinski has argued, "[a]ny subject who claims exclusive possession of language or feels the unease of speaking a language that is 'not my own' might be seen as having internalized this colonizing drive of culture and exhibiting complicity with the order of property and identity. No one can claim 'natural possession' or 'ownership' of language."[9] Over time, this deconstruction of the "natural" possession of a language has opened the path for an understanding of linguistic belonging that rests, instead, on the notion of competence or mastery. In other words, the concept of "mother tongue" gradually loses its Romantic association with the mother, referring instead to the language over which one has the greatest "mastery," that is, one's dominant language. However, the fact remains that we tend to associate ourselves with one (or, sometimes, two or more) distinct language(s), on which we inscribe different positions on a scale of competency—regardless of how the hierarchy is defined, whether by lineage, by national belonging, or according to the chronological order of acquisition. It follows that some of us can then "choose" the language they want to be identified with. Such is the case of Lori Saint-Martin, possibly the most prolific French translator in Quebec these last two decades. In her recent autobiographical book *Pour qui je me prends*, Saint-Martin explains that while she grew up in English-speaking Kitchener, Ontario, the English language never felt "natural" to her, which led her to reinvent herself in French by moving to Quebec City—she speaks of a rebirth in French, comparing

---

[7] Chow, *Not Like a Native Speaker*, 14–15.
[8] Derrida, *Le Monolinguisme de l'autre*, 112, italics original.
[9] Karpinski, *Borrowed Tongues*, 225.

herself to "a language phoenix."[10] Throughout her account, Saint-Martin shows that she has proven herself worthy of being affiliated with French, by virtue of her will, her hard work, and her gift at speaking French without a foreign accent. She can now claim, on the basis of her "mastery" of French, that French is hers, that she *is* French.

However, the notion of language as property—as something that one can claim—is very much related to what Goenpul scholar Aileen Moreton-Robinson calls the "white possessive," that is, "a discursive predisposition servicing the conditions, practices, implications, and racialized discourses that are embedded within and central to white first world patriarchal nation-states."[11] Moreton-Robinson sees whiteness as a form of property, in the sense that "white people are recognized within the law primarily as property-owning subjects";[12] this recognition extends to the grounds of language. As Jonathan Rosa and others have shown, for racialized groups in Western states, neither the use of a particular "national" language nor the standardized variety of that language alone can ensure inclusion, which suggests that Saint-Martin's feat is only possible for white subjects.[13] Indeed, Fanon's exposé on the impossible "possession" of the French language for Black subjects still resonates today:[14] Black Montreal poet Lorrie Jean-Louis states, "if I speak *white*, it doesn't mean anything since I'm Black."[15] Jean-Louis says it makes no difference to her whether she speaks English or French, because neither is hers; both are the master's language. Thus, Black and Indigenous thinkers have shown the extent to which "possessing a national language," even on the grounds of competency, is a possibility foreclosed to nonwhite subjects within white settler nation-states.

In fact, the idea of language as property acquired through genealogical descent is absent from Indigenous knowledge systems, which often articulate Indigenous languages as stemming not directly from the land or one's mother but from the *relations* Indigenous peoples establish and maintain with the land and the forces of nature.[16] For instance, Anishinaabe scholar and writer Kateri Akiwenzie-Damm summarizes the difference

---

[10] Lori Saint-Martin, *Pour qui je me prends* (Montreal: Boréal, 2020), 14.
[11] Aileen Moreton-Robinson, *The White Possessive: Property, Power, and Indigenous Sovereignty* (Minneapolis: University of Minnesota Press, 2015), xxiv.
[12] Ibid., xix.
[13] See Rosa, *Looking Like a Language, Sounding Like a Race*.
[14] Fanon, *Peau noire, masques blancs*, 14–32.
[15] Lorrie Jean-Louis, *La femme cent couleurs* (Montreal: Mémoire d'encrier, 2020), 9.
[16] Leanne R. Simpson, "Anticolonial Strategies for the Recovery and Maintenance of Indigenous Knowledge," *American Indian Quarterly* 28, no. 3–4 (2004): 373–84; Aliana Violet Parker, *Learning the Language of the Land* (master's thesis, University of Victoria, 2012).

in relationships to the land between Western and Indigenous worldviews: "The land does not belong to us; we belong to this land."[17] She explains that for Indigenous peoples, land, community, culture, and spirituality are intricately interconnected. Language is not only a means of expressing this interconnectedness but a necessary performative process for maintaining ongoing connections with the land.[18] Thus, Indigenous languages are crucial to the continuance of Indigenous knowledges and identities because they are designed, through direct relationship to the land, to articulate the worldviews, values, conceptualizations, and knowledge that characterize and inform this relationship. Indigenous languages are not idealized or revered in and of themselves as abstract systems but considered crucial because of the relations they signal and foster with the land and the community at a decidedly more local, embodied, and performative level. Leanne Simpson gives an excellent example of this idea of language as an in situ relation:

> I first encountered the concept of Biskaabiiyang in Wendy Makoons Geniusz's *Our Knowledge Is Not Primitive: Decolonizing Botanical Anishinaabe Teachings*. The concept resonated with me, but because she is from the north-west part of our territory and I do not know her personally, I took the concept first to my language teacher and then to my Elder. I did this because I have learned that unless concepts have local meaning, it is difficult for them to have local resonance. I also thought that, as a Michi Saagiig Nishnaabeg person, I could only really learn to understand this concept from within the web of relations of my existence. While Biskaabiiyang might be an important and powerful cultural way to ground decolonization and resurgence work in other places, it was only going to be useful to me if it had meaning within my current relationships.[19]

In the preceding example, Simpson does not presume she has the inherent right to use an Anishinaabemowin word just because she is Anishinaabe. Furthermore, Anishinaabemowin is framed as fundamentally fluid and flexible in nature, depending on the territory and on own's own personal web of experiences and relations, which opposes its appropriation by any given individual or group. Language—words, concepts—is seen as meaningful

---

[17] Kateri Akiwenzie-Damm, "We Belong to This Land: A View of 'Cultural Difference,'" *Journal of Canadian Studies* 31, no. 3 (1996): 21.
[18] Ibid., 22.
[19] Leanne Simpson, "Gdi-nweninaa. Our Sound, Our Voice," in *Learn, Teach, Challenge: Approaching Indigenous Literatures*, ed. Linda M. Morra and Deanne Reader (Waterloo: Wilfrid Laurier University Press, 2016), 291.

only in relation to the territory on which it is used and to the people who use it to connect to each other and to the land.

Hence, any articulation of exclusive ownership and belonging to any singular language, be it by an individual or a group, needs to be problematized. The meaningfulness and weight of "Biskaabiiyang" in Simpson's community need not be equated with ownership of that word or concept. Even the language that *feels* most familiar to us is never truly "ours," which complicates the intuitive sense that I, for instance, should use "Québécois French" when translating a text. Alongside Derrida, this chapter calls for a radical "dépropriation" of language, a move away from the possessive logics of the white settler nation. This chapter, then, asks: what other ways to relate to language are made possible and visible by this decoupling of language from ownership or exclusive belonging—be it by virtue of race, nativity, location, or even competence? This chapter turns mostly to two writers who, like Derrida, write in "someone else's language," exploring the interconnectedness of their "mother tongues" and the other languages they live in and are surrounded by. They have in common the city of Montreal, with which they are to some extent affiliated and which has shaped their practice in different ways.

Writing and Translating Montreal/ Montréal/Tiohtià:ke/Mooniyang

Similar to Derrida's exceptional yet exemplary positionality as an Algerian Jew, the city of Montreal is neither a monstrous nor a utopic case of linguistic mingling but a place where linguistic difference is both made explicit and blurred in everyday life, illustrating the heteroglossic nature of linguistic landscapes everywhere. Further, Montreal is also a field where people recognize the fraught nature of the ethnonational categories which underlie linguistic categories, that is, the mapping of race from biology onto language. There is in this cosmopolitan, colonial city a kind of learned sensitivity to the fact that languages understood as normative systems and sets of rules are not "objectively observable or embodied phenomena in the first place, but rather ... historically and institutionally constituted subject formations that are rooted in the rearticulation of colonial distinctions between normative Europeanness and Othered non-Europeanness."[20] It is precisely this sensibility, I want to suggest, that prompted the visceral reactions to Christian Rioux's criticism of Dead Obies's or Radio Radio's linguistic practices as illegitimate.

---

[20] Rosa, *Looking Like a Language, Sounding Like a Race*, 3.

This chapter will turn, in a few moments, to two Montreal writers for clues about how to approach language use beyond the notions of mother and foreign tongue. As Sherry Simon has shown, contemporary Montreal has a long-standing history of language contact, leading to a tradition of "experimental interlingual practices."[21] The city has indeed produced a significant number of nonmonolingual writers and writing practices,[22] offering a rich body of work that circumvents or questions the idea of "mother tongue." What is important to keep in mind is that Montreal does not have one "mother tongue," understood as the only possible, legitimate language of its nation/territory, in the first place. As Simon reminds us,

> Montreal is the product of a double colonization, first by the French and then by the British. Each act of appropriation in the history of the city was accompanied by a change in language—from the first encounter of Jacques Cartier with the Iroquois inhabitants of Hochelaga, to the foundation of the French colony, Ville-Marie (Michaud 1992, 28) and the imposition of the English language by the British conquerors of 1759.[23]

Such historical processes underline the artificiality of the imposition of one imperial language or another on a colonized territory, making it clear that neither French nor English can claim a Romantic rootedness or belonging to the island of Montreal—which, of course, does not prevent people from making such a claim. Indeed, the dominance of either English or French over time is only achieved through the violent erasure of various Indigenous linguistic forms, including through the renaming of places and sites in the colonial languages[24]—which, in turn, forecloses the possibility of these linguistic forms appearing in the city, including in its literary practices. As in Derrida's account of the situation of French in Algeria, French and English came from overseas, and the colonial project sought to erase the various linguistic practices that were present in this territory before it was colonized in order to impose, coercively and violently, its own. The heteroglossia that

---

[21] Sherry Simon, *Translating Montreal: Episodes in the Life of a Divided City* (Montreal/Kingston: McGill-Queen's University Press, 2006), 122.
[22] See, for instance, the work of Montreal-based Joséphine Bacon, Natasha Kanapé Fontaine, Gail Scott, Nicholas Dawson, Maude Veilleux, Erín Moure, Alexandre Soublière, Heather O'Neill, and Marco Micone, to name only a few.
[23] Simon, *Translating Montreal*, 21.
[24] The city of Montreal is known as Tiohtià:ke in Kanien'kéha (Haudenosaunee/Mohawk) and Mooniyang in Anishinaabemowin. Both the Haudenosaunee and Anishinaabeg peoples have long ties to what is now the Island of Montreal, the territory's official, commonly known name which replaced and now conceals those Indigenous names.

ensues is thus one that is contained and limited because of Montreal's colonial history and present, for example, in terms of the erasure of Indigenous languages due to the ongoing politics of cultural genocide.

Today, after decades of political struggle on the part of the francophone Québécois majority, the province of Quebec has instituted French as its official language; to argue against the existence of a single legitimate "mother tongue" in the Romantic sense in a place like Montreal is not to deny that a given language holds more power, both material and symbolic, than others. In contemporary Montreal, it is of course easier for white Québécois who were born there to claim the status of native speakers than it is for other types of bodies, and it is in turn easier for (white) French speakers to claim to belong to the Québécois nation, still mainly articulated in ethnocultural nationalistic terms.[25] Still, Montreal's heteroglossia has resisted the forces of monolingualism; it is at its core a city of proliferating differences, historically and currently defined by a variety of (appropriated) competing and intermingling languages, never quite by a singular one. It is in this sense that Simon suggests that a place like Montreal puts translation to the test, since it presents language as more fluid than what the regulatory, dualistic model of translation would allow. Simon sees the "multilingual" city—not only Montreal but also Trieste and Prague, among others—as a "breeding ground for innovative translation practices," for it is populated with "practices of language-crossing that remain incomplete, that defy the regulatory function of translation and result in mixed forms of expression."[26]

Simon has in fact dedicated three whole monographs to the intersections between "polyglot" cities and translation—first with *Translating Montreal: Episodes in the Life of a Divided City* in 2006, followed by *Cities in Translation* in 2012 and *Translation Sites: A Field Guide* in 2019. Simon's approach, or framework, has remained consistent throughout these three publications: understood as a process, translation becomes a tool for analyzing cultural contact in the cities or sites she studies. Translation is thus used as a theoretical framework to study cultural contact and the "interlingual practices" that ensue: "[as] a process that includes direction or vectoriality (always including the 'from' and the 'to' of cultural interactions), it is a dynamic and subtle tool for tracking the elements that come together in cultural contact."[27] In fact,

---

[25] Cultural nationalism in Quebec recently took the form of the controversial *Charte des valeurs québécoises* (2013) and *Loi sur la laïcité de l'État*, also known as Loi 21 (2019). Presented as a bill seeking to enforce the religious neutrality of the state, the law banned the wearing of religious symbols by nurses and teachers, at the same time that it allows the presence of crucifixes in schools and hospitals.

[26] Simon, *Translating Montreal*, 120, 128.

[27] Sherry Simon, *Translation Sites: A Field Guide* (London/New York: Routledge, 2019), 17.

translation appears throughout Simon's project as a synonym for cultural contact, for interactions between different cultural and linguistic groups in a single place. Montreal is seen as a "particularly rich zone of translational activity,"[28] a view that builds on the postcolonial idea that writing between cultures or in several languages is akin to translation. In Simon's account, translation as cultural contact—which produces hybrid, transgressive models of expression and communication that close the gap of difference between languages and cultures—is very different from the monolingual view of translation this book takes as its target.

Simon nevertheless recognizes that

> [t]ranslation can deepen a sense of otherness, reifying the categories of knowledge production. Distancing relegates individual works to their "national" origins. This is the "metaphysics of communication" criticized by Naoki Sakai, according to which the world remains mapped in categories classified in national terms (Sakai 2006: 71). . . . In this context, mediation is a technique aimed at managing difference but not disturbing the categories from which these differences issue. Translation is an act of polite acknowledgement, scarcely disturbing the self-enclosed assurance of each group. This is a small step away from indifference, or gestures of politeness which involve no real engagement—and in fact heighten the sense of distance between cultures.[29]

The regulatory aspect of translation as movement from one language to another, rather than "closing or bridging the gap" between cultures, enacts a *distancing* between cultures, languages, and individuals by cultivating their (fabricated) difference and by producing them as monolingual and thus mutually illegible. Hence, throughout her work Simon focuses on a different kind of translation, one that takes place within linguistic interaction and which enacts *furthering* in the sense that it works against indifference and distancing by transforming the categories it mediates. This approach is a reiteration of the equation between multilingual writing and a poetics of translation that Simon puts forth in *Le trafic des langues*, which enlarges the concept of translation to encompass "interlingual practices" that are not traditionally considered translation per se. Thus, in Simon's writings there is often a tension between a narrower, normative function of translation and a broader, more fluid and creative view of translation understood as

---

[28] Sherry Simon, *Cities in Translation: Intersections of Language and Memory* (London/New York: Routledge, 2012), 148.
[29] Ibid., 13.

"interlingual" writing. She situates the latter in a "third space" between languages and has a preference for this utopic kind of translation, which, through its subversion of normative linguistic categories, reveals the precariousness of our current linguistic regimes and mappings.

However, seeing "interlingual" writing as translational in nature presupposes that writers who write that way move between languages, which presupposes that distinct languages exist in a more or less natural way. The approach chosen here, while it builds on Simon's rich insights, is fundamentally different: rather than using translation as an analytical tool to frame linguistic contact in Montreal, the following sections look at specific forms of "language interaction" to deconstruct the idea that translation is necessarily a movement between languages. In other words, rather than translation being the point of departure for studying cultural and linguistic contact, it figures as the finishing line, having been made impossible by linguistic practices that challenge the regimes of language, which make it imaginable in the first place. Following Myriam Suchet, this chapter understands nonmonolingual, heteroglossic writing practices as instances of *non*-translation,[30] a step which allows us to circumvent the imposition of linguistic categories such as "mother tongue" and "foreign tongue" on writers, since these languages, whatever they might be, are never "theirs" in the first place.

Voices of Montreal: Oana Avasilichioaei and Nathanaël

The two writers who appear in the following pages could theoretically be labeled according to their supposed "mother tongue," prior to the actual reading of their works. For instance, it would be easy to introduce Oana Avasilichioaei as a Romanian immigrant whose learned (thus inauthentic) English is often punctuated by a nostalgic use of her native Romanian. Such a framing would already determine the ways in which readers would or should interpret her works as well as the following analyses around her language use and legitimacy. But, as Simon reminds us, "[i]t is the idiom of origin that best defines distancing, as writers and translators are presented as the representatives of their nation or religion and made to conform to the 'metaphysics of communication.'"[31] This demarcation, not only between languages but also between "native" and "foreign," imposes an already

---

[30] Suchet, *L'imaginaire hétérolingue*, 23.
[31] Simon, *Cities in Translation*, 135.

written, nationalistic script on these writers, obscuring the different kinds of belonging and affiliation they build through language in the various spaces in which they find themselves.[32] With Derrida's insight that no one can ever own or belong to any demarcated, fixed language in mind, it makes no sense to attribute to Avasilichioaei a "mother tongue" that is always imposed by the Other—ironically enough, in this case, the Other being the scholar, the critic, or the reader. Approaching these writers' works without the possessive logics that underlie the notion of "mother tongue" will allow us to explore the various affiliations and identifications they create for themselves through language, without foreclosing any on the basis of their linguistic (and so, implicitly national or geographical) origin.

Particularly telling as to why the identification of a source text's language (commonly understood as the author's mother tongue) matters so much to translators is an exchange that took place in July 2019 at the British Centre for Literary Translation (BCLT) Summer School, where a bilingual French and English translation workshop was held, the objective of which was to translate two excerpts from Nathanaël's writing, one written in "English" and one in "French," into the other language. One of the aims of the workshop was to have participants translate not only into their "mother tongue," as is usually prescribed, but also into their "second" language and to reflect on the prescriptive directionality of translation practice and on the kinds of possibilities that such directionality forecloses. Known for contesting the conventional authorial "I" in her writing, Nathanaël withholds any information, such as biographical details, that could help in identifying her according to commonplace identity labels—gender, religion, ethnicity, origins.[33] Further, she deliberately blurs these cultural and social categories in her extensive body of work. Hence, no one ever really knows which pronoun to use to refer to Nathanaël or if a particular book of hers should be called poetry, creative nonfiction, theory, or all of the above. In short, no one really knows *who* she is or *what* she writes.

Unsurprisingly, then, no one really knows what her "mother tongue" is, either. At the BCLT, when our group began reading and analyzing the

---

[32] In fact, it could be argued that the distinction between "native" and "foreign" is at the very core of the distinction between languages, and that without the first distinction, there would be no need for the second.

[33] Elena Basile has written about the "ongoing inscription of gender indeterminacy, which has consistently characterized the auteure's work from their very first publications." Basile, "A Scene of Intimate Entanglements," 33. I will be using the pronoun "she" to refer to Nathanaël throughout this chapter, since it is the pronoun we both have been using in our correspondence. My use of this pronoun is by no means connected to the author's gender identity.

excerpts, the participants grew unnerved and started complaining about the quality of the author's language.[34] Participants who identified as anglophones thought Nathanaël's English was poor and clumsy, and one participant repeatedly stated something along the lines of: "But that's not English, that's not how you would say this in English." The workshop participants were quick to suppose that English was therefore not the author's "mother tongue," and that this was the reason her English was awkward, full of interferences from the French.[35] This belief was then supported by the fact that Nathanaël was born in Montreal, Quebec: she must have been a francophone growing up. Participants intuitively drew a correlation between the "poor" quality (i.e., its presumed contamination from French) of Nathanaël's English and her place of birth and "mother tongue," what Steven G. Kellman has described as "the equation of locution with location."[36] According to this logic, Nathanaël's performance in French would have to be much better. The problem was, as the workshop participants who identified as francophones quickly pointed out, that it is not. The French excerpt we were working on was also "clumsy" and full of English inflections. Plus, they added, there are many anglophone families in Montreal, and Nathanaël's birth name isn't exactly French— maybe her parents were English, and perhaps she's not francophone after all? Confused, the group, visibly anxious to settle the matter once and for all, then turned to her accent,[37] both in English and in French, for clues: which, exactly, is her mother tongue? This lead also proved inconclusive: Nathanaël's accent, in both languages, is peculiarly unlocal, abstracted, unidentifiable. The workshop participants never found out what her "mother tongue" is.

In her practice, Nathanaël refuses the idea of a mother tongue. She is an "ambilingual" writer, a term Kellman has coined to describe people who write

---

[34] To be fair, Nathanaël's writing is famously opaque and nothing short of difficult for the unaccustomed reader. Reviewing the recent *Hatred of Translation*, Timothy Parfitt observes that "much of [his] reading experience was spent in partial or even total confusion. The author stacks ideas and references so quickly and unconventionally that I often found my head spinning and my fingers a'Googling. Indeed, her thinking rarely follows a straight line that leads to a neat conclusion or unified theory." Timothy Parfitt, "Irresistible Destruction and Building Understanding: A Review of Nathanaël's *Hatred of Translation*," *Newcity Lit*, December 5, 2019, https://lit.newcity.com/2019/12/05/irresistible-destruction-and-building-understanding-a-review-of-nathanaels-hatred-of-translation/.

[35] A different figure is that of Nancy Huston, who has displayed "mastery" in both French and English to the extent that she is recognized as a legitimate speaker of both. Nathanaël, on the other hand, complicates this idea of masterful language, deliberately displaying a lack of mastery in her writings. While Huston could be considered as having two dominant languages, Nathanaël is seen as having none.

[36] Kellman, *The Translingual Imagination*, 18.

[37] We had had a Skype session with Nathanaël earlier that morning.

in more than one language.³⁸ Not only does she simultaneously write and publish in both English and French, refusing to fix her voice in one language or the other, but she also refuses to fix any of her texts in any given language, writing in such a way that both languages touch and interpenetrate each other, always "inviting further confusion into the transferences between languages."³⁹ Nathanaël's writing and translating is thus characterized by a porosity between languages, which structurally refutes the notion of the dominant tongue as fixed origin in a given, recognized, delimited language.⁴⁰ Hence, the ambivalence between English and French does not simply mean going from one to the other; rather, in each language the writing feels ambivalent, strange, unfamiliar—causing a workshop participant to say "this is not English" about a text that is certainly comprised of what are typically recognized as English words. What this anecdote shows is the anxiety that the absence of a clear mother tongue or source language creates for translators, whose habitus is deeply reliant on such categorization, as we saw in the first chapter. For translation to take place, we need to be able to locate the source language unequivocally, if only because it allows us to confidently identify a target language, "our" language, as distinct from the language we are translating. In other words, we need the border to be clear in order to be able to cross it.

Both Nathanaël and Avasilichioaei play with the notion of "mother tongue" to varying degrees in their works. Echoing Derrida's claim that "identity is never given, received or attained, no, only the neverending, indefinitely phantasmatic process of identification endures,"⁴¹ these writers complicate their imposed affiliation with a "mother tongue" and constantly shift their identification to different languages, creating new and surprising affiliations, solidarities, and tensions within and across conventional linguistic borders. First, we turn to Oana Avasilichioaei's 2015 poetry collection *Limbinal*, in which she translates poems written in her "mother tongue" into English, revisiting her relationship to both languages. Compared to water, languages are seen as movements in and of themselves: they remain always out of reach, and Avasilichioaei's relationship to them is not one of belonging or ownership but of further movement, along with the already moving languages, propelled by affection. The chapter continues with a section on Nathanaël's liminal tongue, which is difficult to situate on either side of the linguistic boundary between French and English. I ask what this absence of

---

³⁸ Ibid., 12.
³⁹ Nathanaël, *Asclepias: The Milkweeds* (New York: Nightboat, 2015), 18.
⁴⁰ See Nathanaël, *Alula, de son nom de plume* (Montréal: L'Hexagone, 2018), 256; Nicole Côté, "Nathanaël, ou l'étrange art du déplacement: *Le Carnet de somme* et son apatride traversée de frontières," *Canadian Literature* 224 (2015): 33–45.
⁴¹ Derrida, *Le Monolinguisme de l'autre*, 53.

landmarks implies for translation, focusing on Nathanaël's metaphorical use of the "bridge" to deconstruct the spatial understanding of languages and the corollary understanding of translation as a bridge between cultures. This chapter ends with a discussion of both writers' philosophy of translation as it is articulated in two of their (co)writings.

Ultimately, the writers this chapter thinks alongside seem more interested in encountering the Other, privileging an impersonal, at once delocalized and embodied, use of language in which they give themselves the freedom to experiment with the borders of their own subjectivity. They write against the idea that identity (be it sexual, cultural, linguistic, or otherwise) is something that needs to be closed up, protected, and sheltered from outside interference, exploring instead what happens to an "I" or an "us" when we let the Other transform us. On linguistic grounds, this means that for both Avasilichioaei and Nathanaël, language is not seen as an abstract system we belong to or not but as a set of moving, fluid resources that have different social, political, and affective values in relation to the authors' personal trajectories as well as to their relationships to the discursive spaces in which they write.

Oana Avasilichioaei's *Limbinal*: Language as River, Language as Movement

Montreal-based poet Oana Avasilichioaei is known for interweaving genres and mediums, including photography, moving image, and performance, in her practice. She explicitly engages with "polyglot and polyphonic poetics"[42] and is also a prolific literary translator. Some of her notable works include *Expeditions of a Chimaera*, written collaboratively with Erín Moure (2009), and *Readopolis* (2017), the English translation of Bertrand Laverdure's novel *Lectodôme*, for which Avasilichioaei won a Governor General's Literary Award in 2017. Not unlike Nathanaël, very little biographical information is publicly available on Avasilichioaei, making it difficult to identify her origins as a starting point. I would suggest that, for these two writers, withholding clues that would help us categorize them with labels of mother tongue, place of birth, and so on is deliberate. They remove from our potential gaze the tools with which we could fix them in a given place and consequently police their expression, affiliation, and belonging to other places. That being said, if Avasilichioaei's poetry can be seen as giving any clue as to her life trajectory, there are several passages in her 2015 collection *Limbinal* that allude to a child

---

[42] Author's website, https://www.oanalab.com/.

who is learning English and to Romanian as being the speaker's "familial language."[43] In any case, one can surmise that the poet has a fairly advanced knowledge of the Romanian language, since she translates a series of Paul Celan's Romanian poems into English at one point in the collection. One thing is certain: traces of Romanian and French permeate the collection, most notably in the poems "Borne" and "Coursing Vernaculars." The following pages will focus on these poems to suggest that Avasilichioaei's voice resists boundedness, proposing a view of language as motion instead. As we will see, when language is seen as movement, it becomes impossible to fix and own it; we can only move along with it and participate in its movement.

Limbinal is first and foremost a book about borders and, as the title suggests, liminality; as its publisher's blurb suggests, it "speaks in the porous space between a limb's articulations and a liminal border."[44] The title also suggests liminality on the grounds of language, as *limbă* means "language" in Romanian. Thematically speaking, the border is found throughout most of the collection's poems—with titles such as "Bound," "Partitions," "Thresholds," "The Bo(a)rders," and "On the Threshold." Formally speaking, the border also appears in the formatting of several poems: in "Coursing Vernaculars," the poem is spread across the two open pages, the binding creating a clear line that divides the stanzas in two. Linguistic borders are also materialized, for instance, through the presentation of a Romanian poem by Paul Celan called "Regăsire" on the left-hand page, accompanied by its English translation, "Regain," on the right-hand page:[45]

Regăsire	Regain
Pe dunele verzi de calcar va ploua astănoapte,	Tonight it will rain on the green dunes of limestone.
Vinul păastrat până azi într-o gură de mort	Wine preserved until now in a dead man's mouth
Trezi-va ținutul cu punți, strămutat într-un clopot.	Will awaken the realm of footbridges, displaced in a bell.
O limbă de om va sunar într-un coif cutezanța.	A human tongue will clang courage inside a helmet.
. . .	. . .

This kind of bilingual formatting represents and reifies a strict delimitation between languages. It follows what Naoki Sakai has called the schema of configuration and presents us with two distinct instances of monolingual

---

[43] Oana Avasilichioaei, *Limbinal* (Vancouver: Talonbooks, 2015), 103.
[44] Publisher's website, https://talonbooks.com/books/limbinal.
[45] Avasilichioaei, *Limbinal*, 76–7.

address, where two voices or audiences are "posited as separate from one another in the *representation of translation*."⁴⁶ On these two pages, Paul Celan the poet and Oana Avasilichioaei the translator are posited on either side of the linguistic border between Romanian and English, representing two distinct voices and the imagined linguistic, cultural, and national communities these voices address. At play here is the economy of translational as transactional communication, where languages are presented as a kind of currency and where the process of translation produces an "equivalent" text, an equivalence that is first quantitative—the one-word title is translated by one word in English; the stanzas have the same number of verses—but is also supposed to be qualitative. The author's and the translator's voice are presented as distinct and autonomous, yet equivalent; the two can be compared as products or objects. If a language, a text, or a voice is "fixed," that is, presented as a delimited product, then it can be compared to other similar objects—think of the widespread notions of "gain" and "loss" in translation, not to mention the long-standing concept of equivalence—and, ultimately, it can be owned.

Ironically, this is precisely the view of language as product, which Avasilichioaei plays with and tries to escape from in *Limbinal*. Elsewhere in the collection, the poet produces a kind of language that resists boundedness by mobilizing the border where it would not normally appear and by blending traditionally discrete entities together. The result is sometimes opaque and difficult to grasp, but the experiment succeeds in creating a composite voice that is extremely difficult to identify and thus to objectify. The speaker presents language as something that is always moving, making it difficult to pin down. Indeed, the Celan poem in translation pictured earlier is the only moment in *Limbinal* where a linguistic border shows up where we would normally expect it, aligned with the dominant regime of translation as a schema of configuration.⁴⁷ The dozen or so translations of Paul Celan that follow "Regain" appear without their counterparts in Romanian, suggesting that the two voices join forces and foreclosing the possibility of comparing one to the other. Later, the section "Riverine" takes the form of a dialogue between Avasilichioaei and Celan: first, explicit exchanges between voices assigned to "OA" and "PC" take place in "Overpass"; then, in "Coursing Vernaculars" both voices and languages meet in one poem; and finally, in "Current" and "Overflow," a dialogue between unidentified voices shifts between the use of "you" and "I." There is a gradual shift, then, from the

---

⁴⁶ Sakai, *Translation and Subjectivity*, 5. Emphasis in original.
⁴⁷ Even then, the title "Regain" can be read as a play on the French word "Regain," illustrating how both an English and a French word can have the same spelling and meaning.

presentation of two distinct voices and languages to an explicit melding of the two, where it is impossible to tell when one begins and the other ends.

"Coursing Vernaculars" is a poem where the speaker meets Paul Celan through language. It is also the poem which introduces the idea of language as water:[48]

My river is the language in which we foreign language, obsolete rickety wo estranged. Sometimes strangled.	meet. My familial language, his first od planks to be crossed and re-crossed,
Or the river bowel's to be dredged. Or my ri violence to be resisted. Yet the assigning of affection to bestow upon the river, rather th	ver's surface to will. As Such. A *my* already a first violence. Or an an an articulation of belonging.

The paragraphs that make up the poem are spread on the left and right pages, running across the division between verso and recto. Each paragraph descends into the gutter—the central margin where text is usually absent—and comes out on the other side. Lines and even words are split in two; the poem is not contained on one page but courses across two. Here, language is compared to a river, rather than to a shored territory, and the assignment of the possessive "my" is presented as a violence; can something that moves and flows really be owned? Avasilichioaei suggests that one's possessive articulation of belonging to a language ("my familial language"—note the circumventing, although not entirely successful, of the term "mother tongue") is perhaps misguided; if Romanian is "her" language, then this denies Celan's possible affiliation with it (instead it is "his first foreign tongue"),[49] and it denies, in turn, her own belonging to English or French where she now lives. Against this denial, to engage nonviolently with language is to recognize its fluidity, its nature as something that is collectively transformed, and its resistance to being tamed or fixed by any individual or group. The speaker suggests that her relationship to a language is one not of belonging or property but of affection. Earlier in the collection, she asks, "Should I mention that my frequent crossing is propelled by love not market?"[50] Perhaps this is why Avasilichioaei turns to water as a metaphor for language: water as the ultimate commons, a shared good, along with air, often "regarded as mere externalities in market

---

[48] Avasilichioaei, *Limbinal*, 102–3.
[49] Celan was born in Romania, but he grew up in a German-speaking, Jewish household and went on to be exclusively associated with German, although he occasionally wrote in Romanian as well. This association with German is all the more tragic and paradoxical since Celan's parents died in a Nazi concentration camp, and he himself worked in a forced labor camp for eighteen months.
[50] Avasilichioaei, *Limbinal*, 8.

capitalism and which, because they were shared, were not valued," as Michael Cronin would have it.[51]

The comparison between language and flowing water permeates the end of *Limbinal*, especially the poem titled "Suspension/Sediment":

> The river drifts sediments of loose gravel, live kick of fidgety fish. Syllables unlock the. Mesh of wind gusts. By the river, a girl drifts, sifting a day of pebbles through the mesh of her fingers in her left pocket. The pebbles are syllables leftover from the other language.[52]

This notion of language as water, or language as river, is strikingly different from the idea of language as bounded system or as spatially delimited. In contrast, the metaphor of the "bridge" in translation studies positions the river as the *border* between two different languages, understood as shores on either side, an image we will return to in the next section. The idea of language as a river points to the moving nature of language and to its tendency to vary across space and time. In Avasilichioaei's poetry, language figures itself as movement, as a flow which can never be contained, commodified, or owned. Throughout the poems of *Limbinal* the speaker comes to recognize and embrace the chaos of language, its "flowing, gushing, swelling, evaporating."[53] It is perhaps not a coincidence that several of *Limbinal*'s poems are formatted in a way to create wave patterns (such as the poem "Coursing Vernaculars"), or that the series of photographs in the middle of the book, which begin by showing fences and walls, end with a close-up picture of a body of water. The poetry in itself follows the same sort of progression, starting with relatively straightforward poems that are explicitly about borders, both thematically and visually ("Border," "Partitions," and "Mouthnotes"), moving on to poems which mobilize the notions of threshold and sideline, then to Paul Celan's poems in translation, and finally ending with a series of poems about water, uncertainty, and movement, in which language becomes more and more opaque and unpredictable. The "route of the book" is one that goes from borders as imperialist imperatives, to a "fleshy, abundant, undulating" river which "revel[s] in the fluid silt of its constancy," to an "ebb and flow" that "foliates lavishment."[54] In the movement of the river, words lose their fixed meanings or usage and new associations emerge, such as the verb "foliate"

---

[51] Michael Cronin, "Shady Dealings: Translation, Climate and Knowledge," in *The Dark Side of Translation*, ed. Federico Italiano (London/New York: Routledge, 2020), 103.
[52] Avasilichioaei, *Limbinal*, 114.
[53] Ibid., 118.
[54] Ibid., 123–5.

and the noun "lavishment." Language falls apart, the words overflowing with meaning and possibility.

The idea of language as river—echoing, interestingly, the connection to fluids in the previous chapter—counters the Romantic notion of rootedness in a national territory, complicating the claim that the speaker's familial language is "hers." Furthermore, language also emerges as something that can transform preexisting demarcated territories and their structures of belonging, provided its perpetual movement and flow is embraced: "tidal, swelling, littoral tongues meander / over the volatile landscapes altering riverbeds."[55] Linguistic borders are also mobilized and blurred in "Borne," where English, French, and Romanian share verses and stanzas: "Tu énonces un trajet, tu le suis impassiblement, par la suite tu deviens le trajet, deci dacă inteleg bine, a avea o intentie commits the already intended. La notion oblique of a drunken following."[56] Here, this deterritorialized utterance clashes with the "unisonance" of the national community,[57] suggesting a refusal to participate to the configuration and production of said community and pointing to the performative making of a different, polysonant one. Freeing language from normative containment allows for the embracing of various sounds, voices, and meanings that ultimately enlarge a community's vocabulary and expressive possibilities.

Avasilichioaei likely draws on her own experience of displacement to articulate this view of language as motion, as, in fact, its own kind of displacement. The section "Riverine," in which the poem "Coursing Vernaculars" appears, is introduced by a quote from Ion Caraion: "Language is our first exile."[58] In "Coursing Vernaculars," she compares Celan's exodus to Paris to her own displacement to Montreal:

> Meanwhile the rapid embrace of the urban island occupies, causes the displacement, river of my own, I will not call it exile . . .

> He had called it *ținutul cu punți* anticipating that French city with its undulating river of thirty-seven bridges where he would come to dwell. Where others saw *land*, I saw *a realm of footbridges* transposing my francophone dwelling into a ligament of language aqueducts. I was almost thirty-seven when happened into this thinking. He was just twenty-seven when crossing frontiers to abide by the French tributary.

---

[55] Ibid., 125.
[56] Ibid., 69.
[57] See Anderson, *Imagined Communities*, 149.
[58] Avasilichioaei, *Limbinal*, 95.

Strătumat într-un clopot, he and I were. Or displaced in a bell as my English would later invent it. Melodious and deafening were the new sounds. Disjunctive and disorienting the new tongue, yet exerting an undeniable pull, composing a resonance. In this *there*, which became a *here*, in the new alien *langue*, appropriated though not maternal, we, separately, on our different continents, sought the possibility of a kind of freedom.[59]

To understand language as exile or displacement in itself is of course not the same as stating that someone like Avasilichioaei is at home in Romanian and in exile in English or French; the poet refuses to call her "river" or her current, embodied experience of language, an exile. The speaker is always already exiled in language—echoing Derrida's universal alienation—and, as such, seeks a kind of freedom through the exploration of new languages. Heteroglossia thus appears as its own kind of movement away from the tyranny and fixity of origins, which already constitute an exile in the first place. Of course, the river is also where Celan will find death; displacement can be hopeful, but it can also be violent, opaque, and illegible.

Avasilichioaei's trajectory, at first rooted in a world defined by imperialist borders but eventually emerging in a flowing motion within and outside of these borders, echoes Derrida's claim that our relationship to language is not one of "belonging" but one of "provenance." In this sense, seeing language as movement, as always flowing, allows us to better navigate the constructed, bounded systems we have come to know as "languages" and our sense of belonging to them. Each voice, each utterance is a motion that moves regardless of linguistic borders, which are but one mode of perception imposed on linguistic practices after the fact. Avasilichioaei's "displaced in a bell" recalls the fishbowl metaphor Suchet uses to discuss the artificial borders of language: "It's as if every single one of us were evolving in our language like a goldfish in a fishbowl, having forgotten the contours of this transparent environment that is everything but natural."[60] Avasilichioaei's poetry shows that language as water is only contained by the borders of artificial linguistic categories, and she seeks to shatter the glass panels of the fishbowl in order to let language flow—even though this creates the risk of being misunderstood.

This reading of Avisilichioaei's blurring of linguistic boundaries sees the polyphonic poetic voice as attempting to unbound the languages she writes

---

[59] Ibid., 102–5.
[60] Myriam Suchet, "Le québécois : d'une langue identitaire à un imaginaire hétérolingue," *Quaderna* 2 (2015), https://quaderna.org/2/le-quebecois-dune-langue-identitaire-a-un-imaginaire-heterolingue/.

in, to set them free of their assigned location and set them in movement instead. In the title of the poem "Borne," one single word points to several different possible meanings—borne as in limit, border, or landmark in French, as in transported, as in native—multiplying possibilities and associations across and between different languages and spaces. For rivers are connectors: they connect people and collectivities across space and bounded nations, even when they are enlisted to serve as boundary markers. And water, even if it can be bottled and commodified to a certain extent, remains largely uncommodifiable, free of the constraints of the nation or of identity, even if subject to human agency. As such, seeing language as flowing water, as something that is not fixed or defined spatially but already, always in motion, suggests a new understanding of linguistic belonging.[61] Meeting someone in the river of language means that neither can claim it, and that we can only swim—or drown—together.

Sexual and Linguistic Encounters and the Dissolution of Identity in Nathanaël's Writings

In a recent interview, Nathanaël states that out of the approximately thirty works she has published thus far, she has written very few books in French, maybe four, and only two or three in English, even though they are all marketed as French or English.[62] Indeed, in Nathanaël's works, languages are not seen spatially as "silos"[63] but as performances, a succession and relation of symbols and syntax that aren't constrained spatially. In other words, if the publication of Nathanaël's books follows a monolingual logic, her writing does not. Because French and English function as generic categories which have limited the conceptualization and performance of her voice,[64] she refuses to endorse one or the other, adopting instead a liminal practice that suggests new openings and possibilities outside of what is already authorized. According to Nicole Côté, this liminal practice in Nathanaël's

---

[61] Jon Solomon concludes a recent article by comparing language with water as well. See Jon Solomon, "Beyond a Taste for the Dark Side: The Apparatus of Area and the Modern Regime of Translation under Pax Americana," in *The Dark Side of Translation*, ed. Federico Italiano (London/New York: Routleldge, 2020), 35.
[62] Nathanaël, *Alula, de son nom de plume*, 266. The original words are *vases clos*, literally "closed vases."
[63] Ibid., 255.
[64] Nowhere is this reducing clearer than in the interventions of the BCLT workshop participants, who repeatedly tried to frame her as an illegitimate speaker of the two languages she uses.

works "imagines the self unburdened by its traditional, strictly delimited foundations":

> What makes Nathanaël's posture original, then, is the expansion of her in-between positioning to a statement that both encompasses and destabilizes, as we have seen, various borders, in order to question nothing less than the foundations of the self's representation: thus, both the representation of oneself and of the other are impacted.[65]

Nathanaël's liminal practice—between English and French, as well as at the intersection of other languages—is not only a way of liberating her writing of the constraints of "English" and "French"; by providing us with an ambivalent language, she creates texts that are unlocatable in one or the other, which complicates the idea of translation as movement *from* one language *to* another. The participants at the BCLT Summer School were visibly anxious to locate Nathanaël in a specific, familiar "language," and when they could not, it presented them with a translation problem: if the text/the person we are translating isn't "English" but sitting on the border between English and French, translation as the process of homogenization and establishing equivalence between two linguistic systems is simply impossible. In other words, Nathanaël's writing challenges the notions of "source" and "target" languages, the by-products of the notion of "original" or "mother" tongue. Simply put, one cannot translate something into a "target language" if there is no recognizable "source language" to begin with.

Rather than focusing on specific texts, this section engages with Nathanaël's liminal writing practice and philosophy of translation, as developed in a number of her works since the publication of the seminal *Je Nathanaël* in 2003. Because Nathanaël's oeuvre is best seen as an interrelated whole, where texts echo and answer each other, the following pages engage with the ideas and themes she elaborates in several of her publications, from *Je Nathanaël* to the more recent *Hatred of Translation* (2019). Furthermore, Nathanaël's works represent an interesting case study for overcoming key concepts that underlie the practice of translation—"mother tongue," "source," and "target language"—since she is known for writing two iterations of each text, a practice she has called "traduction soi-disant," or self-called translation.[66]

For instance, *Je Nathanaël* was first published in 2003 by Montreal publisher L'Hexagone, then in a different version by Book*hug in Toronto in

---

[65] Côté, "Nathanaël, ou l'étrange art du déplacement," 44. Emphasis added.
[66] Nathanaël, *Alula, de son nom de plume*, 256.

2006, and both versions were reedited in 2018 and 2019, respectively.[67] One of Nathanaël's most accessible and most discussed books, it is deeply invested in the deconstruction of the authorial "I" along the lines of gender, genre, and language. *Je Nathanaël* also represents a turning point in Nathanaël's oeuvre: it was at the time of the first version of the book that she began purposefully confounding languages in her writing and that she began investigating themes like desire, alterity, and translation. In the author's words, *"Je Nathanaël* [is] a text split across (at least) two languages, and for which neither is a mother tongue, for which neither functions as origin, and by which doubling the text cannot claim itself as antecedent."[68] Both versions exist simultaneously and equally as different ways to articulate the same questions, with different discursive resources that will necessarily create different meanings and aesthetic effects in different locations and bodies. This practice of "traduction soi-disant" is best seen as writing the same book twice, in two different sets of linguistic resources, which by definition results in two different books, neither of which has precedence over the other.

This section analyzes how Nathanaël's writing is situated at the linguistic border, unsettling the idea of distinct source and target languages. The author finds, between presumably fixed and bounded social categories, not a clear boundary that takes the form of a fixed line but rather a foggy interstice where the "I" can dwell in its search (understood as desire) for the Other. By displacing it from its traditional identity (spatial, gendered, linguistic) groundings, this strategic positioning of the "I" not on one side of a border or the other but instead on its threshold presents the subject as plural and equivocal, reminding us that difference is never absolute. Further, the following reading of Nathanaël's works shows that her dwelling on the threshold between artificial boundaries points to a redefinition of translation. Translation becomes more than a matter of transposing/welcoming the Other into our home/culture—where the Other is always represented and

---

[67] L'Hexagone published it in *Alula, de son nom de plume*, an anthology comprised of all three books Nathanaël has published with them, along with a new preface, an interview, and an unpublished text, while Book*hug reedited the book with two new afterwords, one by Nathanaël and the other by Elena Basile.

[68] Nathanaël, "There Is No Capital I," *Lemon Hound*, 2018, https://lemonhound.com/2018/06/22/there-is-no-capital-i-in-conversation-with-nathanael/. Other similar pairs of texts include . . . *s'arrête? Je* (Montréal: L'Hexagone, 2007) and *The Sorrow and The Fast of It* (New York: Nightboat, 2007), *Sotto l'immagine* (Montréal: Mémoire d'encrier, 2014), and *Feder: A Scenario* (New York: Nightboat, 2016), as well as *Le cri du chrysanthème* (Montreal: Le Quartanier, 2018) and *Pasolini's Our* (New York: Nightboat, 2018). These different versions are never posited as either "original" or "translation"; for instance, the 2018 edition of . . . *s'arrête? Je* mentions that the text "exists from Nightboat Books under the title *The Sorrow and the Fast of It*" ("existe chez Nightboat Books sous le titre *The Sorrow and The Fast of It*"). Nathanaël, . . . *s'arrête? Je*, 168.

perceived on the relatively stable terms of the Self—and appears as a process where two already plural and precarious bodies, voices, and languages fall apart and are radically transformed, creating a product that is equivocal, unfamiliar, ambiguous, and ultimately unreliable. Nathanaël's philosophy of translation is a move away from the idea of hospitality in translation[69]— where the translating subject and language remain comfortably at home— and toward a more reciprocal relation where the "I" is radically transformed through translation, possibly violently, as much as the Other is. As a result, the notions of more or less stable "source" and "target" languages lose their integrity: heteroglossic writing gestures toward continual entanglements of linguistic, textual, and bodily materialities. In short, it appears that reading and translating an author/text whose "mother tongue/source language" is unlocatable on a predetermined linguistic map unsettles the "representation of translation as a communicative and international transfer of the message between a pair of ethno-linguistic unities,"[70] forcing the translator to stay in the interstitial zone of linguistic borders rather than simply crossing them. Ultimately, for Nathanaël, meeting the Other outside of conventional categories such as the gendered self involves the refusal to "master" any given language, which ultimately comes with the risk of writing from nowhere.

In *Je Nathanaël, . . . s'arrête? Je* and elsewhere, Nathanaël is concerned with debunking the contours of her subjectivity: "I have no identity. What I have is history's itineraries that pass through me."[71] For instance, in *Je Nathanaël*, the speaker unravels the unicity/unity of the "I," notably through sexual contact with an addressee named Nathanaël. The title of the book first indicates an equation between Nathanaël and the authorial "I," particularly since the book also bears the signature of the author that goes by the same name. However, the book begins with a reference to André Gide's *Les Nourritures terrestres* and one of its characters, Nathanaël, who is referred to in the third-person masculine: "Nathanaël is as absent from the pages of his own book as he will ever be."[72] Nathanaël reappears as the addressee of an epistolary composition a few pages later: "My dear Nathanaël I will not write. / Très cher Nathanaël je ne t'écrirai pas."[73] *Je Nathanaël* is comprised primarily of a series of fragments that play with pronouns and their referents, creating a "shuttle between an I and a You whose referential consistency is utterly confounded."[74] In the

[69] See Paul Ricoeur, *Sur la traduction* (Paris: Bayard, 2004), 18.
[70] Naoki Sakai, "Translation," *Theory, Culture & Society* 23, no. 2–3 (2006): 72.
[71] Nathanaël, *Alula, de son nom de plume*, 249.
[72] Nathanaël, *Je Nathanaël* (Toronto: Book*hug, [2006] 2019), 7.
[73] Nathanaël, *Je Nathanaël*, 11, and Nathanaël, *Alula, de son nom de plume*, 27.
[74] Elena Basile, "Pressing against Tongues: Notes on the Name and Its Ghostly Body," in *Je Nathanaël* (Toronto: Book*hug, 2019), 101.

words of Elena Basile, *Je Nathanaël* creates a scene of "the perception of an entanglement of sorts, a situation comprised of so many knots and twists, so many tangled threads of language(s) and body(ies) that normal (normative) parameters for mapping, orientation, and recognition no longer apply."[75]

In the sexual act, both bodies and selves become entangled: "I fall against you. You against me. . . . Am adrift. Are."[76] Here, the absence of pronouns and the verb conjugations suggest a play between I and you, between self and other. However, when this passage is articulated in the 2003 version, the second iteration of the verb *to be* does not refer to the second-person singular: "Suis la dérive. Sommes."[77] The conjugation "sommes" signals a move away from the I and the you and toward the union of the two, a collective "we," which suggests a new reading of the other iteration: "are" not only refers to "you" but also to "we" and perhaps even to "they." You, we, they are adrift. This mode of writing registers the interstitial moment when bodies, genders, and even languages enter a space of indeterminate, reciprocal delimitation and disintegration. The notion of the threshold continually reappears, under many guises, in Nathanaël's writing as the space that both separates and unites two dissolving entities; echoing Avasilichioaei's insistence on affection, desire is then what brings the narrator to this interstitial moment between herself and the other body/voice: "The intrinsic element to this exchange is desire."[78] In fact, Nathanaël's entire political project of deconstructing monolithic identities emanates from and is based on the desire for a radically transformative alterity.

> "The intersection of the lines of relation" brings the body to one threshold that touches another. In crossing these lines, we transport ourselves into the space of the other. However artificial these boundaries—whose forms are most dramatically, most violently evident at the border crossings between countries . . . —a translation occurs as the body moves over the line, carrying itself as a remnant to be reconstituted on the other, aleatory, side; *the passage threatens always to dissolve what passes,* in the form of time, of space, of body, each in contact with the other, and at times several bodies at once, in just as many directions.[79]

---

[75] Basile, "A Scene of Intimate Entanglements," 27.
[76] Nathanaël, *Je Nathanaël*, 23.
[77] Notice the extra pun here, where "suis" is both the first-person conjugation of the verb "être" and the first- and second-person conjugation of the verb "suivre," to follow. Nathanaël, *Alula, de son nom de plume*, 39.
[78] Nathanaël, *Je Nathanaël*, 88.
[79] Nathanaël, *At Alberta* (Toronto: BookThug, 2008), 19–20. Emphasis added.

The same can be said about linguistic encounters: languages present themselves as available cultural categories as much as gender categories. In Nathanaël's writing and practice of (self-)translation: "Languages and subjects 'come undone' in the sexual and in the translative encounter when the materiality of their intermingling passes a threshold of perception, such that they can no longer be governed by the ideational rule of transparent self-identity."[80] In other words, translation is not merely a process where a source text is transformed but also a process where the translating voice/language is transformed as much as the translated voice/language.

What might such a linguistic encounter look like? Let us look at some examples from the excerpt chosen for the BCLT workshop mentioned earlier, taken from *Asclepias: The Milkweeds* (2015). As we will see, analyzing Nathanaël's writing under the lens of "linguistic interference" or "naturalness"—in other words trying to find "proofs" that her writing is "not natural" or "clumsy," deliberately or not—reveals the difficulty of studying such writing without calling upon predetermined linguistic categories. In any case, here are a few sentences that illustrate Nathanaël's atypical writing:

> It is no secret (to myself, I mean), that in recent years, a kind of German toil, has attempted to insert itself, somewhat infectiously, into my unwitting vocabularies.[81]

Here, the exaggerated use of commas, some of which are "wrong" in English, reads as a parody of the use of commas in German, perhaps even in French. For instance, the comma before "that in recent years" is placed right where one would be in German, exemplifying the "German toil" Nathanaël hints at. Later in this passage we find:

> This "nothing," I would like to hazard, is the condition of a kind of translation which has become a persistent preoccupation.[82]

Here, from a normative point of view, the use of "hazard" without an obvious object (as in "to hazard a guess") is unusual, and one has to reconstruct the structure of the sentence to make sense of it: "I would like to hazard [that] [t]his 'nothing' is the condition of a kind of translation that has become a persistent preoccupation." A simple glitch in syntax complicates a straightforward, transparent production of meaning and requires instead a greater amount

---

[80] Basile, "A Scene of Intimate Entanglements," 30.
[81] Nathanaël, *Asclepias: The Milkweeds*, 69.
[82] Ibid.

of work and concentration on the part of the reader. Nathanaël's writing is populated by this kind of syntactical glitch; in . . . *s'arrête, Je?*, she writes: "Il y a le silence dont."[83] "Dont" is a relative pronoun which connects a subject, here "silence," with a subordinate clause, but here, it does not connect its antecedent "silence" to anything, which creates a gap, an opening in meaning.

> There is an argument to be made for the real. It is made persistently, repeatedly, and with great consequence misapprehended.[84]

While technically not ungrammatical, the second sentence here is functionally a kind of convoluted garden-path sentence. Reading the comma after "repeatedly" as a serial comma leads to a comprehensible but strange parsing: "It is made persistently, [it is made] repeatedly, and [it is made] with great consequence [that is] misapprehended," implying that the significance of making the argument for the real has been understated or underestimated. Only then does the strangeness of this interpretation prompt the reader to go back and reparse the sentence in its more readily comprehensible sense: "It is made persistently [and] repeatedly, and [it is] with great consequence misapprehended."

All in all, even though it remains difficult to point to specific examples because of the fugitive quality of her writing, Nathanaël's style mobilizes linguistic resources in an unusual way, that is, in a way readers of "English" or of "French" are not accustomed to. She often uses the passive voice, typically criticized in both French and English. Commas, meanings, and grammatical categories show up in unexpected places, giving the impression that the writing is "bad," not "mastered," "clumsy." For translation, a problem such as the one presented by the intransitive use of "hazard" is ultimately one of interpretation, as it can't be traced back to a straightforward meaning: what does the author mean by "hazard" if she does not hazard *something* or *someone*? The road "back" to the original meaning "in English" is impossible; we find ourselves in a semantic cul-de-sac. In any case, what appears before the reader is an unfamiliar language, one that does not necessarily conform to the grammatical rules and conventions of English or French. Nathanaël refuses to abide by the so-called consensus that makes up the various rules of these two bounded languages and creates an expression that is "syntactically indefensible."[85] It is in this sense that we can say of such writing that it is written from the threshold of these languages. As such, it operates an

---

[83] Nathanaël, *Alula, de son nom de plume*, 181.
[84] Nathanaël, *Asclepias: The Milkweeds*, 68–9.
[85] Ibid., 68.

unsettling and undoing of the English language as we know it—indeed, how can we translate the excerpts listed above from English and into French if the text is written in a language that constantly unsettles the conventions and meanings associated with English?

The Translation-as-Bridge Metaphor

A figure that can help us better grasp the nature of the linguistic threshold in Nathanaël's oeuvre is that of the river, an often-mobilized metaphor in her work.[86] In *Je Nathanaël*, the river makes several appearances; in her search for Nathanaël, who appears to be calling for her, the author-narrator finds herself at a river:

> Standing on a bridge. I am standing on a bridge. You are not here. You have disappeared. From where you were. The place from which you projected your voice. You are no longer there. You say: Enter. I enter. Say: Here I am. And you are no longer there. So here I am. Standing on a bridge. I straddle a river. Beneath my feet a bridge of concrete and steel connects both river banks. . . . Here-I-am. Knocking up against the water. Here-I-am. Swallowed up and carried away. I come and I go. From one edge from the other I take the bridge. I cross it. Here I am I say. Make myself the echo of my own voice. Yours. Swallowed by the river. With me. Or not. I take my two feet and I leave. I leave the bridge behind me. The water crushes. I touch the bottom. Touch. Here I am. You.[87]

In the above excerpt, the authorial I is not confined to one shore or the other but is capable of moving between the two by way of a bridge, whose constructed nature is made explicit by the presence of "concrete and steel." In search of the Other, wishing for an encounter with a "you," the speaker steps onto a bridge, presumably to leave their shore and move toward the other shore, via the authorized, beaten path that is the bridge. However, once the speaker is on the bridge, the Other has disappeared, asking something else from the speaker: to "come undone" in the encounter as the speaker does—sexual, social, linguistic, or otherwise—the subject needs to leave its boundaries behind in an attempt to move toward the other. But, as the following pages show, using the bridge does not help the narrating I in deconstructing her contours or in meeting the other in a satisfying way—"I

---

[86] See, for instance, Nathanaël, *The Sorrow and the Fast of It*, 1–2, 41.
[87] Nathanaël, *Je Nathanaël*, 39.

cross a bridge. Nothing"—and neither does positioning herself on either bank—"I run along both edges of the river. Nothing."[88] The speaker stands on a bridge, comes and goes between the two banks, only to find out that the other is not there.

Toward the end of the preceding passage, the other voice is swallowed by the river. The speaker decides to leave the bridge behind and goes into the water; it is there that she finds what she was looking for: "I touch the bottom. Touch. Here I am. You." A few pages prior, Nathanaël provides a two-sentence postulate: "One river's edge is but the opposite of the other. What matters is the water that passes."[89] Not only does this constitute a call for leaving the river's (or subject's or language's) edges as we know them behind—since they block any kind of productive proximity and permeability necessary for the subject's undoing—but the focus on the water suggests a redefinition of the contours of cultural categories, similar to Avasilichioaei. The border between two subjects or two languages does not figure as a straight, thin line but appears as a much larger buffer zone that is both constantly in movement and inhabitable: speaking of the intempestive river in *The Sorrow and the Fast of It*, the speaker says, "I could live here I thought."[90] This interstice is not only that which separates two entities but also that which unites them; it is what two people or languages have in common, what they share, and the only place where they can meet; as such, it becomes what we *should* inhabit in the context of a desired, reciprocal, and transformative relation.

Interestingly, in the context of this chapter's argument, the presence of the river and the bridge in Nathanaël's works (as well as Avasilichioaei's notion of language as river) problematizes the translation-as-bridge-building metaphor.[91] In translation, the bridge metaphor indeed links two languages understood spatially and separated by some sort of natural barrier; it usually refers to the *process* of translation, where the translator builds or crosses a bridge between cultures in order to transport some predetermined content from one side to the other.[92] On this front, and echoing Sakai, Suchet has suggested that it is precisely the construction of the bridge that

---

[88] Ibid., 40–2.
[89] Ibid., 24.
[90] Nathanaël, *The Sorrow and the Fast of It*, 2.
[91] For discussions of the translation-as-bridge metaphor, see: James St. André, "Metaphors of Translation and Representations of the Translational Act as Solitary Versus Collaborative," *Translation Studies* 10, no. 3 (2017): 282–95; Myriam Suchet, "Introduction," *Intermédialités* 27 (2016), https://www.erudit.org/en/journals/im/2016-n27-im03060/1039808ar/abstract/; Lieven D'Hulst, "Sur le rôle des métaphores en traductologie contemporaine," *Target* 4, no. 1 (1992): 33–51.
[92] Etymologically speaking, "translation" comes from the Latin "transferre" (past participle, "translatus"), which means "carried over."

produces (or reproduces) opposite shores: "the spatialized image of a bridge produces the existence of two opposite shores that did not exist prior to this representation."[93] As part of her call for the deontologizing of translation, Suchet argues that to represent the practice of translation as bridge building implies that two relatively stable shores exist in the first place. This is not to say that all selves or all languages are commensurable: in Nathanaël's writing, the river does exist, but its edges are unstable and its levels ever-changing according to which subjects, bodies, or voices come into relation. Nor does it create a peaceful, metaphorical in-between zone that creates "hybrid" selves or cultures. Rather, when Nathanaël calls us to move into the water, she invites us to embrace its motion and uncertainty, even its violence: "The river was not wistful as I had imagined it. Intempestif was the word I used. Wind billowing the rapids even whiter. Magisterial."[94]

To practice translation not as bridge building but as dwelling in the troubled waters of intersubjectivity asks us to shift our conversations about translation: instead of asking how to receive or host the Other in our world-culture without transforming the Other in the process, we must ask how touching the Other can transform us as well. Most discussions of the ethics of translation in fact center on the ways in which we can "welcome the other" ethically in the translational gesture, whose aim is typically to "bring back a cultural other as the same, the recognizable, even the familiar."[95] But what Nathanaël's ethics of touch suggests is precisely that in the translational encounter, the translating "I," her language, and her culture, typically defined by available categories such as that of (standard) language, should be radically transformed through her encounter with the Other. That perhaps the translational encounter—jumping into the waters—should be frightening for the translator and dangerous for the "target language." In other words, it does not suffice to "register the linguistic and cultural difference of the foreign text" in a translation.[96] Rather, "to translate is to touch"[97]—to translate not from and into different languages but to stay in the interstice, to let other voices penetrate ours and vice versa, to create an equivocally plural assemblage,

---

[93] Suchet, "Introduction," online.
[94] Nathanaël, *The Sorrow and the Fast of It*, 2.
[95] Lawrence Venuti, *The Translator's Invisibility: A History of Translation* (London/New York: Routledge, 2008), 18. In the words of Sandra Bermann, the ethics of translation usually revolve around the question: "How much of the 'otherness' of the 'foreign' should the translator highlight? How much of the foreign should he mute or erase in order to make texts easier for the 'home' (target) audience to assimilate?" Sandra Bermann, Introduction to *Nation, Language and the Ethics of Translation*, ed. Sandra Bermann and Michael Wood (Princeton: Princeton University Press, 2005), 5.
[96] Venuti, *The Translator's Invisibility*, 20.
[97] Nathanaël, *At Alberta*, 16.

none of whose parts adds up to a familiar, known, already available whole and thus losing one's identity and language in the process.

The idea, then, is not to transpose some predetermined body or meaning or content from one side of the border to the other but to create a relation between two already equivocal bodies/texts that ultimately dissolves any presumed fixity in both, creating a further assemblage in the process. Ultimately, what this dwelling in the threshold celebrates is the porosity of bodies and texts, which necessarily come undone when touching one another. During the encounter, be it sexual or linguistic, the "I" (body/voice/text) takes on a plurality through its dissolution and its contact with the Other. Whether in the form of "your voice on my tongue" or of "I become your voice,"[98] the voices of self and Other—and the languages they speak—come together to the point where they cannot be distinguished. Further, this meeting of two voices on the threshold of the encounter suggests that one's voice is already plural, having already lived in the many thresholds of previous encounters. "The voice is but the echo of a voice,"[99] says the speaker of *Je Nathanaël*. And, later: "One voice carries another. The echo is insurgent. Bones knock together denying the text its impermeability."[100] According to Cécile Canut,

> To acknowledge the Other within ourselves, to acknowledge heterogeneity as constitutive for the subject, pushes speakers to let go . . . of fences, enclosures, homogeneity, the exhibition of borders, the measuring of difference, etc., as well as of what metaphorizes to the highest degree the mythical figure of origins, of an originary, fixed, immutable, pure language.[101]

In short, the self is always already in the water, constantly reinventing and redefining itself in the singularity of the encounter. The building of a bridge and the subsequent naturalization of two opposite edges is revealed as an illusion that hides the plurality of selves, voices, and languages.

Herein lies the potential of translation as an exemplary gesture that deals very explicitly with the border between categories and identities—not only between languages but also between selves (author/translator) and bodies (texts). As Nathanaël's use of the bridge shows, translation is not inherently

---

[98] Nathanaël, *Je Nathanaël*, 17, 45.
[99] Nathanaël, *Alula, de son nom de plume*, 72.
[100] Nathanaël, *Je Nathanaël*, 83.
[101] Cécilel Canut, "Le nom des langues ou les métaphores de la frontière," *Ethnologies comparées* 1 (2000): 15.

subversive, since it can easily adopt the national regime of translation and reify linguistic difference and the idea of an originary tongue, a communicative approach Nathanaël calls the "permanent work of repatriation which governs so much of what calls itself translation."[102] But translation can participate in the dissolution of languages, provided it dwells in their interstices rather than simply crossing them. It was Spivak who said that translation, since it entails in the manner of someone else, is one of the ways to get around the confines of one's identity: in a sense, translation is a "miming of the responsibility to the trace of the other in the self."[103] The only way to access this trace, Nathanaël tells us, is to dissolve our own contours in the encounter with alterity. As Vicente L. Rafael has pointed out, this search for otherness, this "you" that constitutes the "I," never totally arrives: "It is precisely this otherness, both inside and outside of oneself . . . that translation promises to bring forth. But just as every translation is essentially incomplete, the arrival of otherness will always be deferred, disguised, and displaced."[104] Translation is thus best seen as a never-ending relation between two already plural voices, rather than as a movement or transportation of one singular voice through another singular voice, from one side of a linguistic border to the other.

In this light, each translation is a singular encounter between two plural selves/voices that are traversed by the itineraries of history. In this context, the figure of the translator "reveals the profound polyphony of any speaking subject, typically hidden behind a first-person singular pronoun."[105] The translated text is the result of a relation between one (already plural) voice and another, an assemblage of bodies that denies the singularity of both the translation and the "original" text as it posits them as relations with other voices, texts, and bodies. Translation, because it adds a body/voice between the author's and the reader's bodies, sheds light on the relational nature of any act of writing or reading. This recognition of the plurality inherent to any act of speaking or writing suggests a redefinition of translation, away from the classical notion of equivalence: "it seems to me that, rather than seeing these repetitions, which always cause some kind of disjunction, as equivalences, it would be more apt, when speaking of this kind of writing, to acknowledge its equivocity."[106]

---

[102] Nathanaël, *Hatred of Translation* (New York: Nightboat, 2019), v.
[103] Gayatri Chakravorty Spivak, *Outside in the Teaching Machine* (London/New York: Routledge, 2009), 200–1.
[104] Vicente L. Rafael, *Motherless Tongues: The Insurgency of Language Amid Wars of Translation* (Durham: Duke University Press, 2016), 16.
[105] Suchet, "Introduction."
[106] Nathanaël, *Alula, de son nom de plume*, 256.

In the end, Nathanaël's dwelling in the doorway between languages creates a highly abstracted and unlocatable voice, as illustrated by the BCLT anecdote earlier in this chapter. The workshop participants' reaction also tells us that it is difficult, perhaps impossible, to relate linguistically to Nathanaël's writing, that is, to recognize it as our own, as familiar, since it is so far removed from any geographic, cultural, or social specificity. Abstraction thus appears as the cost of writing between languages—in other words, in no language in particular. Nathanaël's unmarked and opaque voice figures, then, not as matter out of place but as matter from nowhere. In Nathanaël's oeuvre, language is unterritorialized, making it more difficult, perhaps impossible, for readers to engage with her writing with preconceived ideas and within predetermined categories. By uncoupling her writing from any easily recognizable, delimited language, she also severs any potential ties to any kind of already delineated community. This is, of course, the point: Nathanaël's writing resists translation in its dominant form, and the only way of engaging with her writing is to meet it on its own terms. Nathanaël's unmarked, interstitial language thus also causes the loss of linguistic landmarks usually needed during the practice of translation.

This absence of a familiar whole brings us back to the question of "mother tongue." Put in conversation, Nathanaël's liminal mode of writing and her philosophy of translation—translation as relational encounter where the desire for alterity and an ethics of touch cause subjects in their bodily or linguistic fixity to dissolve—point to a theorization of translation beyond the source language/target language dichotomy. Her "mother tongue" or the SL of her texts is unidentifiable according to conventional linguistic categories, as creating a recognizable or familiar whole was never the point. For translation, this absence of SL requires an approach that also creates an absence of "target language" in the strict linguistic sense. What Nathanaël's refusal of the mother tongue shows is that the "foreign" or "second" tongue was always already in the translating voice/language, as a trace or specter: "You do not come to me. You need not come to me. You are already in me."[107] A liminal writing practice (or liminal practice of translation) simply exposes this presence, whereas the movement between relatively fixed "source" and "target" hides the inherent plurality of linguistic practices.

In other words, fixing oneself in one's mother tongue or labeling a text, especially a translated one, as written in "French" or "English" is a profoundly reductive gesture that occludes the materiality of these interstitial moments that are linguistic encounters, as well as the plurality and equivocity we find

---

[107] Nathanaël, *Je Nathanaël*, 36.

within any voice or text. Perhaps the solution is to keep translation in the water between (artificial) linguistic shores for a bit longer, rather than constructing a bridge between the two. This liminal practice, where the translating self and language dissolve as much as the translated ones would, could, certainly, create opaque, mind-boggling textual results—as Nathanaël's writing does— that would nevertheless bring the author, the translator, and the reader into the river, rather than placing them on either side of it, as in Schleiermacher's famous dilemma between "bringing the reader to the author" and "bringing the author to the reader."[108] Translation's political potential for the deconstruction of linguistic difference, as Nathanaël obliquely tells us, lies precisely in its work at and from the border, not in its crossing.

Experiments in Unfamiliar Translation

The refusal to limit oneself to one's mother tongue (or any tongue, for that matter), for both Avasilichioaei and Nathanaël, is perhaps nowhere more palpable than when they explicitly write about translation. Both translators themselves—Avasilichioaei has translated a number of Quebec writers and poets such as Catherine Lalonde, Daniel Canty, and Bertrand Laverdure, while Nathanaël has translated Édouard Glissant, Hervé Guibert, Hilda Hilst, Gail Scott, and Sina Queyras, to name only a few—they have in fact each dedicated books or sections of books to the concept, practice, and philosophy of translation.

In *Expeditions of a Chimaera*, cowritten with fellow Montreal poet Erín Moure (as well as with interferences from Elisa Sampedrín, Moure's Galician literary alter ego, and with an epilogue from what appears to be a fictional academic, suspiciously named Otilia Acacia), Avasilichioaei explicitly tackles the work of translation from a decidedly postmodern, polyphonic, and heteroglossic perspective. The book opens on a loose sheet of paper, with a series of affirmative questions titled "How": "How to language. How its wealth. How to find language in life's commonplaces and have it mean. How to live in language that opens language to language, opens us to one another, language that humanes us." These are followed by: "How to not monopolize, monospeak, monouse, monothink, monobe" and, finally, "How to unborder a border. How to unmean, unwar, unnormalize a border. How to unborder

---

[108] Schleiermacher, "On the Different Methods of Translating."

a language's borders."[109] The book's statement could not be clearer, and the two (four?) writers embark on a collaborative and polyphonic translational enterprise that seeks to create meaning as much as it seeks to complicate it.

Expeditions of a Chimaera starts with translation: the very first section of the book, titled "Prank!," begins with a poem called "The Roost, *translated by E.S. from Nichita Stănescu.*" On the following page, we learn that Elisa Sampedrín has no knowledge of Romanian whatsoever, but that she felt compelled to translate (into English, another language she is unfamiliar with) some of Nichita Stănescu's poems when she briefly visited Romania in the 1990s. The poem is, of course, erroneously translated, which means that the translation's corresponding original is a poem that has not been written and thus does not exist. On the next page, Oana Avasilichioaei then translates Sampedrín's translation backward, into Romanian, so as to "create the original Stănescu poem" that will function as the translation's original.[110] However, as the following page states, the problem with Avasilichioaei's backward translation is that it renders Sampedrín's purported translation accurate (which is impossible, since Sampedrín does not know either Romanian or English). Thus, Sampedrín retranslates Avasilichioaei's translation of her translation of Stănescu's poem, again erroneously. This confusing and comical back and forth between "originals" and "translations" and "mistranslations" between Romanian and English (as well as between English and English) by E. S., O. A., and E. M. goes on for six more pages.

From one version of the poem to another, most translations that appear in this section seem to have been done on the basis of a similarity between words in terms of sound or spelling. For instance, Sampedrín translates the Romanian verse "în spate la fabrica de tricotaje, am gasit un camp" with "spit on the fabric of tractors, there's gas in a camp."[111] What guides the translation is not the meaning of the words in Romanian, words for which translation would typically find "equivalents" in English, since Sampedrín does not know either language, but the similarities in form (either visual or oral) between lexical units in both languages, regardless of what they may mean. What is interesting about these translations is that they are not done *from one language into another* (i.e., by translating something which means X in Romanian by something which means X in English)—in other words, they do not follow the usual directionality or rules of translation. Rather, "fabrica" is translated by "fabric" solely on the basis of the homonymic relation between the two

---

[109] Oana Avasilichioaei and Erín Moure, *Expeditions of a Chimaera* (Toronto: BookThug, 2009), no page number.
[110] Ibid., 13.
[111] Ibid., 13–14.

words. Because she does not take into account the definitions of these words in Romanian, Sampedrín cannot be said to translate "from the Romanian"; in other words, the linguistic system to which these words belong does not matter. She could learn Romanian along the way or at least consult the definitions of the words she is translating in a Romanian dictionary (which is what most translators would do in such instances), but she decides not to. Sampedrín actively refuses to ground her translation in the "mastery" or "correctedness" of either Romanian or English and actively seeks to translate otherwise. Translation becomes not a matter of carrying meaning across languages but rather of carrying the materiality of words into new utterances, which creates an entirely new version with new associations and new meanings. "Mastering" "a language" is of no importance, and anyone can take part in this kind of translation, whatever their linguistic affiliation or competence might be.

Later in the book, Sampedrín reappears, this time translating into English a Romanian poem by Paul Celan. Her translation is followed by an English translation of the same poem by O. A., then by a Galician translation by E. M. from the English translation of O. A., then eventually by a Romanian translation by O. A. from the Galician translation of E. M., and so on and so forth. The directionality of translation is constantly confounded, reversed, played with: the poets and translators translate from and into different languages at different times, going as far as translating from or into languages they do not know. At some point, the poets also provide us with a "dictionary of equivalences," in which "unable to resist = i touched your wrist," "poor = pour," "hammering = . . .," and "myrrh = mere (lake)."[112] Uncoupling translation from rigid notions of "meaning" and "languages," Avasilichioaei and Moure's playful game of translation shows us what kinds of associations, connections, and inventions translation can produce when it is not done across languages and according to fixed semantic equivalences and rules.

Even if Sampedrín's translations are deemed "impossible" by Moure, they are still, materially and undoubtedly, (mis)translations, if only because of the performative declaration that they *are* translations.[113] A footnote added to one of Sampedrín's impossible translations even states: "The original of the

---

[112] Ibid., 74.
[113] On the performative power of the speech act that declares "this text is a translation," see Kate Brigg's discussion of Theo Hermans's insights on the matter, where she quotes him saying: "a translation comes into being when a text that has been written alongside another text is declared to be a translation of that other text. The declaration is an illocutionary speech act. . . . I regard a translation as initially being merely another text until it is declared to be a translation." Kate Briggs, *This Little Art* (London: Fitzcarraldo, 2017), 45, 370.

copy is here originated in translation by Elisa Sampedrín, who still does not know any Romanian but won't desist. We don't know how E.S. got hold of the work of O.A., unless she found it in a book by Stănescu, where it hadn't, at that moment, been written. Yet the unruliness has a ring of truth to it, and it cuts to the bone."[114] This teasing "prank" that plays with translation and its underlying ideas of equivalence, mastery of language, legibility, and legitimacy illustrates that translation can be more than the simple, mechanical rendering of a text from one mastered language to another, and that the "mastery" of a language is not necessarily a prerequisite for translation, erroneous or not. As delusional as she might be, Elisa Sampedrín keeps translating "from Romanian" and "into English" and offering us versions that sometimes make sense, that are either interesting or beautiful or funny. Even though her translations are "erroneous" and "impossible," Sampedrín keeps going, resisting the idea that one must "know" the languages from and into which we translate, suggesting that one never truly, fully knows a language anyway. At the end of the section, we still do not know what the original poem is and which translation is "adequate" or "correct." And yet, it is also in Sampedrín's unmasterful and unruly translations that we may be able to find some type of "truth."

In *Expeditions of a Chimaera*, translation figures as the "how" that allows Avasilichioaei and Moure "to live in language that opens language to language, opens [them] to one another, language that humanes [them]." But the kind of translation they practice and embody in no way resembles the conventional, structural understanding of translation this book has sought to challenge. The following excerpt, which I take as a tentative definition of translation, makes no mention whatsoever of language in the structural sense, as a countable, bordered system:

> At once necessary and impossible, the question of translation renders the impossible possible regarding an inaudible and disconcerting event, a particular experience of language. We are called by language itself to do this impossible, a politics of force and openness to the future, a politics of friendship whose end is to try to resist the inaudible pressure of History and to make signs to the distance in the plurality of voices where knowing is operatively inoperative.[115]

Translation becomes the rendering of a particular *experience* of language, regardless of one's mother tongue or of one's linguistic competency. Of course,

---

[114] Avasilichioaei and Moure, *Expeditions of a Chimaera*, 17.
[115] Ibid., 82.

the degree to which a translator is familiar with the linguistic forms that make up the text they are translating will influence this particular translator's particular experience of that particular text's particular language, as we saw with the translations by Sampedrín, for whom the experience of Stănescu's poems was radically different than for Avasilichioaei. But, as *Expeditions of a Chimaera* playfully and convincingly shows, the mastery of either source or target languages by no means guarantees the "truth" or the relevance or the quality of one translation over another, and translating according to similarities in sound or spelling is no more random than translating according to similarities in meaning.

Nathanaël makes a similar case for the uprooting of translation in the 2019 collection of essays *Hatred of Translation*. A play on Bataille's 1947 book *La haine de la poésie*, which he retitled *L'impossible de la poésie* for its republication in 1962 (and which is, by all accounts, a book of poetry), *Hatred of Translation* is extremely critical of the diplomatic, normative regime of translation as well as of common celebrations of translation as subversive border-crossing. Nathanaël's view of translators as border control agents is made clear when she states that "one should not overlook blaming translators themselves for the rehabilitation of their image from traitorous, loose-moralled floozies of language, to accredited diplomatic ambassadors, authorized foreign agents devoted to the open smuggling of precious cultural goods across otherwise inhospitable limits."[116] She reminds us that crossing linguistic and cultural borders in ways that reproduce, solidify, and legitimate these borders participates to the violence of bordering: "For as many borders as are crossed there are bodies left hanging."[117] Throughout the book, Nathanaël speaks harshly of translation, comparing the activity to a straightjacket, to murder, and to destruction, echoing Tiphaine Samoyault's recent call to reframe translation as conflict.[118] However, recognizing, much like Avasilichioaei and Moure, that translation is at once impossible and necessary, Nathanaël goes on to explore the ways in which translation can resist the dominant ideology of immediately legible and transparent communication.

Hatred of Translation thus makes a case for the traitorous, illegible translator and does so by rejecting the idea of rootedness, which, as we have seen earlier in this chapter, is an important underlying aspect of the notion

---

[116] Nathanaël, *Hatred of Translation*, 49.
[117] Ibid., 5.
[118] Samoyault, *Traduction et violence*, 10–14. Samoyault writes: "We have to stop seeing translation as the exclusively positive operation of welcoming of the Other. . . . Translation can also become the main crutch for walking towards an isolated world" (Samoyault, *Traduction et violence*, 10).

of mother tongue. For Nathanaël, translation fundamentally dislodges "a conviction resting in an idea of *radicality*."[119] It is a matter of refusing both the idea that the source text is rooted somewhere and the idea that the translator and their translation are (or should be) rooted elsewhere. Moving past Deleuze and Guattari's concept of deterritorialization, where a language becomes unrooted (which presumes that it was rooted in the first place), Nathanaël's philosophy of translation (and, more generally, of language) posits language as essentially unterritorialized, never rooted in the first place. This radical uncoupling from a bounded territory (in the national sense) allows translation to become something other than a border-crossing enterprise: "In the absence of a single place, one may not lay claim to a single origin. And in the absence of a country against which to align one's proclivities, there persist the intimate traversals of continents and the constant threat of drowning (being drowned)."[120] Here we find the image of the intempestive river once again, the river into which *Je Nathanaël*'s speaker jumps (like the one in which Avasilichioaei's Celan does in fact drown).

Always looking to push against and blur the borders and the limits of the self, including on linguistic grounds, Nathanaël has translated various texts in what we would typically call different language pairs—notably "from English into French" and "from French into English," already challenging the idea that one should translate toward one's native language. Interestingly, Nathanaël has also translated a novel by Brazilian writer Hilda Hilst, *A Obscena Senhora D*. The novel is published in Portuguese, a language that is mostly absent from both Nathanaël's oeuvre—whereas she often quotes German writers and philosophers and discusses German words or excerpts, for instance—and her repertoire as a translator.[121] In *Hatred of Translation*, she explains coming to the translation of Hilst's novel via its French version, *L'obscène Madame D.*:

> Coming to *A Obscena Senhora D* by way of *L'obscène Madame D.* it is immediately clear that the effort demanded of us is a *dispersive* more than a *discursive* one. Perhaps it is that the emotional demand implicates a language in the flesh—kneaded, knotted and bruised—that belies *comprehension*. What I mean is that a translator's pretense to *fluency* is corrected when faced with the evidence of exclusion. The multiplication

---

[119] Ibid., ii.
[120] Ibid., i.
[121] Nathanaël is credited as the sole translator of *The Obscene Madam D.*, although a review of the book in the *LA Review of Books* mentions that the translation was done in collaboration with Rachel Gontijo Araújo.

of versions decorticates the so-called original to the point of burning out the incumbent text . . . In the third instance, a distortion occurs, which simultaneously renders visible *all three languages at once,* by virtue of none of them arriving at themselves.[122]

It is clear here that Nathanaël did not translate exclusively *from the Portuguese,* nor exclusively *from the French,* but rather from both. And she is careful not to label the third version, the one she wrote, as "in English," as this would embed the text within a delimited history, canon, and territory; rather, her version carries all three languages at once.

Nathanaël's praxis goes beyond making "the source language" of "the original" visible in her translation, in the sense that it even brings a third one into the mix, with her particular experience of the novel having been influenced by the French version as well. Rather than positing translation as the rendering of one text from one language to another, Nathanaël proceeds to write her version, *The Obscene Madam D.*, by drawing on multiple sources, which are always already plural, and by inscribing these sources in the translated text. Translation is seen not as a matter of fluency—in either Portuguese or English, the supposed source and target languages—but as a process that seeks to disperse meaning and language(s) rather than to bring everything into a fixed, recognizable whole.

This experience of feeling excluded from the Portuguese version because of its illegibility or opacity is what allows Nathanaël to see that her "fluency" in either English or French is also an illusion, a deception. The fact is, even texts written in a language which we believe we "master" contain passages or words that are opaque, that present us with the evidence of exclusion, regardless of the language to which they supposedly belong. Thus, "[i]f one begins with the pretext that the glass is *never clear,* then one begins to escape (maybe) the trappings of the occidental ideology of *intelligibility,* which lead invariably to a tendency toward *correction*."[123] Translating in an unrooted manner means taking nothing for granted—neither the source text nor our mother tongue—and refusing to "correct" either our subjective experiences of given texts or the ways in which we might want to write these texts again.

Ultimately, *Hatred of Translation* shows hostility only toward the normative, bordering kind of translation this book has set out to problematize. Nathanaël does not *hate* translation so much as she hates the need, ongoing and sweeping, for translation. Seeing the mere fact of communication as an a priori failing of truth, following Spinoza who "regarded it as a 'universal failing in people that

---

[122] Ibid., 66, italics original.
[123] Nathanaël, *Hatred of Translation*, 66. Emphasis in original.

they communicate their thoughts to others,'"[124] and realizing that "there is no obvious equivalency between truth and language,"[125] Nathanaël admits that translation cannot, by its very nature, be anything but a failure. The question, for Nathanaël, becomes how to inscribe translation's very impossibility and failure into its practice and how to expose in the process not only "the *foreignness* of every culture" but also and most importantly "their distance from what they might be inclined to call their *own*."[126]

Motherless Tongues

In the final pages of *Borrowed Tongues: Life Writing, Migration, and Translation*, Eva C. Karpinski concludes that the concept of "borrowed tongue," defined as a language on loan from someone else, is inadequate: "The texts I have analyzed unsettle any claims of the law of the 'proper' in more than one sense, engaging the questions of 'propriety' and 'property' in politicized ways, by foregrounding issues of competence in a language that is supposedly 'not one's own.'"[127] However, the language of competence, far from being neutral or apolitical, still only seems to grant recognition to certain speakers—such as Lori Saint-Martin, as opposed to Frantz Fanon and Lorrie Jean-Louis—as legitimate users of a given language. What the writers in this chapter have in common is that they refuse to play the game of linguistic legitimacy altogether, refusing to be perfectly legible subjects, whether they could be granted legitimacy on the basis of competence or not.

In her writings, Oana Avasilichioaei invites everyone to participate in the collective movement of languages, while Nathanaël deliberately displays a twisted, unmastered language that emerges out of a series of singular, relational, transformative encounters. These writers, thus, challenge the ownership of language not only according to race or birth but also according to the measurement of competence, by actively working against legibility and linguistic legitimacy—usually attained by a proper, monolingual performance of the standard language by white subjects. These writers recognize that the question of linguistic competence and of who can achieve it is still fundamentally tied to the recognition, by the very people or group who set the norm, of their legitimacy. In turn, "proper," monolingual writing only serves to reproduce and maintain the normative category of language, which

[124] Ibid., 13.
[125] Ibid., 14.
[126] Ibid., 50.
[127] Karpinski, *Borrowed Tongues*, 226.

operates as a unifying, homogenizing address to the national community that supposedly shares a "common language." But Avasilichioaei and Nathanaël, having been shaped by Montreal, know very well that their community does not really share "one" language. They refuse to write in the "mother tongue" of the state, producing instead voices whose forms are not recognizable or containable by the state. They are not so much excluded from the national community on the grounds of their linguistic (in)competence as they actively disidentify with said national community.

In retrospect, all the "different languages" used by the two writers who make up this chapter are "theirs," in the sense that they use them. Naturally, if any language can be "ours" by the simple fact that we use it, it follows that no language ever belongs to anyone. This brings us back to Derrida: every single word in these books is coming *from* these writers, but these writers do not *own* those words. Language always comes from its speakers, it is from/of us, but it is never ours. The concept of a "motherless tongue" moves away from any identification between social agents and a language seen as a fixed system. Importantly, the concept appears in the title of Vicente L. Rafael's *Motherless Tongues*; surprisingly, however, the book is only very obliquely about the notion of "mother tongue"—the expression "motherless tongue" appears only twice throughout the book, with no definition provided.

However, Rafael's account does suggest something in line with this current chapter: he claims that whenever he speaks or writes in what appears to be "coherent English," it is only because he has managed to momentarily repress his own history and legacy of linguistic pluralism. The writing and speaking in a coherent tongue thus amounts to an act of translation of this linguistic plurality or chaos into a recognizable, delimited language—resembling what Scofield and Daigle do in their works, as shown in the second chapter. Monolingual utterances are what require translation—not "multilingual" or heteroglossic ones. What the two writers analyzed in this chapter do is precisely to refuse this kind of translation; they provide a demonstration of the "irreducibly insurgent element in every language that undermines such attempts at mastery."[128] De- or unterritorializing language in order to explore the potentialities that lie *elsewhere*, these writers open up language(s) to possibilities that are usually foreclosed in the name of linguistic purity. Similarly, Mehmet Yaşın has coined the expression "stepmother tongue" to break the bonds between languages and enforced national communities and to embrace linguistic impurity; he uses the concept to refer to the unbiological and "contaminated" nature of languages in the context of

---

[128] Rafael, *Motherless Tongues*, 9.

the multiple Turkishes and Greeks of Cyprus.[129] But "step-mother," while it signals a move away from the idea of biological inheritance, is still imbued with the notions of filiation and parental authority and raises the specter of the "wicked step-mother."

Motherless, on the other hand, does more than merely break the link between a language and the community, national or otherwise, that it is typically associated with; it also does away with the normative and hierarchical notion of authority. Breaking the association between a language and a group of people—be it on biological/national grounds or according to an assessment of linguistic competence, although the latter is always shown not to suffice when it comes to racialized speakers—undoes the grounds on which "languages" were created, constructed, and delimited in the first place. A language without a mother—defined here broadly as the imagined community to which it supposedly belongs—loses its limits, as these limits were never linguistic in the first place. A language without an owner becomes a collective process, rather than a fixed product that we inherit, and if it is collectively "owned," it becomes something that can be used and transformed by anyone, regardless of one's place of birth, familial ties, or even linguistic competence. Here we circle back to the idea of language as system, which is at the very basis of the problem of the "mother tongue."

One way to challenge this delimited view of language, then, might be to take away its owners. As we have seen in this chapter, particularly in the example of Nathanaël, the problem of "mother tongue" in translation stems first and foremost from the very labeling and reading of texts according to their "source language." In other words, it is only through the categorization of a given text as "English" that translation into "French" is made possible. A good place to start, then, is perhaps to stop labeling texts according to their supposed language of publication, thus decoupling them from a presupposed collective body demarcated by ethnonational lines. This deterritorialization—that is, the uncoupling of a set of linguistic practices from national borders—would reveal the ways in which writers call upon various expressive tools to address, and thus create, other kinds of (potential) communities. For the practice of translation, this means moving away from the idea that we transpose something that is "foreign" into something that is "ours." For these writers, language is not something that exists prior to us and that we share; rather, we construct what we share as we go along, through writing and reading one another, in ways that are not necessarily decided for us in advance.

[129] See Mehmet Yaşın, "Introducing Step-Mothertongue," in *Step-Mothertongue: From Nationalism to Multiculturalism: Literatures of Cyprus, Greece and Turkey*, ed. Mehmet Yaşın (London: Middlesex University Press, 2000), 1–24.

Conclusion

Toward a Postlingual Approach to Translation: Translating (in) the Twenty-First Century

> On ne peut plus écrire une langue de manière monolingue.
> —Édouard Glissant, *L'imaginaire des langues*

This book has explored the various linguistic cartographies drawn by six writers who all write and publish within the context of the settler colonial state of Canada. What these cartographies have in common is that they are all, to some extent, postnational, in the sense that they deliberately transgress the national, colonial order to which they are supposed to adhere, particularly in terms of language. In distinct yet analogous ways, the writers analyzed here all choose not to map linguistic practices according to dominant national-linguistic borders, which amounts to a refusal to address the imagined communities of Canada and/or Quebec according to their settler monolingual modes of expression. To echo Audra Simpson, these writers refuse to play the game of language according to the settler nation's rules.[1] Writing this way in present-day Canada, as the preceding chapters have shown, is a way for marginalized speakers—be they Indigenous, queer, immigrants, Acadian, or Québécois—to escape the fixed linguistic identity they are supposed to perform and, by the same token, to counter the colonial and heteronormative linguistic narratives that characterize present-day Canada. This book has argued that these writers, rather than identifying with the languages in which they publish, undertake a constant, active disidentification with said languages, opting to open their expression to a multiplicity of linguistic forms instead. They write against the idea that our identities— gendered, cultural, or linguistic—are fixed containers that we must close up, secure, and barricade. The main lesson of this book is, crucially, that the work of translation must reenact the same kind of disidentification and refusal within its own context of production.

---

[1] Simpson, *Mohawk Interruptus*, 25.

Texts that are decidedly and explicitly written in nonnormative, heteroglossic ways, such as the ones that were featured throughout these pages, force translators to practice translation outside of the idea of "standard languages" or even outside the idea of "languages" tout court. This is what I call a postlingual paradigm, where the notion of language as fixed, bounded, countable system is discarded altogether. As Walkowitz and elhariry remind us, "the verbal arts and all literature are postlingual."[2] It is about time we start treating them as such, through literary histories, critique, and theories that are also post(mono)lingual, that is, that do not impose predetermined linguistic grids on creative and moving expression. Only through a postlingual approach which uncompromisingly refuses to reproduce the idea of named languages can the entire regime of translation as currently constituted be reconsidered and its practice reinvented. From a postlingual perspective, translation becomes "an operation that doesn't anchor itself in one single language in order to succeed in producing another single language."[3]

Indeed, from such a perspective, translation cannot be the rendering of a text *from one language to another*; it is, rather, the revoicing of a text from one linguistic subjectivity (or repertoire) to another, where both subjectivities draw on specific linguistic landscapes, real or imagined. The "trans" in translation remains, but the idea of movement or displacement concerns physical, material, and/or virtual selves and places, rather than abstract languages. Etymologically speaking, translation is after all a "carrying across" or "bringing across": the Latin translation derives from *transferre* (*trans*, "across" + *ferre*, "to carry" or to "bring").[4] But the carrying need not occur across a linguistic border; *across* can also be understood as "from one end of something to the other," as in "across the city," across the territory that both separates and unites the writer and the translator. The thing to be "crossed" is not a border but a distance, which can be measured in terms of space and time, two factors that can be and frequently are inscribed in translation. A postlingual approach to translation does not impose normative linguistic categories on any text, not only on those that draw explicitly on heteroglossia. A postlingual approach understands translation as a fundamentally social practice that does not necessarily need to happen along the preestablished lines of available "languages." A postlingual approach shifts our gaze away from abstracted, idealized, disembodied categories of language ("French," "slang") and concentrates instead on subjective, embodied, affective,

---

[2] Walkowitz and elhariry, "The Postlingual Turn," 3.
[3] Samoyault, *Traduction et violence*, 135.
[4] See Christopher Kasparek, "The Translator's Endless Toil," *The Polish Review* 28, no. 2 (1983): 83.

minoritized experiences of language, which are always specific (to a time, a place, an individual, a community). A postlingual approach has as its guiding principle not fidelity or equivalence to an original but making visible the encounter between translator and text, keeping a trace of the relationship a specific translator formed, in a specific time and a specific place, with a specific text. A postlingual approach recognizes that there could be as many translations of one text as there are translators at any given time, and that this unicity of translations relationships should be encouraged and celebrated. A postlingual approach recognizes that the power of minoritized linguistic forms is not simply that they enable resistance to domination but that they also forge "a space for alternative cultural production and alternative epistemologies—different ways of thinking and knowing that [are] crucial to creating a counter-hegemonic worldview."[5]

The idea becomes, rather than mobilizing the authorized resources of "the French language," to draw from the resources that make up the translator's immediate linguistic, communicative, and expressive environment—physical, virtual, imagined—in order to produce translations that will resonate in that place at the same time that they reproduce the source text's heteroglossia and undermine the (national) language of publication's monopoly and dominance. This echoes the ethical considerations of critical place inquiry, a set of methods put forth by Eve Tuck and Marcia McKenzie to attend more responsibly to the specificity of place. Specifically, critical place inquiry calls for a focus on community and place as the main geographic unit of account or concern, rather than on the nation-state.[6] Tuck and McKenzie show that it is especially salient for decolonizing perspectives and Indigenous epistemologies, which are always spatially and temporally specific, since relationships to land are diverse, specific, and ungeneralizable.[7]

A postlingual approach to translation replaces the typical question, "how do I translate this English sentence into French?," with a set of questions that ask: What does the linguistic landscape around me look like, in this place where I translate from, and how does it compare to the landscape from which the author writes—what forms are valued there, and what forms are not? What are the linguistic resources available to me, in my surroundings, to replicate the ones the author chooses from their own linguistic landscape? What linguistic practices are obscured by the dominant, national, public language, and how can I engage them in my work? How can this text or sentence be

---

[5] bell hooks, "Language: Teaching New Worlds/New Words," in *Teaching to Transgress: Education as the Practice of Freedom* (New York: Routledge, 1994), 171.
[6] Tuck and McKenzie, *Place in Research*, 7.
[7] Ibid., 48, 55.

spoken, and written, *here*, *now*, *by my body*? What are the different, multiple ways in which this text or sentence is or can be spoken or written? What does it mean when I say/write this like that? How do other people with whom I share my city, or the land, or an online space, say or write this? And how can my gesture of translation include, rather than exclude, minoritized linguistic practices and forms? How can I address a community that is not yet fixed, a community-in-the-making, a community of my own making? What kind of community do I want to invoke in my own translation work?

Noopiming: A Postlingual Attempt at Translation

We now circle fully back to translation, by way of my own practice. In September 2021, my translation of the novel *Noopiming: The Cure for White Ladies* by Anishinaabe writer Leanne Betasamosake Simpson was published by Montreal-based publisher Mémoire d'encrier. Having already cotranslated (with Natasha Kanapé Fontaine) two of Simpson's previous books, namely *Islands of Decolonial Love* (2013) and *This Accident of Being Lost* (2018), this was the third time I found myself faced with the challenge of transposing Simpson's heteroglossic, postlingual, decolonial prose into a new context. Considering, in light of the arguments made throughout this book, that *Noopiming* is not written in "English," let alone "standard English," nor in a combination of "English" and "Anishinaabemowin," and that in any case it is not written in Leanne's "mother tongue," it follows, then, that what I should aim to do is neither to translate the novel into "French"—or into a combination of "equivalent" languages—nor into the "standard," nor into whatever it is I could call my "mother tongue." Returning to my translation of *Noopiming* today, I realize that some of my translation choices, detailed later in the chapter, are decidedly postlingual.

Take this short excerpt from *Noopiming*, which features both the narrative voice and some dialogue between the narrator and a character called Mindimooyenh:

> Nothing drives Mindimooyenh more crazy than "self-care."
> "We are self-caring our way to fascism," they yell.
> I try and explain.
> "That's not a thing," they reply. "It is just care."[8]

---

[8] Leanne Betasamosake Simpson, *Noopiming: The Cure for White Ladies* (Toronto: House of Anansi, 2020), 86.

Such an excerpt would not be typically included in a discussion on "multilingual" or "translingual" texts, since it appears to be comprised exclusively of English linguistic forms. However, from a postlingual point of view, an excerpt like the one above is as relevant as any, since a postlingual perspective does not posit that this text is written in English in the first place. What's more, this seemingly monolingual excerpt, even though it does not mobilize elements from "different languages," nevertheless resists to the differential, structural regime of translation, since even two standardized, naturalized linguistic systems do not ever completely overlap in terms of all potential meanings.

Indeed, two aspects of the excerpt would pose problems if we were to translate it according to a (dual) monolingual perspective, in other words into "(standard) French": first, the words *care* and *self-care*, for which there are no readily equivalent solutions in French, and second, the gender-neutral singular pronoun "they," which again has no equivalent that is officially sanctioned in French.[9] For demonstration purposes, here is an attempt at translating the above excerpt into what would be commonly perceived as "proper French."

Rien n'agace Mindimooyenh autant que les « soins personnels ».
— Les soins personnels nous conduisent droit au fascisme, s'exclame-t-elle.
Je tente de la raisonner.
— Cela n'existe pas, répond-elle. Il s'agit tout simplement de soins.

Such a translation, while it conforms to a unitary language and therefore would be considered an acceptable translation according to most linguistic standards, contains a few supralinguistic problems. First, "soins personnels"—or other potential solutions such as the theoretical "souci de soi," the technical "soins auto-administrés," and the more theoretical "sollicitude," an equivalent sometimes seen in lieu of "care" in scholarly literature in French—is relatively adequate semantically speaking, in the sense that it means, roughly and depending on context, the same thing as

---

[9] My translation of *Noopiming* came out in September 2021, two months before the online version of the *Robert* dictionary, whose mission is primarily descriptive, announced the inclusion of the gender-neutral pronoun "iel," sparking a worldwide controversy. Prescriptive dictionaries and linguistic institutions such as *Le Petit Robert* (the Académie française dictionary's print version) in France or the Office québécois de la langue française in Quebec do not yet catalogue the pronoun, going as far as to recommend against its use in the case of the OQLF—its absence from *Le Petit Robert* serving as a de facto disapproval of its usage.

"self-care." However, it is not in circulation on social media, where self-care discourse is prevalent these days, especially among younger people; in other words, it is not used to refer to the current discourses and practices of "self-care" as it is collectively articulated and understood, and so it does not, in fact, refer to the same thing at all.

Further, the gender-neutral pronoun "they" is translated by the feminine third-person singular pronoun "elle" in the standard translation earlier, since neologisms used in queer circles such as "iel," "ul," or "al" are not yet sanctioned by French-language institutions. For instance, in a 2019 blog post on the topic, the Office québécois de la langue française paradoxically states, in an entry titled "How to Refer to Non-Binary People": "The Office does not recommend the use of these writing practices. No general change whatsoever related to the grammatical distinction between masculine and feminine in French is in sight,"[10] adding that the French language is "rich" and that it already allows for neutral formulations to refer to nonbinary people, which is objectively false. In fact, there is no readily equivalent formulation in French that allows me, here, to translate in a gender-neutral way the excerpt—let alone the entire novel, in which the twelve or so characters are each referred to as "they." Further, it should be noted that the quasi-total absence of gender in *Noopiming* stems from the absence of gender markers in Anishinaabemowin; hence, the translation of "they" is also the translation of the gender-neutral aspect of the author's ancestral worldview. Finally, in the standard translation offered earlier, the dialogues and narration, which draw on both vernaculars and Anishinaabemowin's syntax in Simpson's works, are rendered in a belle-lettrist style, according to traditional French literary conventions which are still arguably predominant in French publishing worldwide.

Later in the text are two examples of what a postlingual translation strategy, that is, one that does not follow the contours or the grammatical rules of (standard) French, might result in, according to two different translators who inhabit two different places and subject positions in the world. The first is my own translation and the second is courtesy of Sonya Malaborza, a translator based in Moncton, New Brunswick. While both of us—as well as any French translator, regardless of where they should find themselves in the world—are very much capable of coming up with a "standard" version that would resemble closely the one drafted earlier, once we move away from the idea of "proper French," we come up with translations that are highly localized, subjective, and embodied—in other words that reflect our own linguistic practices and the ones in our immediate surroundings.

[10] Office québécois de la langue française, Government of Quebec. "Désigner les personnes non binaires," 2019, http://bdl.oqlf.gouv.qc.ca/bdl/gabarit_bdl.asp?t1=1&id=5370.

My translation:

Y'a rien qui fait capoter Mindimooyenh autant que le « self-care. »
« À force de self-care on s'en va tout droit dans gueule du fascisme, » iel me crie après.
J'essaie d'expliquer.
« Ça existe pas, ton truc, iel répond. C'est du care tout court. »

Sonya Malaborza's translation:

Y'a rien qui chavire plus Mindimooyenh que l'idée du « self-care. »
— Nos histoires de self-care sont après nous driver à venir fascistes, qu'iel me dit en criant.
J'essaie d'expliquer.
— C'est pas vraiment une thing, qu'iel répond. C'est juste carer.

We see earlier two translations that draw from the translators' local linguistic repertoires, regardless of how they conform to the borders of "proper" French. "Self-care" appears in both translations, the term being one that is presumably used and circulated in both translators' feeds on social media. "They" is translated by "iel," a relatively new pronoun that some nonbinary people use in real life, regardless of what linguistic institutions have to say about it. Reproducing the author's intention to not gender her characters—and to reflect the absence of gender markers in Anishinaabemowin—seems in these excerpts more important than the need to conform to presumed French readers' habits or expectations. "Iel" is not *the* right answer, as there is no singular "right answer" (and no right way to find the right answer), but it nevertheless represents an attempt to reproduce an effect found in the source text that is impossible to achieve if we stay within the confines of "French." Both translations have social and/or geographical markers—capoter, chavire, self-care, iel, crie après, sont après, driver, dans gueule, une thing, carer—drawing on spoken and heard forms that echo the source text's orality and heteroglossia. There are, if we look at the excerpts from a normative, standard French perspective, a number of grammatical "mistakes," such as using the verb "expliquer" with neither a direct or an indirect object, the gender-neutral pronoun "iel" and its many (supposedly ungrammatical) agreements throughout the novel, and so-called anglicisms.

Another example taken from the translation of *Noopiming* relates to the several references to Canada geese Simpson makes throughout the book. From a conventional -lingual perspective, there "exists" in "French" a "proper" equivalent to translate the "English term" *Canada goose*: the term "bernache du Canada," an expression I almost never hear or use, despite growing up and living in a place where I see hundreds of them every year. The term I'm most familiar with—the term everyone around me uses—is "outarde." "Outarde" in French actually refers to a different bird, native to North Africa, but it was used to denote the Canada goose by French colonizers, notably Jacques Cartier, when they first set foot on Turtle Island in the 1500s. The term has stuck on this side of the Atlantic, despite "bernache du Canada" being the standardized term adopted in French by the Commission internationale des noms français des oiseaux and other works of reference. In my translation of *Noopiming*, I could use either the correct translation, in strictly denotative and referential terms from an abstracted, normative, "neutral" (read: European) point of view, or I could use the incorrect term, the one that I use, regardless of what it might possibly mean to other people elsewhere. In the end I opted for "outarde," since it carries the history of colonization and French settlement on Turtle Island and because it points to a linguistic history, tradition, and usage that departs from a certain official, canonized linguistic history and use. Consequently, this nonstandard, postlingual choice situates my translation in North America, as coming from my specific body and subjectivity, and as such, it points to my own linguistic and affective relationship to this bird, as well as to the colonial encounter, through naming, between that bird and French colonizers. All of these histories, trajectories, and relations would be lost in the "correct" linguistic equivalent from a normative, metropolitan standpoint. Again, this echoes the theories of critical place inquiry, which insist that ethical practices must be "place-specific, place-responsive, place-resonant,"[11] rather than abstracted and generalized so as to appear "neutral." The gesture of translation goes from being perceived as an operation of substitution or replacement to thinking communally about language, names, and how we relate to each other and the land.

In short, Simpson's linguistic choices from the resources of her own linguistic landscape should inspire our own from the multiple resources we each have access to, rather than confining ourselves to the supposedly neutral, universal resources of "French," because after all, Simpson does not limit herself to the confines of proper English, either. Further, a postlingual approach to translation means that the linguistic landscape from elsewhere, that of the author for instance, might be "carried across" as well—what we carry in translation is not just the meaning or content of words but perhaps also their form, as is the case with certain words in Anishinaabemowin (or even English) for instance. Both my and Malaborza's translation of the

---

[11] Tuck and McKenzie, *Place in Research*, 161.

Noopiming excerpt earlier feature the sentence "J'essaie d'expliquer," which reproduces the initial syntactic structure of "I try and explain" without an object that follows the second verb, even if this is "improper." Throughout the novel, this will produce, similar to Nathanaël's and Avasilichioaei's writing, as well as to Scofield's translations for the names of his ancestors, unexpected, peculiar formulations and turns of phrase. My previous translations of Leanne Betasamosake Simpson's work have in fact been described as "not completely lucid,"[12] and Kevin Lambert has said of my translation of *Jonny Appleseed*: "I find it extremely refreshing that the language in which these texts are made available to us is not a rigid, ossified French... Your rendering of the language is strange, playful, funny, dynamic!"[13] Upon reading such descriptions of my work, I remember thinking that I had done something right—even though, in my experience, "not lucid" and "strange" are usually pejorative comments made to discredit a translation. But the fact is, these texts that I have translated are precisely that, "not completely lucid" and "strange" in their own ways, since they pull away from the centrifugal force of unitary language. Honoring their strange postlingual effects by translating them with a voice that does not correspond to any fixed language but that draws on a linguistic landscape where multiple traditions, voices, and communities interact and blend together should in fact be at the center of these translation projects.

This book's focus has been on texts that force a postlingual redefinition of translation precisely because they are themselves written in explicitly heteroglossic and postlingual ways. From a postlingual perspective, however, *no* text is written in one single, unitary language: all texts are heteroglossic and postlingual, and their monolingual classification (English, French, etc.) is always imposed after the fact. Nonetheless, some texts are written in decidedly normative ways, that is, in ways that conform to, rather than transgress, exogenous linguistic norms and ideals, thereby reproducing these norms and ideals to some extent. Can a postlingual approach to translation be applied to such texts, seemingly written in "one language," in other words to texts that espouse a normative or standard view of language? I want to suggest that, since a postlingual approach not only focuses on the translator's linguistic landscape, regardless of linguistic borders, but also encourages, for political reasons, the blurring of these borders in the rewriting of a text, any text can (and should) be translated in a postlingual manner. A recent

---

[12] Camille Toffoli, "*Quand je lis je m'invente suivi de D'elles et autres textes* de Suzanne Lamy/*Cartographie de l'amour décolonial* de Leanne Betasamosake Simpson," *Spirale* 268 (2019): 24.
[13] Personal correspondence with the author.

translation, published in 2020 in Canada by Acadian poet Georgette LeBlanc, is a fascinating case in point.

Océan: A Masterclass in Postlingual Translation

Raised in Baie Sainte-Marie, a rural francophone community in the otherwise anglophone province of Nova Scotia, Georgette LeBlanc is twenty-first-century Acadia's most renowned poet. A two-time finalist at the Governor General's Literary Awards for Poetry and the Canadian Parliamentary Poet Laureate in 2018 and 2019, LeBlanc now lives in Moncton, New Brunswick. She has published five poetry collections to date, including the acclaimed *Alma* (2006), *Prudent* (2013), and *Petits poèmes sur mon père qui est mort* (2022). Her works are all written in what critics and scholars have described as a variety of Acadian French from southwestern Nova Scotia—typically considered different from other Acadian Frenches, such as the one spoken in Moncton or in Louisiana—also known as "Acadjonne," which is to say that LeBlanc's poetry consistently deviates from the French linguistic norm in a number of ways. In her own words: "It is obvious that I write in a French that is *other*."[14]

In 2020, Moncton-based publisher Perce-Neige published LeBlanc's translation of *Ocean*, by Halifax-based poet Sue Goyette—LeBlanc's first literary translation to be published. The poetry collection, shortlisted for the prestigious Griffin Poetry Prize in 2014, is comprised of fifty-six numbered poems with no titles. Together, the poems tell the story of the ocean, of its consciousness, and of human relationships with it. The collection takes as its stage the moving boundary between ocean and land, where the shore dwellers live. To give an idea of the language, or repertoire, in which the collection was originally written, here is a poem that is somewhat representative of the book as a whole, titled "Eight":

> The trick to building houses was making sure
> they didn't taste good. The ocean's culinary taste
>
> was growing more sophisticated and occasionally
> its appetite was unwieldy. It ate boats and children,
>
> the occasional shoe. Pants. A diamond ring.
> Hammers. It ate promises and rants. It snatched up

---

[14] Georgette LeBlanc, "Ce qui ne se dit pas," *Lettres québécoises* 181 (2019): 47.

names like peanuts. We had a squadron of cooks
specifically catering to its needs. They stirred vats

of sandals and sunglasses. They peppered their soups
with pebbles and house keys. Quarts of bottled song

were used to sweeten the brew. Discussions between
preschool children and the poets were added

for nutritional value. These cooks took turns pulling
the cart to the mouth of the harbour. It would take four

of them to shoulder the vat over, tipping the peeled
promises, the baked dreams into its mouth.

And then the ocean would be calm. It would sleep. Our mistake
was thinking we were making it happy.[15]

This excerpt does not contain much deviation from the common idea of standard English. Few elements, if any, are marked in terms of class, race, gender, or geographical location, except for the Canadian (versus US) spelling of "harbour." The poem is characterized by a conversational orality and simple, effortless syntax, but apart from the contraction in the second verse, it is written in what would generally be analyzed as a somewhat formal literary register—as opposed to slang or popular speech, for instance. As such, this poem, and *Ocean* as a whole, does not challenge the traditional regime of translation as much as the other texts presented throughout this book do. Most translators would probably choose an "equivalent" register such as standard, literary French to translate Goyette's collection. Georgette LeBlanc, however, is not most translators.

LeBlanc's version of *Ocean* is in fact written in a language that is highly reminiscent of her own creative work as a poet, in what some of us would describe as a kind of "Acadian French," or "Acadjonne." Here is her translation of the poem "Thirteen":

L'idée de *dater*[16] braquit quand ce que y en a
qui fumirent l'exhaust d'une troupe d'enfants

---

[15] Sue Goyette, *Ocean* (Kentville: Gaspereau Press, 2013), no page numbers.
[16] The italics throughout LeBlanc's translation of *Ocean* serve not so much to signal that the words are "foreign" than to signal a change in pronunciation, since there are several "English" words that appear without italics in the collection (such as "job"). Here, for instance, the italics signal that the word *dater* is intended to be heard or pronounced /deɪ.te/ rather than /da.te/.

en se disant qu'ils étiont des lions. J'aurions point normalement fumé
tcheque affaire d'aussi fort, mais la nuit avait braqué

à prêcher, à radoter comme un politicien
qui promettait plus de jour. Y en a qui se sentiont une miette ourlés.

Le plus fort que j'avions l'habitude de fumer, c'était l'écho
d'un bon rire, ça fait que la *feeling* d'avoir des pattes pis un logis, creux,

était de quoi de neuf. J'étions une miette gênés de rôder.
La manière que j'nous nudgions

un dans l'autre. Ej rougissions aux dents pointues
du toucher. Mais tout ça changit

quand j'découvrirent nos ronronnements.[17]

The purpose of this discussion is not to document and index all the ways in which LeBlanc's language deviates from standard French and, by the same token, the ways in which it constitutes "Acadian French"—that would be contrary to a postlingual approach—but to reflect on what it means to translate a seemingly monolingual text postlingually, that is, by drawing on the linguistic resources and forms that are available to the translator, regardless of how they correspond (or not) to a given linguistic system. If we take for granted that Goyette's *Ocean* was not, in fact, written in English, then it follows that its translation does not have to be written in French—or in any fixed, delimited variety, for that matter.

LeBlanc's original translation strategy for rendering *Océan* was first to rewrite it in "standard French," in a recognizable register and variety equivalent to those created by Sue Goyette in the first place. This amounted to producing a conventional translation, in other words the rendering of Goyette's poetry collection from English into French. However, LeBlanc felt deeply unsatisfied with this first rendering and thought the poems lacked something, that they were not alive enough. LeBlanc thus decided to start over, this time with a new strategy, which I interpret as being profoundly postlingual, where she takes up a variety of linguistic forms from her own oral, embodied, and subjective surroundings, which happens to be various places in Acadia, including but not limited to the Baie-Sainte-Marie, Moncton, the Acadian Peninsula, and even Louisiana. Moving away from a mimetic, identitarian representation of a specific "variety" spoken in a specific place, LeBlanc picks and chooses

---

[17] Sue Goyette, *Océan*, trans. Georgette LeBlanc (Moncton: Perce-Neige, 2020), "Treize" (no page number).

certain forms that made up her own personal linguistic landscape over time. For instance, she describes having foregone the -onne pronunciation that is typical of Acadjonne, the brand of Acadian French spoken in Baie-Sainte-Marie, but having decided to keep other, localized pronunciations or expressions, such as "djetter" (for "guetter/attendre," meaning to wait).[18] Thus there seems to be no "rule" or external dictate (such as a dictionary or a glossary of Acadian terms) according to which certain things should be included or excluded from the language of the translation. It is LeBlanc's own creative process of assemblage from what she hears (or reads or speaks) that leads to the inclusion (and exclusion) of given linguistic forms. As the poet-translator said herself: "It isn't the language that writes the poem; it's the poet's body that molds language so as to let the experience of the body, which has lived in a community, speak."[19] Translation, in this view, is driven by a "relational ethics of accountability to people and place,"[20] rather than to a regulatory, idealized, supposedly neutral category (French).

LeBlanc has written about the reasons motivating her choice of writing and translating in ways that center her own material linguistic surroundings, saying that her intention is not necessarily political, or at least not in a deliberate, activist way. She says: "I write this language down because it exists, because it's my language, the code that is the closest to my own sensory experience of the world."[21] In evoking "her" language here, LeBlanc is not calling upon a fixed mother tongue that she owns but a subjective and profoundly sensory experience which she is able to translate into words. The poet-translator attends to linguistic specificities—their sonority, their taste, their texture—and shows that the forms spoken in her communities can and do express things that are poetic, profound, and intellectual at once. It is through this specificity, which comes directly from an embodied relation and a lived experience with an actual community in an actual place, that LeBlanc addresses her not-so-imagined community, both in her poetry and in her translation. Not-so-imagined, in the sense that her community is already there, around her: by choosing to write not in French but postlingually, LeBlanc addresses (maybe) her children, the cashiers in grocery stores in Moncton, her parents in Baie-Sainte-Marie, her colleagues at the University

---

[18] See Georgette LeBlanc, Sonya Malaborza, and Arianne Des Rochers, "La traduction littéraire en Acadie," Université de Moncton, November 23, 2021, https://www.youtube.com/watch?v=iGznMZ7ZnaU.

[19] Georgette LeBlanc, "L'Océan de la langue: à la rencontre du français en Acadie," Monument Lefebvre, August 3, 2021, https://www.facebook.com/MonumentLefebvre/videos/causerie-du-mardi-georgette-leblanc/550251299504699, 35:30.

[20] Tuck and McKenzie, *Place in Research*, 19.

[21] LeBlanc, "Ce qui ne se dit pas," 47.

of Louisiana, her neighbors, and perhaps no one else—which is not to say that no one else is welcome to read or listen. By drawing on what she *hears* around her and wherever she goes, LeBlanc creates an assemblage of "sounds that link us together."[22] This "us" is not some imagined national or supranational community (e.g., the francophone world) but an actual neighborhood, an actual network of relationships. What links this "us" together, what resonates *here* and *now* is not some abstracted, delocalized, standardized, faraway language but a heterogeneous, fluid, changing, live, very real, and immediate linguistic landscape from which translators can draw.

That LeBlanc does not directly address a wide, imagined community such as "the francophone world," or that she does not directly address readers from Quebec or from France (where the various linguistic landscapes are quite different than the one(s) she herself inhabits), does not mean that readers from Quebec, France, or elsewhere in the world cannot or should not read her translation or her works. On the contrary, LeBlanc's version of *Océan* offers to these readers from elsewhere, on its own terms, a window onto linguistic and expressive practices that are both similar to and different from their own, because they are uttered and written away from the centers. There is no pretense to universality, abstraction, or generalization: the value of postlingual writing lies precisely in its capacity to let place- and time-specific heteroglossia emerge out of the refusal to reproduce an abstracted norm, on the one hand, and in its potential to expose the artificiality of the norm (as well as the violence inherent to its naturalization) to the very people who believe or seem to hold it, on the other hand. Thus, postlingual practices, such as the ones at play in *Océan*, reveal two things: the potential of marginalized linguistic practices to express anything that a "standard language" might, especially for people who embody these practices, and the empirical reality of linguistic variability, especially for people who embody or believe in the norm. In short, postlingual writing *diffracts* language, to borrow Myriam Suchet's wording,[23] and as such it is a constant reminder of the inherent heteroglossia of any language, which is to say that no "language" exists in a singular way, that language is always already plural and never neutral.

Perhaps the most radical and empowering aspect of LeBlanc's version of *Océan* is that she allows herself to do precisely what the writers analyzed throughout this book do—write postlingually—in *translation*. Indeed, LeBlanc actively refuses to follow all three axioms we have been deconstructing: she refuses to translate into a "standard language," she

---

[22] LeBlanc, Malaborza, and Des Rochers, "La traduction littéraire en Acadie," 44:00.
[23] Myriam Suchet, *Traduire du français au français* (Rennes: Éditions du commun, 2021).

refuses to translate into her "mother tongue" (actively rejecting some of the linguistic forms she grew up with, instead picking and choosing things as she goes along), and, ultimately, she refuses to engage in translation as "the rendering of a text from one language to another," since the final product is not written in a unitary, recognizable language but in a language that emerges from, has ties to, and points to a certain landscape or set of landscapes. More radically, perhaps, for LeBlanc the "source language" (i.e., the relatively standard English of Goyette and what it means socially) is of no importance: she does not aim to reproduce the original's register but rather to convey her own sensory experience of Goyette's poems. Yet, what LeBlanc has given us with *Océan* is still very much a translation, a postlingual one that shows us that standard French does not have a monopoly on translation and that heteroglossic, minoritized, decentered forms can and do express poetry, research, narrative, and more. It shows us that drawing from a linguistic landscape, rather than from a linguistic system, can produce lively, relational, playful, and highly enjoyable translations, even for speakers who do not share the same landscape and therefore are not directly addressed—after all, LeBlanc's translation won the Governor General's Literary Award for Translation in 2020, a Canada-wide award for which none of the jury members were Acadian. Finally, it shows us that what is most important in translation is the encounter between a text and a translator's voice, and that translators have so much more to offer than merely following a dictionary or a set of grammatical rules.

Postlingual Futures

What is now clear is that translation, both as a field and a practice, must be redefined outside of the structural and national-linguistic paradigm. Translation, this book has argued, is best understood as a social practice which deals with and draws from at least two sets of socially meaningful linguistic, communicative, and expressive resources. Such a move away from abstract linguistic entities and national communities and toward local linguistic landscapes and communal, embodied, and subjective linguistic practices has several implications for the field, the practice, and the teaching of translation. First, it opens the field to translators from minoritized linguistic backgrounds, as the focus moves from solely or at least predominantly the "mastery" of the "standard language" (to which only certain speakers are afforded access and accorded legitimacy in the first place) to encompass a broader linguistic range. The normative and structural understanding of language and translation is exactly what produces linguistic insecurity for marginalized, racialized, and/or Indigenous people and, consequently, what prevents them from entering the field of translation altogether.[24] A postlingual, heteroglossic view of translation frames minoritized speakers' linguistic repertoires and ranges as an asset, rather than as something they need to overcome in order to practice translation "properly." It also creates challenges for settler or hegemonic translators, as it forces us to inquire, explore, and engage with social voices outside of the standard, or dominant, language.

Second, the move away from the transparent, rational, logical, and universal thrust of standard languages reveals the profoundly relational nature of translation by making the translator's linguistic subjectivity visible. Translation into vernaculars and other linguistic forms associated with social positions (class, race, gender, age, etc.) has historically been frowned upon—and even outright rejected as an option—precisely because it makes the translator—especially the queer translator or the racialized translator or the poor translator—visible and locatable, both geographically and socially.[25] Making the translator visible through the use of the various social voices and linguistic resources that make up their linguistic landscape makes the work of translation visible, revealing the fundamentally relational aspect of translation as a space where two subjectivities and sets of embodied experiences meet. Perhaps it is worth noting that it would also make the work of translation visible precisely *as work* and translators legible as laborers. A postlingual strategy of translation reveals the conditions under which translations are made and sees

---

[24] The lack of diversity in Canadian literary translation remains a pressing problem. For instance, the Literary Translators' Association of Canada has a predominantly white membership, with only a handful of translators of color out of some 200 members. Further, Indigenous writers are almost exclusively translated by white settler translators (such as myself) in Canada, with the exception of Natasha Kanapé Fontaine and Charles Bender, who both came to translation outside of formal training.

[25] Lawrence Venuti, on the cultivated illusion of the translator's invisibility: "A translated text ... is judged acceptable ... when the absence of any linguistic or stylistic peculiarities makes it seem transparent, giving the appearance that it reflects ... the essential meaning of the foreign text—the appearance, in other words, that the translation is not in fact a translation, but the 'original.' The illusion of transparency is an effect of a fluent translation strategy, of the translator's effort to insure easy readability by adhering to current usage, maintaining continuous syntax, fixing a precise meaning. But readers also play a significant role in insuring that this illusory effect occurs because of the general tendency to read translations mainly for meaning, to reduce the stylistic features of the translation to the foreign text or writer, and to question any language use that might interfere with the seemingly untroubled communication of the foreign writer's intention. What is so remarkable here is that the effect of transparency conceals the numerous conditions under which the translation is made, starting with the translator's crucial intervention. The more fluent the translation, the more invisible the translator, and, presumably, the more visible the writer or meaning of the foreign text." Venuti, *The Translator's Invisibility*, 1.

the translator's subjectivity and linguistic landscape as equally important as the author's. In other words, translation is an expression of the self, at the same time as it forces the self to dislocate in the encounter. The translated text is revealed as the outcome of the relation between two social actors, as the product of the translator's subjective choices among a set of linguistic resources, inspired (or not, as we have seen with LeBlanc's translation) by the choices the writer made within a different set of resources, rather than as the more or less transparent carrying of some content (which stems solely from the author's subjectivity and which the translator has to "discover") from one "neutral" language to another. In this view, translation as relation, rather than as equivalency, opens up new grounds on which to articulate an ethical practice of translation centered around the deliberate relations that the translator initiates, builds, and maintains—not only with the source text but also with the author, the language of publication, their linguistic landscape, their own linguistic practices, and so on. The illusion of transparency is gone, and the translator must fully assume responsibility for their choices. The focus moves from the "fidelity" or the "correspondence" of a translation in comparison with its source text to the staging of the distance, and of the difference, between both texts.

Finally, a postlingual approach to translation, by countering state monolingualism, forces us to reconsider the ties between the field of translation and the demands of the nation-state for homogeneous publics. Indeed, drawing postnational cartographies of language in our translations points to the creation of new, different publics than the ones we often take for granted when we translate.[26] What would our translations look like if we stopped addressing imagined national (and sometimes, supranational) communities on the grounds of a shared, abstract language? What kinds of publics do we create through an explicitly heteroglossic address? What grounds does a postlingual approach to reading, writing, and translation provide for the production of communities, real and imagined, free of exclusions based on language use? The texts analyzed in this book participate in the making of communities across and beyond linguistic and national borders and, through their address, work for the creation of alternative communities. In the untranslated, postlingual words of Édouard Glissant: "Quel est ce 'on' qui intervient? Celui de l'Autre, celui de voisinage, celui que j'imagine pour tenter de dire? Ces 'nous,' ces 'on,' sont un devenir."[27] In

---

[26] I am often asked, for instance, to cater my translations to a "metropolitan readership," as my translations are also distributed in Europe. Another recurring question in translation and in publishing is how to produce translations that will be immediately "understood" in all of la Francophonie, as if this were possible, let alone desirable.

[27] Édouard Glissant, *Poétique de la Relation* (Paris: Gallimard, 1990), 222.

any case, what is shared in these works is not a common language but the inherent difference and variability within language and the will to create "des nous qui seraient des nous de consentement à l'ouvrage des différences."[28] Perhaps translation does not need a border after all. Perhaps it can instead be one of the key sites for the unmapping of borders and the cultivating, rather than the overcoming, of difference, not only in relation to the Other but also within ourselves.

In the end, there is nothing subversive about the crossing of linguistic borders when we are authorized to do so and, most importantly, when these borders remain intact after we have crossed them. Perhaps translators should take some cues from the language smugglers who have prompted the writing of this book. Perhaps translators, who are tasked with the revoicing of texts in new and ever-changing linguistic landscapes, should smuggle unauthorized, queer, abject, decolonial, disruptive, strange, beautiful forms into their writing practice, so as to participate to the creation, already underway, of a more welcoming, less hierarchical postlingual present.

---

[28] Édouard Glissant, *L'imaginaire des langues : Entretiens avec Lise Gauvin (1991–2009)* (Paris: Gallimard, 2010), 92.

Works Cited

Adese, Jennifer. "The New People: Reading for Peoplehood in Métis Literatures." *Studies in American Indian Literatures* 28, no. 4 (2016): 53–79.
Agha, Asif. "Enregisterment and Communication in Social History." *Registers of Communication* 18 (2015): 27–53.
Akiwenzie-Damm, Kateri. "We Belong to This Land: A View of 'Cultural Difference.'" *Journal of Canadian Studies* 31, no. 3 (1996): 21–8.
Aléong, Stanley. "Discours nationalistes et purisme linguistique au Québec." *Culture* 1, no. 2 (1981): 31–41.
Anderson, Benedict. *Imagined Communities: Reflections on the Origins and Spread of Nationalism*. New York: Verso, [1983] 2016.
Andrews, Jennifer. "Irony, Métis Style: Reading the Poetry of Marilyn Dumont and Gregory Scofield." *Canadian Poetry* 50 (2002): 6–31.
Attig, Remy. "Transnational Translation: Reflections on Translating from Judeo-Spanish and Spanglish." *TTR* 32, no. 2 (2019): 61–80.
Austen, Ian. "Law Requiring French in Quebec Becomes Stricter." *The New York Times* (New York), May 24, 2022, https://www.nytimes.com/2022/05/24/world/canada/quebec-language-bill-96.html.
Avasilichioaei, Oana. *Limbinal*. Vancouver: Talonbooks, 2015.
Avasilichioaei, Oana and Erín Moure. *Expeditions of a Chimaera*. Toronto: BookThug, 2009.
Baer, Brian James. *Queer Theory and Translation Studies: Language, Politics, Desire*. New York: Routledge, 2020.
Bakhtin, Mikhail. *The Dialogic Imagination: Four Essays*, translated by Caryl Emerson and Michael Holquist. Austin: University of Texas Press, 1982.
Balibar, Renée. *L'Institution du français: Le colinguisme des Carolingiens à la République*. Paris: Presses Universitaires de France, 1985.
Balibar, Renée. *Les français fictifs: Le rapport des styles littéraires au français national*. Paris: Hachette, 1974.
Barrett, Rusty. "The Emergence of the Unmarked: Queer Theory, Language Ideology, and Formal Linguistics." In *Queer Excursions: Retheorizing Binaries in Language, Gender, and Sexuality*, edited by Jenny L. Davis, Lil Zimman, and Joshua Raclaw, 195–223. Oxford: Oxford University Press, 2014.
Basile, Elena. "A Scene of Intimate Entanglements, or Reckoning with the 'Fuck' of Translation." In *Queering Translation, Translating the Queer*, edited by Brian Baer James and Klaus Kaindl, 26–37. New York: Routledge, 2018.
Basile, Elena. "Pressing Against Tongues: Notes on the Name and Its Ghostly Body." In *Je Nathanaël*, 97–102. Toronto: Book*hug, 2019.
Bataille, Georges. *Œuvres complètes, tome II, Écrits posthumes 1922–1940*. Paris: Gallimard, 1970.

Bauman, Richard and Charles L. Briggs. *Voices of Modernity: Language Ideologies and the Politics of Inequality*. Cambridge: Cambridge University Press, 2003.

Baynham, Mike and Tong King Lee. *Translation and Translanguaging*. New York: Routledge, 2019.

Belcourt, Billy-Ray. *A History of My Brief Body*. Toronto: Penguin Random House, 2020.

Belcourt, Billy-Ray. "Can the Other of Native Studies Speak?" *Decolonization: Indigeneity, Education, Society*, 2016, https://decolonization.wordpress.com/2016/02/01/can-the-other-of-native-studies-speak/.

Berman, Antoine. "La traduction comme épreuve de l'étranger." *Texte* 4, no. 1 (1985): 67–81.

Berman, Antoine. "Translation and the Trials of the Foreign," trans. Lawrence Venuti. In *The Translation Studies Reader*, ed. Lawrence Venuti, 284–97. London: Routledge, 2000.

Bermann, Sandra. Introduction to *Nation, Language and the Ethics of Translation*, edited by Sandra Bermann and Michael Wood, 1–10. Princeton: Princeton University Press, 2005.

Bernabé, Jean, Patrick Chamoiseau, and Raphaël Confiant. *Éloge de la créolité*. Paris: Gallimard, 1989.

Bex, Tony and Richard J. Watts. Introduction to *Standard English: The Widening Debate*, edited by Tony Bex and Richard J. Watts, 1–15. London: Routledge, Taylor & Francis e-library, 2002.

Bonfiglio, Thomas. "Language, Racism, Ethnicity." In *The Handbook of Language and Communication: Diversity and Change*, edited by Marlis Hellinger and Anne Pauwels, 619–50. Berlin: De Gruyter Mouton, 2007.

Bonfiglio, Thomas. *Mother Tongues and Nations: The Invention of the Native Speaker*. Berlin: De Gruyter Mouton, 2010.

Bouchard, Chantal. *La langue et le nombril: Une obsession québécoise*. Montréal: Fides, 1998.

Bouchard, Chantal. *Méchante langue: La légitimité linguistique du français parlé au Québec*. Montréal: Presses de l'Université de Montréal, 2012.

Boudreau, Annette. *À l'ombre de la langue légitime: L'Acadie dans la francophonie*. Paris: Classiques Garnier, 2016.

Boudreau, Raoul. "Le rapport à la langue dans les romans de France Daigle: du refoulement à l'ironie." *Voix et Images* 29, no. 3 (2004): 31–45.

Boudreau, Raoul. "Les français de *Pas pire* de France Daigle." In *La création littéraire dans le contexte de l'exiguïté*, edited by Robert Viau, 51–63. Montréal: Publications MNH, 2000.

Bourdieu, Pierre. *Langage et pouvoir symbolique*. Paris: Éditions du Seuil, [2001] 2014.

Briggs, Kate. *This Little Art*. London: Fitzcarraldo, 2017.

Butler, Judith. *Bodies That Matter*. New York: Routledge, 2011.

Butler, Judith. *Gender Trouble*. New York: Routledge, [1990] 2008.

Cabajsky, Andrea. "The Vivid Feeling of Creating: An Interview with France Daigle." *Studies in Canadian Literature* 39, no. 2 (2014): 259–69.

Cameron, Deborah and Don Kulick. *Language and Sexuality*. Cambridge: Cambridge University Press, 2003.
Campbell, Maria. *Halfbreed*. Toronto: Penguin Random House, [1973] 2019.
Canadian Broadcast Corporation. "Beyond 94," updated June 8, 2022, https://www.cbc.ca/newsinteractives/beyond-94?&cta=1.
Canagarajah, Suresh. *Translingual Practice: Global English and Cosmopolitan Relations*. New York: Routledge, 2013.
Canut, Cécile. "Le nom des langues ou les métaphores de la frontière." *Ethnologies comparées* 1 (2000): 1–18.
Chapdelaine, Annick and Gillian Lane-Mercier. *Faulkner: Une expérience de retraduction*. Montréal: Presses de l'Université de Montréal, 2001.
Chazan, May, Lisa Helps, Anna Stanley, and Sonali Thakkar. "Labour, Lands, Bodies." In *Home and the Native Land: Unsettling Multiculturalism in Canada*, edited by May Chazan, Lisa Helps, Anna Stanley, and Sonali Thakkar, 1–11. Toronto: Between the Lines, 2011.
Choi, Don Mee. *Translation is a Mode: Translation is an Anti-Neocolonial Mode*. Brooklyn: Ugly Duckling Press, 2020.
Chow, Rey. *Not Like a Native Speaker: On Languaging as a Postcolonial Experience*. New York: Columbia University Press, 2014.
Côté, Nicole. "Nathanaël, ou l'étrange art du déplacement: *Le Carnet de somme* et son apatride traversée de frontières." *Canadian Literature* 224 (2015): 33–45.
Coulthard, Glen Sean. *Red Skin, White Masks: Rejecting the Colonial Politics of Recognition*. Minneapolis: University of Minnesota Press, 2014.
Cronin, Michael. "Shady Dealings: Translation, Climate and Knowledge." In *The Dark Side of Translation*, edited by Federico Italiano, 95–110. London/New York: Routledge, 2020.
D'Hulst, Lieven. "Sur le rôle des métaphores en traductologie contemporaine." *Target* 4, no. 1 (1992): 33–51.
Daigle, France. *For sure*, translated by Robert Majzels. Toronto: House of Anansi, EPUB e-book, 2013.
Daigle, France. *Pour sûr*. Montréal: Boréal, 2011.
Davis, Hailey. "Typography, Lexicography and the Development of the Idea of 'Standard English.'" In *Standard English: The Widening Debate*, edited by Tony Bex and Richard J. Watts, 69–88. London: Routledge, Taylor & Francis e-library, 2002.
Davis, Jenny L. "More than Just 'Gay Indians': Intersecting Articulations of Two-Spirit Gender, Sexuality, and Indigenousness." In *Queer Excursions: Retheorizing Binaries in Language, Gender, and Sexuality*, edited by Jenny L. Davis, Lil Zimman, and Joshua Raclaw, 62–80. Oxford: Oxford University Press, 2014.
Deerchild, Rosanna. "Poet Joshua Whitehead Redefines Two-Spirit Identity in *full-metal indigiqueer*." CBC Radio, *Unreserved*, 2017, https://www.cbc.ca/radio/unreserved/from-dystopian-futures-to-secret-pasts-check-out-these-indigenous-storytellers-over-the-holidays-1.4443312/poet-joshua

-whitehead-redefines-two-spirit-identity-in-full-metal-indigiqueer-1.4447321.

Del Valle, José and Luis Gabriel-Stheeman. "Nationalism, Hispanismo, and Monoglossic Culture." In *The Battle Over Spanish between 1800 and 2000: Language Ideologies and Hispanic Intellectuals*, edited by José Del Valle and Luis Gabriel-Stheeman, 1–13. London: Routledge, 2002.

Deleuze, Gilles and Félix Guattari. *Kafka: pour une littérature mineure*. Paris: Éditions de Minuit, 1975.

Delisle, Jean. *La traduction raisonnée: Manuel d'initiation à la traduction professionnelle de l'anglais vers le français*. Ottawa: Presses de l'Université d'Ottawa, 2013.

Denti, Chiara. "L'hétérolinguisme ou penser autrement la traduction." *Meta* 62, no. 3 (2017): 521–37.

Derrida, Jacques. "Des Tours de Babel." In *Difference in Translation*, edited and translated by Joseph F. Graham, 165–207. Ithaca: Cornell University Press, 1985.

Derrida, Jacques. *Le Monolinguisme de l'autre, ou la prothèse d'origine*, 72. Paris: Galilée, 1996.

Douglas, Mary. *Purity and Danger: An Analysis of Concepts of Pollution and Taboo*. London: Routledge, Taylor & Francis e-library, [1966] 2001.

Dowling, Sarah. "Conflicting Englishes: Cheap Signaling and Vernacular Poetry." *Jacket2*, January 20, 2015, https://jacket2.org/commentary/conflicting-englishes.

Dowling, Sarah. *Translingual Poetics: Writing Personhood Under Settler Colonialism*. Iowa City: University of Iowa Press, 2018.

Driskill, Qwo-Li, Chris Finley, Brian Joseph Gilley, and Scott Lauria Morgensen. Introduction to *Queer Indigenous Studies: Critical Interventions in Theory, Politics, and Literature*, 1–28. Tucson: University of Arizona Press, 2011.

Dubuc, Robert. *En français dans le texte*. Montréal: Linguatech, 2000.

Edelman, Lee. *No Future: Queer Theory and the Death Drive*. Durham: Duke University Press, 2004.

Fanon, Frantz. *Peau noire, masques blancs*. Paris: Éditions du Seuil, [1952] 1971.

Felski, Rita. *Uses of Literature*. Hoboken: Wiley-Blackwell, 2008.

Flaherty, Peter. "Langue Nationale/Langue Naturelle: The Politics of Linguistic Uniformity during the French Revolution." *Historical Reflections/Réflexions Historiques* 14, no. 2 (1987): 311–28.

Gal, Susan. "Sociolinguistic Regimes and the Management of 'Diversity.'" In *Language in Late Capitalism: Pride and Profit*, ed. Monica Heller and Alexandre Duchêne, 22–37. London: Routledge, 2012.

García, Ofelia and Li Wei. *Translanguaging: Language, Bilingualism and Education*. London: Palgrave Macmillan, 2014.

Gauthier, Alex. "These foreign c*nts've goat trouble wi the Queen's f*ckin English, ken, our é-énoncer la voix scots de *Trainspotting* au moyen du Québec et de la (socio-)linguistique." *TTR* 28, no. 1–2 (2017): 207–37.

Gauvin, Lise. *Les langues du roman: Du plurilinguisme comme stratégie textuelle*. Montréal: Presses de l'Université de Montréal, 1999.
Giroux, Dalie. *L'œil du maître*. Montréal: Mémoire d'encrier, 2021.
Giroux, Dalie. *Parler en Amérique: Oralité, colonialisme, territoire*. Montréal: Mémoire d'encrier, 2019.
Glissant, Édouard. *L'imaginaire des langues: Entretiens avec Lise Gauvin (1991–2009)*. Paris: Gallimard, 2010.
Glissant, Édouard. *Poétique de la Relation*. Paris: Gallimard, 1990.
Goeman, Mishuana. *Mark My Words: Native Women Mapping our Nations*. Minneapolis: University of Minnesota Press, 2013.
Goyette, Sue. *Ocean*. Kentville: Gaspereau Press, 2013.
Goyette, Sue. *Océan*, trans. Georgette LeBlanc. Moncton: Perce-Neige, 2020.
Grutman, Rainer. *Des langues qui résonnent: L'hétérolinguisme au XIXe siècle québécois*. Montréal: Fides-CÉTUQ, 1997.
Halberstam, Jack. *The Queer Art of Failure*. Durham: Duke University Press, 2011.
Hall, Kira and Rusty Barrett (eds.). *The Oxford Handbook of Language and Sexuality*. New York: Oxford University Press, 2018.
Haque, Eve. *Multiculturalism within a Bilingual Framework: Language, Race, and Belonging in Canada*. Toronto: University of Toronto Press, 2012.
Haque, Eve and Donna Patrick. "Indigenous Languages and the Racial Hierarchisation of Language Policy in Canada." *Journal of Multilingual and Multicultural Development* 36, no. 1 (2015): 27–41.
Heller, Monica. "Bilingualism as Ideology and Practice." In *Bilingualism: A Social Approach*, edited by Monica Heller, 1–24. London: Palgrave Macmillan, 2007.
Heller, Monica. "Socioeconomic Junctures, Theoretical Shifts: A Genealogy of Language Policy and Planning Research." In *The Oxford Handbook of Language Policy and Planning*, edited by James W. Tollefson and Miguel Pérez-Milans. Oxford Handbooks Online, 2018, https://www.oxfordhandbooks.com/view/10.1093/oxfordhb/9780190458898.001.0001/oxfordhb-9780190458898-e-6.
Heller, Monica and Bonnie McElhinny. *Language, Capitalism, Colonialism*. Toronto: University of Toronto Press, 2017.
Higonnet, Patrice L.-R. "The Politics of Linguistic Terrorism and Grammatical Hegemony during the French Revolution." *Social History* 5, no. 1 (1980): 41–69.
Hobsbawm, Eric. *Nations and Nationalism since 1780: Programme, Myth, Reality*. Cambridge: Cambridge University Press, 1990.
hooks, bell. "Language: Teaching New Worlds/New Words." In *Teaching to Transgress: Education as the Practice of Freedom*, 167–76. New York: Routledge, 1994.
Jakobson, Roman. "On Linguistic Aspects of Translation." In *On Translation*, edited by Reuben A. Bower, 232–9. Cambridge, MA: Harvard University Press, 1959.

Jean-Louis, Lorrie. *La femme cent couleurs*. Montréal: Mémoire d'encrier, 2020.
Jewell, Eva and Ian Mosby. "Calls to Action Accountability: A Status Update on Reconciliation." The Yellowhead Institute, December 17, 2019, https://yellowheadinstitute.org/2019/12/17/calls-to-action-accountability-a-status-update-on-reconciliation/.
Jones, Ellen. *Literature in Motion: Translating Multilingualism Across the Americas*. New York: Columbia University Press, 2022.
Justice, Daniel Heath. *Why Indigenous Literatures Matter*. Waterloo: Wilfrid Laurier University Press, 2018.
Justice, Daniel Heath, Bethany Schneider, and Mark Rifkin. "Introduction." *GLQ: A Journal of Gay and Lesbian Studies* 16, no. 1–2 (2016): 5–39.
Kamboureli, Smaro. *Scandalous Bodies: Diasporic Literature in English Canada*. Waterloo: Wilfrid Laurier University Press, 2009.
Karpinski, Eva C. *Borrowed Tongues: Life Writing, Migration, and Translation*. Waterloo: Wilfrid Laurier University Press, 2012.
Kasparek, Christopher. "The Translator's Endless Toil." *The Polish Review* 28, no. 2 (1983): 83–7.
Kellman, Steven G. *The Translingual Imagination*. Lincoln: University of Nebraska Press, 2000.
Kristeva, Julia. *Pouvoirs de l'horreur*. Paris: Éditions du Seuil, collection Points, 1980.
Lalonde, Catherine. "Littérature: Querelle de Paris." *Le Devoir* (Montréal, QC), September 14, 2019, https://www.ledevoir.com/lire/562617/litterature-querelle-de-paris.
Lambert, Kevin. "Faut-il 'bien' écrire?" Centre de recherche interuniversitaire en sociocritique des textes, Université de Montréal, 2017, http://oic.uqam.ca/fr/communications/faut-il-bien-ecrire.
Lambert, Kevin. *Querelle*. Paris: Nouvel Attila, 2019.
Lambert, Kevin. *Querelle de Roberval*. Montréal: Héliotrope, 2018.
Lambert, Kevin. *Querelle of Roberval*, translated by Donald Winkler. Windsor: Biblioasis, EPUB e-book, 2022.
Landry, Rodrigue. "Légitimité et devenir en situation linguistique minoritaire." *Linguistic Minorities and Society* 5 (2015): 58–83.
LeBlanc, Georgette. "Ce qui ne se dit pas." *Lettres québécoises* 181 (2019): 47–9.
LeBlanc, Georgette. "L'Océan de la langue: à la rencontre du français en Acadie." Monument Lefebvre, August 3, 2021, https://www.facebook.com/MonumentLefebvre/videos/causerie-du-mardi-georgette-leblanc/550251299504699.
LeBlanc, Georgette, Sonya Malaborza, and Arianne Des Rochers. "La traduction littéraire en Acadie." Université de Moncton, November 23, 2021, https://www.youtube.com/watch?v=iGznMZ7ZnaU.
LeBlanc, Matthieu. "Traduction, bilinguisme et langue de travail: une étude de cas au sein de la fonction publique fédérale canadienne." *Meta* 59, no. 1 (2014): 537–56.

Leclerc, Catherine. "Between French and English, Between Ethnography and Assimilation: Strategies for Translating Moncton's Acadian Vernacular." *TTR* 18, no. 2 (2005): 161–92.
Leclerc, Catherine. *Des langues en partage? Cohabitation du français et de l'anglais en littérature contemporaine.* Montréal: XYZ, 2010.
Leclerc, Catherine. "Hiérarchies et inhibitions francophones: quelques exemples empruntés à France Daigle et à Jacques Poulin." *Zizanie* 1, no. 1 (2017): 26–47.
Leclerc, Catherine and Robert Majzels. "In Conversation: Catherine Leclerc and Robert Majzels." *Lemon Hound*, 2013, https://lemonhound.com/2013/09/27/in-conversation-catherine-leclerc-robert-majzels/.
Lennon, Brian. *In Babel's Shadow: Multilingual Literatures, Monolingual States.* Minneapolis: University of Minnesota Press, 2010.
Lepschy, Giulio. *Mother Tongues and Other Reflections on the Italian Language.* Toronto: University of Toronto Press, 2002.
Leroux, Daryl. *Distorted Descent: White Claims to Indigenous Identity.* Winnipeg: University of Manitoba Press, 2019.
Lewis, Rohan Anthony. *Creolising Translation, Translating Creolisation.* Doctoral thesis, Université de Montréal, 2004.
Lewis, Rohan Anthony. "Langue métissée et traduction: quelques enjeux théoriques." *Meta* 48, no. 3 (2003): 411–20.
Mackey, Eva. *The House of Difference: Cultural Politics and National Identity in Canada.* Toronto: University of Toronto Press, 2002.
Maracle, Lee. *My Conversations with Canadians.* Toronto: Book*hug, 2017.
McCall, Sophie. "Diaspora and Nation in Métis Writing." In *Cultural Grammars of Nation, Diaspora, and Indigeneity in Canada*, edited by Sophie McCall, Christine Kim, and Melina Baum Singer, 22–63. Waterloo: Wilfrid Laurier University Press, 2012.
McCan, Yes. "Dead Obies et le franglais: La réplique aux offusqués." *Voir* (Montréal, QC), July 23, 2014, https://voir.ca/jepenseque/2014/07/23/la-replique-aux-offusques/.
Melançon, Benoît. "Un roman, ses langues. Prolégomènes." *Études françaises* 52, no. 2 (2016): 105–18.
Merkle, Denise and Gillian Lane-Mercier. "Towards an Ethos of Diversity." In *Minority Languages, National Languages, and Official Language Policies*, edited by Denise Merkle, Gillian Lane-Mercier, and Jane Koustas, 3–32. Montreal/Kingston: McGill-Queen's University Press, 2018.
Meylaerts, Reine. "Heterolingualism in/and Translation: How Legitimate are the Other and His/Her Language?" *Target* 18, no. 1 (2006): 1–15.
Milroy, James. "The Consequences of Standardisation in Descriptive Linguistics." In *Standard English: The Widening Debate*, edited by Tony Bex and Richard J. Watts, 16–39. London: Routledge, Taylor & Francis e-library, 2002.
Moreton-Robinson, Aileen. *The White Possessive: Property, Power, and Indigenous Sovereignty.* Minneapolis: University of Minnesota Press, 2015.

Motschenbacher, Heiko. "Language and Sexual Normativity." In *The Oxford Handbook of Language and Sexuality*, edited by Kira Hall and Rusty Barrett. Oxford Handbooks Online, 2018, https://www.oxfordhandbooks.com/view /10.1093/oxfordhb/9780190212926.001.0001/oxfordhb-9780190212926-e -14.
Muñoz, José Esteban. *Cruising Utopia: The Then and There of Queer Futurity*. New York: New York University Press, 2009.
Nathanaël. *Alula, de son nom de plume*. Montreal: L'Hexagone, 2018.
Nathanaël. *Asclepias: The Milkweeds*. New York: Nightboat, 2015.
Nathanaël. *At Alberta*. Toronto: BookThug, 2008.
Nathanaël. *Feder: A Scenario*. New York: Nightboat, 2016.
Nathanaël. *Hatred of Translation*. New York: Nightboat, 2019.
Nathanaël. *Je Nathanaël*. Toronto: Book*hug, [2006] 2019.
Nathanaël. *Le cri du chrysanthème*. Montréal: Le Quartanier, 2018.
Nathanaël. *Pasolini's Our*. New York: Nightboat, 2018.
Nathanaël. *s'arrête? Je*. Montréal: L'Hexagone, 2007.
Nathanaël. *Sotto l'immagine*. Montréal: Mémoire d'encrier, 2014.
Nathanaël. *The Sorrow and The Fast of It*. New York: Nightboat, 2007.
North, Michael. *The Dialect of Modernism*. Oxford: Oxford University Press, 1998.
Office québécois de la langue française, Government of Quebec. "Désigner les personnes non binaires," 2019, http://bdl.oqlf.gouv.qc.ca/bdl/gabarit_bdl.asp ?t1=1&id=5370.
Okimāsis, Jean and Arok Wolvengrey. "How to Spell It in Cree: The Standard Roman Orthography," 2008, http://resources.atlas-ling.ca/media/How_To _Spell_It_In_Cree-Standard_Orthography-Plains-Cree.pdf.
Otheguy, Ricardo, Ofelia García, and Wallis Reid. "Clarifying Translanguaging and Deconstructing Named Languages: A Perspective from Linguistics." *Applied Linguistics Review* 6, no. 3 (2015): 281–307.
Paré, François. *Les littératures de l'exiguïté*. Ottawa: Le Nordir, 1992.
Parfitt, Timothy. "Irresistible Destruction and Building Understanding: A Review of Nathanaël's *Hatred of Translation*." *Newcity Lit*, December. 5, 2019, https://lit.newcity.com/2019/12/05/irresistible-destruction-and-building -understanding-a-review-of-nathanaels-hatred-of-translation/.
Parker, Aliana Violet. *Learning the Language of the Land*. Master's thesis, University of Victoria, 2012.
Patrick, Donna. "Indigenizing Language Policy in Canada: Redressing Racial Hierarchies in Language and Education." In *Minority Languages, National Languages, and Official Language Policies*, edited by Denise Merkle, Gillian Lane-Mercier, and Jane Koustas, 201–27. Montreal/Kingston: McGill-Queen's University Press, 2018.
Pelletier, Francine. *La bataille pour l'âme du Quebéc*. Périphéria, https://ici.tou.tv /bataille-pour-lame-du-quebec, 2022.
Piotte, Jean-Marc and Jean-Pierre Couture. *Les Nouveaux visages du nationalisme conservateur au Québec*. Montréal: Québec-Amérique, 2012.

Pokorn, Nike. *Challenging the Traditional Axioms: Translation into a Non-Mother Tongue.* Amsterdam: John Benjamins, 2005.

Proulx, Gilles. "L'anglicisation, cette autre épidémie." *Le Journal de Montréal* (Montréal, QC), January 28, 2021, https://www.journaldemontreal.com/2021/01/28/langlicisation-cette-autre-epidemie.

Prudent, Lambert-Félix. *Des baragouins à la langue antillaise.* Paris: L'Harmattan, 1999.

Quebec Government. "Projet de loi sur la langue officielle et commune du Québec, le français," 2022, http://www2.publicationsduquebec.gouv.qc.ca/dynamicSearch/telecharge.php?type=5&file=2022C14F.PDF.

Rafael, Vicente L. *Motherless Tongues: The Insurgency of Language Amid Wars of Translation.* Durham: Duke University Press, 2016.

Ricoeur, Paul. *Sur la traduction.* Paris: Bayard, 2004.

Rioux, Christian. "J'rape un suicide." *Le Devoir* (Montréal, QC), July 18, 2014, https://www.ledevoir.com/opinion/chroniques/413795/j-rape-un-suicide.

Rioux, Christian. "Radio Radio." *Le Devoir* (Montréal, QC), October 26, 2012, https://www.ledevoir.com/opinion/chroniques/362441/radio-radio.

Robinson, Douglas. *Transgender, Translation, Translingual Address.* London/New York: Bloomsbury, 2019.

Rosa, Jonathan. *Looking Like a Language, Sounding Like a Race: Raciolinguistic Ideologies and the Learning of Latinidad.* Oxford: Oxford University Press, 2019.

Rosa, Jonathan and Nelson Flores. "Unsettling Language and Race: Towards a Raciolinguistic Perspective." *Language in Society* 46, no. 5 (2017): 621–47.

Rouleau, Maurice. *Pratique de la traduction. L'approche par questionnement.* Montréal: Linguatech, 2007.

Saint-Martin, Lori. *Pour qui je me prends.* Montréal: Boréal, 2020.

Sakai, Naoki. "Translation." *Theory, Culture & Society* 23, no. 2–3 (2006): 71–86.

Sakai, Naoki. *Translation and Subjectivity: On Japan and Cultural Nationalism.* Minneapolis: University of Minnesota Press, 1997.

Samoyault, Tiphaine. *Traduction et violence.* Paris: Éditions du Seuil, 2020.

Sarkar, Mela. "'Ousqu'on chill à soir?' Pratiques multilingues comme stratégies identitaires dans la communauté hip-hop montréalaise." *Diversité urbaine,* Special Issue (2008): 27–44.

Schleiermacher, Friedrich. "On the Different Methods of Translating," trans. Susan Bernofsky. In *The Translation Studies Reader,* edited by Lawrence Venuti, 43–63. London/New York: Routledge, 2012.

Scofield, Gregory. *kipocihkân.* Gibsons: Nightwood Editions, 2009.

Scofield, Gregory. "On Poetry as Testimony, Interview with Shelagh Rogers." CBC Radio, *The Next Chapter,* December 20, 2016, https://www.cbc.ca/radio/thenextchapter/gregory-scofield-noah-richler-and-the-year-s-best-thrillers-1.3886040/gregory-scofield-on-poetry-as-testimony-1.3886101.

Scofield, Gregory. *Singing Home the Bones.* Vancouver: Raincoast Books, 2005.

Scofield, Gregory. *Thunder Through My Veins.* Toronto: Penguin Random House/Anchor Canada, Kindle edition, [1999] 2019.

Scofield, Gregory. *Witness, I Am*. Gibsons: Nightwood Editions, 2016.
Scott, James C. *Seeing Like a State: How Certain Schemes to Improve the Human Condition Have Failed*. New Haven: Yale University Press, 1998.
Scudeler, Jane. "'The Song I Am Singing': Gregory Scofield's Interweaving of Métis, Gay and Jewish Selfhoods." *Studies in Canadian Literatures* 31, no. 1 (2006): 129–45.
Shadd, Deborah. "Language, Education, and the Structuring of Canada's Social Sphere." In *Minority Languages, National Languages, and Official Language Policies*, edited by Denise Merkle, Gillian Lane-Mercier, and Jane Koustas, 187–209. Montreal/Kingston: McGill-Queen's University Press, 2018.
Simon, Sherry. *Cities in Translation: Intersections of Language and Memory*. London/New York: Routledge, 2012.
Simon, Sherry. *Le trafic des langues: traduction et culture dans la littérature québécoise*. Montréal: Boréal, 1994.
Simon, Sherry. *Translating Montreal: Episodes in the Life of a Divided City*. Montreal/Kingston: McGill-Queen's University Press, 2006.
Simon, Sherry. *Translation Sites: A Field Guide*. London/New York: Routledge, 2019.
Simpson, Audra. *Mohawk Interruptus: Political Life across the Borders of Settler States*. Durham: Duke University Press, 2014.
Simpson, Audra. "The State Is a Man: Theresa Spence, Loretta Saunders and the Gender of Settler Sovereignty." *Theory & Event* 19, no. 4 (2016), https://muse.jhu.edu/article/633280/.
Simpson, Leanne Betasamosake. "Anticolonial Strategies for the Recovery and Maintenance of Indigenous Knowledge." *American Indian Quarterly* 28, no. 3–4 (2004): 373–84.
Simpson, Leanne Betasamosake. *As We Have Always Done: Indigenous Freedom through Radical Resistance*. Minneapolis: University of Minnesota Press, 2017.
Simpson, Leanne Betasamosake. "Gdi-nweninaa. Our Sound, Our Voice." In *Learn, Teach, Challenge: Approaching Indigenous Literatures*, edited by Linda M. Morra and Deanne Reader, 289–300. Waterloo: Wilfrid Laurier University Press, 2016.
Simpson, Leanne Betasamosake. *Islands of Decolonial Love*. Winnipeg: ARP Press, 2013.
Simpson, Leanne Betasamosake. *Noopiming: The Cure for White Ladies*. Toronto: House of Anansi, 2020.
Solomon, Jon. "Beyond a Taste for the Dark Side: The Apparatus of Area and the Modern Regime of Translation under Pax Americana." In *The Dark Side of Translation*, edited by Federico Italiano, 19–37. London/New York: Routleldge, 2020.
Spivak, Gayatri Chakravorty. *Outside in the Teaching Machine*. London/New York: Routledge, 2009.
St. André, James. "Metaphors of Translation and Representations of the Translational Act as Solitary Versus Collaborative." *Translation Studies* 10, no. 3 (2017): 282–95.

Steiner, George. *After Babel: Aspects of Language and Translation*. Oxford: Oxford University Press, 1975.
Stigter, Shelley. "The Dialectics and Dialogics of Code-Switching in the Poetry of Gregory Scofield and Louise Halfe." *American Indian Quarterly* 30, no. 1 (2006): 49–60.
Stratford, Madeleine. "Au tour de Babel! Les défis multiples du multilinguisme." *Meta* 53, no. 3 (2008): 457–70.
Suchet, Myriam. "Introduction." *Intermédialités* 27 (2016), https://www.erudit.org/en/journals/im/2016-n27-im03060/1039808ar/abstract/
Suchet, Myriam. *L'horizon est ici: Pour une prolifération des modes de relations*. Paris: éditions du commun, 2019.
Suchet, Myriam. *L'imaginaire hétérolingue: Ce que nous apprennent les textes à la croisée des langues*. Paris: Classiques Garnier, 2014.
Suchet, Myriam. "Le québécois: d'une langue identitaire à un imaginaire hétérolingue." *Quaderna* 2 (2015), https://quaderna.org/2/le-quebecois-dune-langue-identitaire-a-un-imaginaire-heterolingue/.
Suchet, Myriam. *Traduire du français au français*. Rennes: Éditions du commun, 2021.
Swiggers, Pierre. "Ideology and the 'Clarity' of French." In *Ideologies of Language*, edited by John E. Joseph and Talbot J. Taylor, 112–30. London: Routledge, 1990.
Tardif, Dominic. "Les nouveaux mâles de la littérature québécoise." *Le Devoir* (Montréal, QC), September 29, 2018, https://www.ledevoir.com/lire/537851/les-nouveaux-males-de-la-litterature-quebecoise.
Taylor, Talbot J. "Normativity and Linguistic Form." In *Redefining Linguistics*, edited by Talbot J. Taylor and H. G. Davis, 118–48. London: Routledge, 1990.
Taylor, Talbot J. *Theorizing Language: Analysis, Normativity, Rhetoric, History*, 156. Oxford: Pergamon, 1997.
Toffoli, Camille. "*Quand je lis je m'invente suivi de D'elles et autres textes* de Suzanne Lamy/*Cartographie de l'amour décolonial* de Leanne Betasamosake Simpson." *Spirale* 268 (2019): 22–4.
Trerice, Spencer and Catherine Léger. "*Pour sûr* de France Daigle: un miroir des représentations linguistiques à l'égard du chiac." *Revue de l'Université de Moncton* 50, no. 1–2 (2019): 171–212.
Trudgill, Peter. "Standard English: What It Isn't." In *Standard English: The Widening Debate*, edited by Tony Bex and Richard J. Watts, 117–28. London: Routledge, Taylor & Francis e-library, 2002.
Tuck, Eve and Marcia McKenzie. *Place in Research: Theory, Methodology, and Methods*. London/New York: Routledge, 2015.
Venuti, Lawrence. *The Translator's Invisibility: A History of Translation*. London/New York: Routledge, 2008.
Vinay, Jean-Paul and Jean Darbelnet. *Stylistique comparée du français et de l'anglais*. Montreal: Beauchemin, 1958.
Vizenor, Gerald. *Survivance: Narratives of Native Presence*. Lincoln: University of Nebraska Press, 2009.

Walia, Harsha. *Border and Rule: Global Migration, Capitalism, and the Rise of Racist Nationalism*. Halifax/Winnipeg: Fernwood Publishing, 2021.

Walkowitz, Rebecca and yasser elhariry. "The Postlingual Turn." *SubStance* 50, no. 1 (2021): 3–9.

Watts, Richard J. "The Social Construction of Standard English: Grammar Writers as a 'Discourse Community.'" In *Standard English: The Widening Debate*, edited by Tony Bex and Richard J. Watts, 40–68. London: Routledge, Taylor & Francis e-library, 2002.

Whitehead, Joshua. *full-metal indigiqueer*. Vancouver: Talonbooks, 2017.

Whitehead, Joshua. *Jonny Appleseed*. Vancouver: Arsenal Pulp Press, 2018.

Wolfe, Patrick. *Settler Colonialism and the Transformation of Anthropology: The Politics and Poetics of an Ethnographic Event*. New York: Cassell, 1999.

Yaşın, Mehmet. "Introducing Step-Mothertongue." In *Step-Mothertongue. From Nationalism to Multiculturalism: Literatures of Cyprus, Greece and Turkey*, edited by Mehmet Yaşın, 1–24. London: Middlesex University Press, 2000.

Yildiz, Yasemin. *Beyond the Mother Tongue: The Postmonolingual Condition*. New York: Fordham University Press, 2011.

Index

abjection   41–3, 112–14, 132, 136
   Indigenous abjection   152–4
   Indigiqueer abjection   139–40, 151
   in Lambert   119–20, 132
   linguistic abjection   43–4, 112–13, 116–17, 145–6, 151, 157 (*see also* linguistic abject)
   queer abjection   111–12, 116, 119–22, 124, 136–43
   in Whitehead   141–8, 151
Acadian French   92–3, 96–8, 214–17, *see also* Acadjonne, Chiac
Acadian people   67, 84–6, 88, 214–17, 219
Acadjonne   214–15, 217, *see also* Acadian French, Chiac
accents   50–1, 173
Akiwenzie-Damm, Kateri   165–6
alterity   57, 186, 193–4
ancestry   23 n.2
   and language   164–5 (*see also* genealogy and language)
   Métis ancestry   68–71, 99
Anderson, Benedict   35, 46, 52
anglicisms   87, 127–8
Avasilichioaei, Oana   162, 171–2, 175–81, 195–200
axioms of translation   15, 21, 29

Bakhtin, Mikhaïl   61–2, 88
Balibar, Renée   33–5, 43
Bataille, Georges   41 n.56, 114, 132, 199
Belcourt, Billy-Ray   138, 153–4
belle-lettrist style   89
Berman, Antoine   37, 54–6

bilingualism   10, 38, 40, 58
   official bilingualism   5, 9–10, 38, 49–50
Bonfiglio, Thomas   45, 46 n.75, 48–9
borders   2, 41, 195–6, 198–200
   bordering   2, 29, 112, 199, 201
   linguistic borders   7, 29, 52, 77–8, 174, 213
   in Avasilichioaei   176–7, 179–81
   in Nathanaël   183–6, 190
   and translation   18, 25, 52, 192–3, 200, 206, 221–2
Boudreau, Annette   86
Bourdieu, Pierre   19, 101
Butler, Judith   41–2, 114, 151–2

Canada geese   211–12
cartographies of language   31, 62–4, 221, *see also* linguistic cartographies
Celan, Paul   176–81
Chiac   84–7, 92–101, *see also* Acadian French
   examples of   87, 90–1, 94, 95
   in translation   106–8
Chow, Rey   46, 50, 163–4
class markers   124–5, 129–36, 220
code-switching   72
critical place inquiry   207, 212

Daigle, France   65–8, 84–109
Dead Obies   4, 30, 44
death drive   114–15, 124
decoloniality   83–4, 140 n.65, 140–2, 149, 153–4
Derrida, Jacques   1, 162–4, 181, 203
desire   184, 186, 194

deterritorialization   62–4, 200, 204
differentiation (of identity
    categories)   41–2, 113–15,
    152, see also linguistic
    differentiation
directionality of translation   18, 64,
    161–2, 172, 196–7
dominant understandings of
    translation   23–8
Dubuc, Robert   22–3, 27–8, 30,
    42, 50

Edelman, Lee   114–16, 139
    critique of   116 n.15
emergence of the nation-state   36,
    38, 46, 52
enregisterment   8
ethics of translation   191 n.95,
    191–4, 217, 221
Expeditions of a Chimaera   195–9

Franglais   4–5, 131 n.41
    example of   126
French Revolution   34–5, 37
full-metal indigiqueer   137, 140–3,
    145–8, 151, 153

Gauvin, Lise   87–8, 93
gender-neutral pronouns   209–10
Giroux, Dalie   117, 126, 128–9,
    157

Halberstam, Jack   114–15
Haque, Eve   9, 49–50
    and Donna Patrick   146
Hatred of Translation   173 n.34,
    199–202
Heller, Monica   38, 44–5
    and Bonnie McElhinny   34, 146
heteroglossia   61–3, 82–3, 102–5,
    117, 151, 181, 218–21
    and Montreal   167–9
    and translation   67–8, 78–80,
    107–8, 158

heteroglossic address   118, 221, *see
    also* multilingual writing,
    heterolingual address
heterolingualism   54, 56–8, 60, 62,
    see also translingualism
heteronormativity   40–2, 114,
    119–21, 124
    and settler colonialism   138–40
Hobsbawm, Eric   34
homolingual address   53–4
homosexuality (representations
    of)   118–19, 121–2
hybridity   70–2, 99

identity categories   40–2, 51, 71–2,
    136, 137
ideology of the dialect   86, 96, 98
ideology of the standard   36, 66, 86,
    96, 98
    and translation   36–8
illegibility   118, 157, 201, *see also*
    unreadability
Indigeneity   71–2, 137–9, 152–4
    fraudulent claims to   69 n.10
Indigenous knowledge
    systems   165–6
Indigenous languages   10–11, 50,
    82–3, 149–50, 165–6
    Anishinaabemowin   166–7,
    210–12 (*see also*
    Indigenous languages,
    Ojibway)
    Cree   69, 72–83, 104–5, 148–51
    Ojibway   149–51 (*see also*
    Indigenous languages,
    Anishinaabemowin)
Indigenous resurgence   142, 150,
    153
Indigenous Studies   137–9
indigiqueerness   137, 139–40, 151

Jakobson, Roman   27
Jonny Appleseed   116, 137–8, 142–5,
    149–51

Justice, Daniel Heath   82–3,
    137 n.51, 139, 152–3

Karpinski, Eva C.   47 n.80, 50, 164,
    202
Kristeva, Julia   41, 113–14, 123

Lambert, Kevin   44, 118–20, 213
language and colonization   168–9
language and race   49, 68, 146, 164
    racialization of language   48–50,
        73
language as bounded system   28–30,
    39–44, see also structural
    understanding of language
language as exile   180–1
language as social practice   93–4,
    97–100, 103
language institutionalization
    in Canada   5–6, 9, 49, 97, 210
    in France   35, 209 n.9
language standardization   31–9,
    44, 66
La traduction raisonnée   24–5
LeBlanc, Georgette   214–19
legitimate language   19, 35, 45, 132,
    151, 168, see also legitimate
    speaker; linguistic
    legitimacy; mother tongue
legitimate speaker   95, 117,
    173 n.35, see also legitimate
    language; linguistic
    legitimacy; native speaker
Le Monolinguisme de l'autre   162–4
Lennon, Brian   75
liminality   176, 182–3, 194–5
linguistic abject   132, 146–7, 157,
    see also abjection, linguistic
    abjection
linguistic autonomy   28, 39, 111–12,
    155
linguistic boundaries   29, 39–44,
    see also borders, linguistic
    borders

and translation   25, 111–12
linguistic capital   19, 101
linguistic cartography   8, 31, 161,
    205, see also linguistic
    mapping; mapping of
    language
linguistic categories   8, 13, 57, 64,
    112–13, 167
    in literary critique   59–61, 171
    naturalization of   30
    reproduction of   44
linguistic competence   95, 101,
    163–5, 197–8, 202–4
linguistic difference   26, 27, 53,
    57, see also linguistic
    differentiation
linguistic differentiation   31, 39,
    43, 52–3, 57, 128, see also
    linguistic difference
linguistic insecurity   67, 86, 131–2
linguistic interference   25–6, 187
linguistic landscape   206–7, 212–13,
    217–22
linguistic legitimacy   45, 67–8, 101,
    202, see also legitimate
    language; legitimate
    speaker
linguistic normativity   5, 40, 61,
    125, 128–9, 136
    and translation   7, 30
linguistic ownership   48, 163–4,
    167, 202, see also linguistic
    property
linguistic performance   38, 51, 91,
    182
linguistic property   35–6, 45–6,
    162–5, see also linguistic
    ownership
linguistic symmetry   27, 29, 36–7
literary diglossia   87–8
Luther, Martin   37–8

Majzels, Robert   105–8
mapping of language   8, 44

masculinity 119–21, 124, 145
matter out of place 113, 194
metaphors
   bridge metaphor 175, 179, 189–92
   metaphors for language 126, 178–82
   metaphors for translation 25, 179, 190–2
   metaphors of nativity 23 n.2, 45
Métis identity 70–4, 76, 82–3
Métis people 69–70, 76
monolingualism 9–10, 12, 44, 118, 176
   in Derrida 162–3
   monolingual paradigm 45–6, 60
   parallel monolingualisms 38
   settler monolingualism 77 n.32
   and translation 28, 54, 169–71
Montreal 3–6, 27, 131 n.41, 167–71, 203
Moreton-Robinson, Aileen 165
motherless tongue 202–4
mother tongue 45–9, 161–4, 168, 171–4, *see also* native language
Moure, Erín 195–9
multilingual writing 10, 13, 112, 116–17, 169–70
   heterolingual address 54 (*see also* heteroglossic address)
   as a problem for translation 54–6, 59–61
Muñoz, José Esteban 115, 116 n.15, 154–6

Nathanaël 172–5, 182, 195, 199–202
nationalism 34
   cultural nationalism 4–7, 169 n.25
   ethnolinguistic nationalism 45–8
   French nationalism 113

Quebec nationalism 3, 5–6 (*see also* Québec, Québécois nation)
national language 8, 34–5, 45, 52–3, 165
nation-building 6, 9, 34, 49
native language 29, 45, 47–9, 171–2, *see also* mother tongue
native speaker 48, 163–4, *see also* legitimate speaker
New Brunswick 10–11, 84–5
Noopiming: The Cure for White Ladies 208–13
normativity
   heteronormativity 114–15, 124–5, 129
      settler heteronormativity 138–9
   linguistic normativity 16, 40, 124–5, 128–9, 136
      and translation 7
   sexual normativity 13, 119, 136
   violence of 78, 124–5, 128–9, 135–6

Ocean 18, 214–16, 218–19
Office québécois de la langue française 5, 6 n.12, 97, 209 n.9, 210
one nation, one language model 8, 34, 113
orality 67, 86, 88, 126–7

parallel monolingualisms 38
pedagogy of translation 26, *see also* translation training
polyphony 193
positionality 2, 104 n.95, 105
postlingual paradigm 59–60, 64, 206–9, 212–13, 216–19
   postlingual approach to translation 18, 20, 206–8, 210–13, 219–22

Pour sûr 84–6
  translation of 105–9
Pouvoirs de l'horreur 41, 113–14
prescriptivism 7, 30, 33, 50–2, 91–3
  and translation 23, 26–8
purism 6–7, 22–3, 146

Québec
  Québécois French 97, 117, 126,
    135–6
  Québécois identity 3, 120,
    134–5 (*see also* Québec,
    Québécois nation)
  Québécois nation 3–6,
    169 (*see also* Québec,
    Québécois identity, Quebec
    nationalism)
  Québécois vernacular 125, 129–
    32, 135 (*see also* Québec,
    Québécois French)
queering of language 17, 151, 159
queer studies 114, 137 n.51, 138–9,
  see also queer theory
queer theory 40–1, 112, 114,
  116 n.15, 137, *see also*
  queer studies
Querelle de Roberval 118–20
  French adaptation of 127–9

Rafael, Vicente L. 193, 203
refusal 17–19, 59–62, 151, 205–6
  politics of 153–5
  of translation 80–1
registers 8, 130, 135, 140, 215–16,
  see also enregisterment
  formal register 87–8, 93, 130
relationality 153, 193–4
  relations to the land 165–6
  and translation 20, 104 n.95,
    217, 220–1
reproductive futurism 114–16
residential school system 10–11,
  146

Rioux, Christian 4–5, 30–1, 44, 50,
  131 n.41
Rosa, Jonathan 49, 71, 73, 112

Saint-Martin, Lori 164–5
Sakai, Naoki 52–4, 170
Sampedrín, Elisa 195–9
Scofield, Gregory 68–70
settler colonialism 3, 9–10, 138–9,
  147 n.91, 168
Simon, Sherry 7, 25, 42, 168–71
Simpson, Audra 138, 153, 205
Simpson, Leanne
  Betasamosake 138, 153,
    166–7, 208
social categories 40–2, 51, 71–4,
  112–13, 136, 170
  ethnic categories for Indigenous
    peoples 152
sociolinguistics 32
standard languages 31–9, 45, 65–6,
  86
  and translation 55, 218–20
structural understanding of
  language 21, 23, 26–9, 39,
    103, 219
structural understanding of
  translation 15, 21, 26,
    28–9, 38
*Stylistique comparée du français et de
  l'anglais* 26–7
survivance 145, 145 n.85, 151

translanguaging 58–9, 59 n.111
translation as relation 194, 221
translation textbooks 22–5, 27
translation training 7, 22–3, *see also*
  pedagogy of translation
translator's habitus 21, 28, 174
translingual 58, 60, 209
Truth and Reconciliation
  Commission of
  Canada 11–12

unreadability 147, 156, *see also* illegibility
untranslatability 35, 54, 65

vernaculars 51, 54–5, 128 n.37, 135
    in literature 54–5, 88–9, 124–5
    translation into 220
Vizenor, Gerald 145

Whitehead, Joshua 111–13, 116–17, 137, 139–41

www.ingramcontent.com/pod-product-compliance
Lightning Source LLC
Chambersburg PA
CBHW050325020526
44117CB00031B/1799